Grief, Loss and Pain in Churches

A handbook for understanding
and advising in a Christian context

Bill Merrington

MINNEAPOLIS

GRIEF, LOSS AND PAIN IN CHURCHES
A handbook for understanding and advising in a Christian context

© Copyright 2011 Bill Merrington

Original edition published in English under the title GRIEF, LOSS AND PAIN IN CHURCHES by Kevin Mayhew Ltd, Buxhall, England.

This edition published in 2020 by Fortress Press. All rights reserved. Except for brief quotations in critical articles articles or reviews, no part of this book may be reproduced in any manner without prior written permission from the publisher. Email copyright@augsburgfortress.org or write to Permissions, Fortress Press, PO Box 1209, Minneapolis, MN 55440-1209.

Cover image: © iStock 2020: Inside view of a church in Saint-Emilion, France stock photo by MarioGuti

Cover design: Emily Drake

Print ISBN: 978-1-5064-5997-4

*To all the people who graciously allowed me
to minister to them in God's name.
To listen, weep, pray, give glimmers of reflection
and to hope for a better future.*

About the author

Bill Merrington has been an Anglican priest for over 25 years. Originally an analytical chemist, after a serious illness he retrained in ministry and has since led churches in city, town and countryside in the West Midlands. Bill has a PhD in Psychology specialising in the understanding of the longterm impact on parents when a child dies. He has carried out research in Britain, Lebanon and Africa, looking at the cross-cultural impact of death. He has spoken at a number of national and international conferences, and lectures regularly at universities. Bill has written a number of books for both adults and children. He is currently the Lead Chaplain at Bournemouth University and runs Counselling Care, a support organisation for bereaved parents and children. Bill is married with three grown-up children.

Other books by Bill Merrington

Death, Funerals and Heaven
Coping when your parents separate
When Someone Dies
101 ways to cope with grief and loss
The Hideway
Alice's Dad

Contents

Introduction		9
Change in a parish		15
Part One		**17**
1.	You can't avoid the loss issue	19
2.	Why is grief so important?	25
3.	When loss occurs	35
	The bereaved	38
	The type of bond	41
	Previous losses	44
	Age	45
	Gender	46
	Personality type	51
	Complicated grief	53
	The deceased	55
	The culture and environment	57
	Miscellaneous factors	60
4.	Making the issue real	63
5.	Anticipatory grief	67
6.	The journey of grief	75
	Emotional reactions	78
	Physical reactions	87
	Cognitive reactions	88
	Behavioural encounters	90
	Social impact	92

		Intellectual adjustment	94
		Spiritual reflection	95
	7.	The history of grief theories	97

Part Two   109

	8.	The role of faith	111
		So what is a healthy Christian grief?	113
	9.	Ministering to the bereaved in a Christian way	119
		Opening phase	120
		Intermediate phase	122
		Is there a time to talk theology?	124
		Final phase	128
	10.	Observe the expert at work	131
	11.	When does a person need to be referred?	143
	12.	Grief factor assessment	151
		Grief factor case studies	152
	13.	The role of prayer	155
	14.	When faith hits the rocks	163
		Can I forgive?	170
	15.	Life after death?	175
	16.	Funerals	185
		Memorial services in church	190
		Roadside memorials	191

Part Three   195

	17.	The loss of a child in a modern society	197
	18.	Miscarriage, stillbirth, abortion and infant death	203
		Miscarriage	205
		Stillbirth	207
		Abortion	209
		Prenatal Loss	210

		Cot deaths	213
		Pastoral implications for the loss of a baby	216
19.		The death of children	221
20.		The death of teenagers	229
21.		The death of young adults	237
22.		Common issues the church needs to be aware of with the loss of children	241
		The need not to forget	241
		Dreams	242
		The wish to die	243
		A change of values	245
		Shadow grief	246
		A strategy of support	259
23.		Supporting children in grief	267
		Infants	270
		Older children	271
		Adolescents	273
		Techniques that children/youth workers can use	279
24.		The death of friends	287

Part Four — 293

25.	Suicide	295
	Pre-suicide events	296
	Caring for the survivors	298
	The suicidal event	299
	Suicide notes	300
	Long-term effects	300
26.	Murder	305
27.	Disaster – post-traumatic stress debriefing	311
	What do families need?	313
	The complexity of disasters	314

	A strategy of help	315
	Debriefing	316

Part Five   323

28.	Coping with divorce and complex relationships	327
29.	The loss attached to parenthood	331
30.	Singleness in church	335
31.	The problems of age	341
32.	The rich, the poor and the unemployed	345
33.	When abuse lives in the church	351
34.	Christian hopes unfulfilled	357
35.	When the minister moves on	361
36.	Disenfranchised grief	367

Part Six   371

37.	When the pastor weeps	373
38.	Support and supervision	387
39.	Know yourself	393
40.	Developing a pastoral policy	397
41.	A time to listen	403
42.	Conclusion	407

Resources	411
Glossary	413

Introduction

> Spirituality is like a river flowing through every person
> Unfortunately, it can be dammed
> in times of illness, dying
> or bereavement with
> Pain, fear, and loneliness.
> However, a compassionate,
> caring presence can prevent
> The dam from forming and
> keep the river flowing.
> Lord, teach us together how to keep the river flowing. Amen.
>
> *Steven Jeffers*

In a typical church somewhere in England, there was a new minister of the church. He had only been in post for 18 months but he was finding it hard going. His family hadn't settled in the new area, the schools weren't as good and his wife missed her friends. They weren't the only ones. The minister had wanted to move on to this church and had felt God was in the move, but he had mixed feelings. Yes, he was glad to get away from some of the issues in the other church, but he had also made some really close friends. He valued their support and now felt rather isolated in a church that seemed to be still wrapped up in praising the name of the last minister. His church though was a fairly typical congregation regardless of its size. There was a good number of elderly coping with old age, aches and pains and a few living with widowhood. Two or three people unemployed, one critically ill and a few with long-term illnesses. There was a good number of young families present with their variously aged children and a couple of mums-to-be. It all looked healthy on the surface. But with a little bit of scratching, one soon found that several couples were coping with children with either learning or behaviour difficulties and one couple struggling to have children. There were also one or two marriages that looked shaky as well as the usual number of divorced people in the church. All in all, a typical church of any denomination. On first visiting, it appeared to be a happy thriving community; it was only as he got to know the people that he began to realise how many issues, particularly loss issues, were present waiting to be recognised and supported.

Being a minister or pastoral worker in a church is both demanding and costly. The good news is that we mainly enter the ministry because of our own positive faith experiences. This usually comes from finding support and wisdom from within the church. Our faith is finely honed as we share our testimonies, painful experiences, loves, pleasures and hopes. We begin ourselves to care for others in need and personally reap the joy of servanthood. Eventually, we find ourselves heading for full-time ministry or giving much of our spare time in a caring capacity to the church. However, the honeymoon doesn't last forever. Before you know it, the joy of entering ministry can quickly become a burden. You can easily find yourself carrying people's stories, struggles, worries and fears.

One of the greatest issues we will have to face is handling loss issues in people's lives. It is here that our own values, beliefs and personal experience will influence our perceptions and actions. But how will we adapt if the events of people's lives challenge our own understanding of our mortality, our faith and what we think we have to offer those in need? How will we cope over a period of time with our emotions, our beliefs and our actions? How many of us give time to stop, reflect and adjust our ministry according to our evolving faith? It is so easy to end up working in the way of the past, even though our views and beliefs have adjusted and changed. To be truly present in our ministry, we have to learn how to dovetail effectively our developing beliefs and experiences with how we minister and care for others. This is the only way to be truly congruent in our ministry.

The aim of this book is to make ministers and pastoral workers more prepared and equipped in their working context to handle loss issues in such a way that we can maintain a long enduring ministry over many years. This includes understanding the variety of loss events in a parish, getting alongside the bereaved and those carrying loss issues, understanding the variety of grief reactions, preparing a policy within the church and recognising one's own losses in life.

First, I'll put the case that so much of ministry in God's kingdom and the world is handling loss issues. I believe this was at the heart of Jesus' ministry, whether it be to individuals, groups, nations or the whole of mankind. Any ministry therefore needs to have a strategy of how we handle loss both in individuals' lives and in the church or parish. This inevitably raises the question of how we handle our own losses and how they impact upon our ministry.

Secondly, I will begin by looking at who we are and what makes us tick. So much of our personal make-up goes back to early childhood beginnings. We will look at our early attachments and how they influence us in regard to how we cope and adjust to change and loss issues. We will reflect upon our own beginnings and whether we think they still affect us in our ministry today.

The book is divided up into six parts, of which each can be read individually.

Part One outlines the reason why grief is such an important issue in the life of a church and its ministry. We will look why we bother to grieve in the first place and what makes it so complex at times. We will go on a journey of trying to perceive what it is like to be bereaved and we will then relate this to the many grief theories that have developed over the last century.

Part Two looks at the role of faith and we how we can bring our own Christian approach to this rewarding ministry. We will gain a picture of what might be called a healthy Christian grief approach and will reflect upon the example that the expert in ministry, Jesus, showed in handling grief.

Part Three looks at specific types of losses. We will see how society has changed over the years and how this has impacted upon how we grieve. We will hear different stories helping us to be aware of the differences between having a miscarriage, neo-natal death, abortion and a cot death. We will then journey to see what it is like for parents to lose a young child to a young adult. Finally, we will read about how death affects children and how important it is that we help them to grieve in a way that allows them to carry as little baggage in life as possible. We will conclude with a range of ideas to help pastors, children workers and youth workers to work effectively with bereaved children.

Part Four first looks at the subject of suicide and its particular impact upon the bereaved. We will then compare the difference when a murder occurs and how it affects the family and community. So far we have only looked at singular deaths, so we will then look at what might occur in a parish if a disaster strikes at the heart of the community. We will see what a strategic role the church can play and learn a simple technique called 'post-traumatic distress debriefing' which can be such an effective tool to deploy.

In Part Five, we will consider how not all loss experiences are related to death. So often we have people suffering in church with loss issues that are often unrecognised by the church. This might include recognising long-term problems with partners or children, or living with singleness or handicap of some description. There is also the complex reaction that occurs when a minister moves on and leaves a congregation and parish behind. This is a period that we often fail to address which also brings complexities for the incoming minister. There are at times so many multiple losses in a church that people can accumulate and go unrecognised. This is call 'Disenfranchised Grief'.

Finally, Part Six will look at how pastors and churches can survive being involved in this kind of exhausting ministry. We see the importance of understanding ourselves and being willing to seek help that will sustain us in our ministry, so that we ourselves do not end up ill and worn out. To assist us in this, guidance is given into how to formulate a healthy grief-loss policy within the church that both cares for the carers and those being cared for. This policy will affect the whole life of the church. It will encourage the church to be pastorally minded in such a way that it will produce an outreaching congregation that people in the community will hopefully want to be a part of.

Change in a Parish

'I'm on the last great journey here…and people want me to tell them what to pack'

Morrie Schwartz in 'Tuesdays with Morrie'.

In the first six weeks of being ordained in the Church of England, I found myself having to adjust to a barrage of change. Leaving theological college and all my friends, losing my anonymous identity in the crowd as I adjusted to people staring at me with my new white dog collar on and being upfront in a church rather than in the pews. I was in a large city church where there were several clergy staff. We lived next to a fellow curate. In my third week, the curate's wife giving birth to their third child, only to see him die within hours of birth. My wife gave birth to our first child days later and only four weeks after ordination. I soon found that the vicar had planned a Scandinavian tour with the choir, which left me to run a large church. So here I was, six weeks into my new post, when I heard that a fellow ordinand that I had trained with for three years had been killed in a car crash. It was all a baptism of fire. I recall meeting after the funeral with other friends from the theological college. We were dazed, confused, and theologically perplexed. What was all of the training for, if it could end so suddenly without rhyme or reason?

All of these changes affected me emotionally, socially and spiritually. Of course, I recognise that there were also many positive changes going on at the same time; being surrounded by a caring community who instantly knew you, the respect that people gave you as a clergyman, being wanted and needed, growing through being 'thrown in the deep end' of problems and the wonder of being a father for the first time.

Now after nearly thirty years of ministry, I can look back and see how these and so many more events have shaped my ministry and personal life. Some have scarred me deeply, other have led me onto a journey of discovery and growth; some have broken my spirit while others have led to a discovery of new gifts and talents. In the end I hope they have broken the arrogance within and led to a greater humility. However, many of my contemporary colleagues have not been so fortunate. Some have left the ministry with deep anger, others have lost their faith altogether, a few have found that their family life couldn't cope with the pressures put upon them and some, I guess, have learned to survive, often with tainted enthusiasm. Yet others have blossomed and couldn't ever see themselves doing anything other than being a minister in a church.

Is all of this just a game of chance, God-directed, or could we have been given better skills for the trade we embarked upon? It is easy to criticise theological colleges, but they have in reality a short period to train ordinands for all that life can throw at them.

This handbook attempts to combine many years of ministry in city, town and countryside along with my own reading and learning in the field of grief and loss issues. I hope it will at least provide a useful tool of reflection for ministers who find themselves immersed in people's lives who have to handle some of the world's most tragic situations. Most of all, I hope it will assist ministers and pastoral workers to at least protect themselves in their calling, so that they can use all their God-given talent for a full and long ministry in the Church.

Part One

In the first section of this book we will look at the basic human reactions to grief. This begins with recognising that grief is very much hard wired into human beings, it's something we simply can't avoid. We will see what lies underneath grief and why we bother to grieve at all. We will then look at the various components that affect how we cope with loss. Finally we will compare the various grief theories that exist and see which one feels most appropriate to our Christian perspective.

ONE

You can't avoid the loss issue

'Almighty means that there is no evil from which good cannot be brought.'

From the moment you are appointed to a parish, you and those around you are encountering an experience of loss. You are having to leave a home, church and community behind you while taking on a new church and community full of unknowns. The new church and community, however successful the last minister might have been, are adjusting to the loss of someone who takes with them a baggage of information and experience. At key times, the minister is very involved in people's lives. Baptism, weddings, personal problems, illnesses, funerals, and in the midst of grief, the minister is there. The new minister arrives with no history of these people or the key events in their lives. No wonder therefore there is a sense of sadness in the loss of the minister. It is inevitable that people will want to ask the previous vicar to return for a baptism, wedding or a funeral. I'm not suggesting this should or shouldn't be allowed; the point is that we need to recognise why people make such requests and not make the issue personal. It is not surprising that clergy often resent the previous minister that they have replaced only to discover, when they leave, the process begins all over again.

It is inevitable that ministers tend to reproduce in the new parish what they did previously elsewhere. This can create an emotional reaction where one is endlessly drawing comparisons between the two communities. A reaction that the new parish can begin to resent.

We see this often enough with bishops bringing in people from their previous diocese, much to the annoyance of the local clergy. Now it is very natural to bring our experience to bear upon our present situation. However, we do need to recognise why we tend to reproduce the past in our ministries, rather than develop new styles and discern more what God might want for us in our new situation.

If I reflect upon the eight communities I have ministered in over my ministry, I have to recognise that having been highly engaged in peoples' lives, it is natural that I seem to leave a part of my inner being in each community. I can look back with moments of joy and sadness, success and failure; wondering what is happening in people's lives now and whether the new ministers are building upon my ministry or tearing it down. You can't be engaged at such a deep level in people's lives without becoming bonded to them in some form. As you move on and inevitably struggle to hold on to the contacts, there is a natural grief reaction to the loss. How much consideration ministers allow themselves to acknowledge and experience is unknown, but I suspect a good number of ministers in their first few years in a parish are often tinged with pain and a sense of unsettledness.

This is not only true of individual lives but also of a corporate identity of a community. When I became a minister of six rural churches, it was clear that each community had its own unique sense of identity. It is only by understanding something of their history, that I could begin to see how to minister most appropriately to each community. It was certainly no good trying to treat them all the same. If I did, they would resent it and be hesitant about any change I suggested. I think of one of the churches where the vicar left under a cloud. Half the village loved the man but the other half had done all they could to make his life hell. Someone even presented him with the *Church Times* each week and informed him there was a job in it for him. How to feel unwanted! So when I arrived, I had a choice; either to ignore the past and push forward or spend some time listening and understanding the community's divisions and hurts on both sides. Only by recognising the hurt, anger, guilt and fear that the community felt was I able to attempt to move individuals and the community as a whole forward.

Once in the parish, loss issues surround a minister. Just look at some facts:

- Just over half a million people die each year in England and Wales.
- Approximately 1.5 million people lose someone close to them through death.
- There are approximately 6 per cent of the population widowed.
- Approximately 53 children a day are bereaved of a parent, equating to 20,000 children and young people each year in the UK (data from Winston Wish, a child bereavement agency).
- 1 per cent of males and 0.8 per cent of females die before the age of 15 years.
- Approximately 4,000 people commit suicide each year.
- Nearly 4,000 people die as a result of a road accident each year.

Office of National Statistics

When a death takes place, it is like a pebble being dropped into a pond. Ripples of grief go out in ever increasing circles affecting people at a variety of levels. On top of this, grief reactions occur far more through general life events than just when death occurs. Grief is something we all experience in life:

- Infants grieve at the loss of a breast or a bottle of milk.
- Children grieve when they can't find their favourite toy.
- Teenagers grieve at the break-up of their first love relationship.
- Couples grieve when they get the divorce papers.
- Adults grieve when unemployed.

- Families grieve when relocated.
- Individuals grieve when they experience the loss of health.

Since the heart of ministry is relating to people, it is therefore inevitable we are going to face loss issues on a daily basis in our ministries.

There will also be very specific loss issues we will have to face relating to our religious belief. We are told that today there are more people who have left churches sitting at home on a Sunday than are actually worshiping in church. Whatever the reasons that lie underneath this, it is clear that people have had a link with the church generally and specifically with key individuals, which have since been severed. We will hear in Chapter 28 what occurs when such relationships break. If we have any desire to win people back into our worshiping communities, it is essential that we understand what has happened to them and how they might be feeling. Only when people have had the opportunity to have their voice heard and worked through their issues, will they be ready to re-engage with a Christian community. To do this we need to not only understand their emotional reactions when they leave a church, but also be equipped to re-engage with them in a creative, healing way.

Our coping mechanism of dealing with our own losses in life will clearly have an impact upon our own pastoral care within the Christian community and with those estranged from the church. Nancy Cramp recognises this not only with ministers but also in many professions.

> The greatest deterrent to helping grieving people is the fact that many professionals have never dealt with their own losses or have never had a person close to them die. Thus it becomes too painful to reach out to others, and they simply hide behind 'professionalism'.[1]

---

1. Crump, N. in Jeffers, S. and Smith, H. (2007). *Finding a Sacred Oasis in Grief.* Abingdon: Radcliffe Publishing.

So what we need in ministry is a decisive leadership in ministering with grieving people. For the most part, this will relate to death issues. This needs to take place before a loved one dies, at the time of death, during the post-death rituals and in times of transition that lead to reconciliation with the death. But for those with eyes and ears open to perceive, there will be many more opportunities in daily ministry to care and support people who are dealing with loss issues. No other opportunity in life gives the pastor a better opportunity to minister to people. Indeed, this ministry is at the heart of mission. In Chapter 10, we will see how often Jesus engaged with such people.

- Reflect upon your own church experience, how have you felt when you have moved from church to church?
- What strategy have these churches developed to handle loss issues?
- How do you think your own experience of loss affects your ministry?

TWO

Why is grief so important?

'I'm like a grain of sand tumbling about in the sea.'

Why are some people in grief strengthened, others strained, depressed and anxiety-ridden?

Grief is a natural, normal healthy response to life events, which allow traumatised people to move through times of difficulty with minimum lingering unhealthy effects.

But why do we bother to grieve or mourn? We can lose our job because of it, we can become physically ill and we can lose friends because of it. In evolutional terms we should get back out and form new relationships as quickly as possible.

Grief is hard-wired into us and it goes right back to our early childhood relationships and attachments. We come into the world as strangers when we are newborn as we leave the security of the womb. We are not like baby lambs that emerge from the womb with four legs that work and grass ready to eat. Others must welcome us or else we will perish within hours. We depend utterly upon our main caregiver; this is usually a parent who meets our most elementary needs of food, water, clothing, shelter, comfort, warmth, touch, attention, affection and love. We know how to cry for these things, but we don't know self-consciously that we need them. We have no self-awareness to ground self-understanding as we lack the ability to distinguish between ourselves and the world around us. As we look at our caregiver, we see ourselves, this is who we are. It is from this person we begin the journey of finding out who we are.

We extend our knowing in small incremental steps through infancy. At first we are confined to the arms around us but gradually we establish a foothold on the world. With the attention to our basic needs, we begin to feel safe, secure, and at home in the world. Our caregivers attract our attention and fascinate us. We cling to them and grow attached to them.

The first attachment is focused on survival, but gradually the child forms other affectionate bonds with the wider family, then at the first school with teachers and peer groups. This continues throughout his or her life. As we form secure attachments, we are then able to feel secure and relaxed enough to learn and pursue new developments. It's what we see in students in their first few weeks at university; they quickly find people around to relate to and it's from these new affectionate bonds that they feel secure enough to begin to concentrate on their academic subject. This is where websites like Facebook are proving to be helpful. Students make contact with fellow students on their courses well before they arrive at college. This allows friendships to form so that it is not such an alien environment when they arrive in freshers' week.

The key thing here is what it tells us, that the bond between the caregiver and the child has strong biological roots and is imbued with very strong emotion. The bond is deeply influenced by experimental learning; in particular, the mother's own experience of being parented.

When we are born, we know nothing about our own identity. There are many questions to be answered about our selves.

Who am I?
Am I good?
Am I bad?

Am I lovable?
Am I unlovable?
Am I competent?
Am I helpless?
Is the world safe?
Is life is worth living?

Our caregiver either builds our self-esteem through their love and consistency or else they neglect us and give us a negative message that we are not important.

Let's imagine I'm standing with my daughter when she was 14 months old. She was a bottom shuffler that walked late, but was very content with her books and toys around her. She has a healthy relationship with me, I've fed her, changed her nappies, picked her up when she cries. I have provided protection; she in turn clings because she can't feed or protect herself, she needs a caregiver to help her survive. So she has a secure attachment to me (and her mum). Let's imagine this attachment to me is an elastic band. As the relationship develops, so does the complexity of the bond, the elastic band thickens. As we develop abilities to move on our own, to reach and grasp, to hold our heads up, sit, crawl, walk, we bring more and more things, people and places into the range of our experience. We begin to venture out into the world on our own, if at first very tentatively. Gradually we form new bonds of affection with many people, things and experiences. All of these are like tiny elastic bands that form a greater affectionate bond of identity that make up who we become.

So my daughter is secure, happy to play with me standing near her. She's near me, can smell me, she can hear my voice and keeps looking in my direction. She's secure so she is free to get on with learning. And throughout her life she will move on to form new bonds of affection with people and things that will allow her to be secure enough to explore, learn and develop.

Attachment is just one half of the child's relational development. Gradually, the child has to achieve a feeling of independence. To feed oneself, walk, dress, is all a form of independence. In each stage there is a dilemma to resolve. How can you have a feeling of trust and hope while moving on into independence? We do it with a sense of what is called 'optimum distancing', where we have to balance security with adventure. Life is a series of developmental crises, where in each situation we have an emotional dilemma to resolve. We need security in life but also a sense of independence.

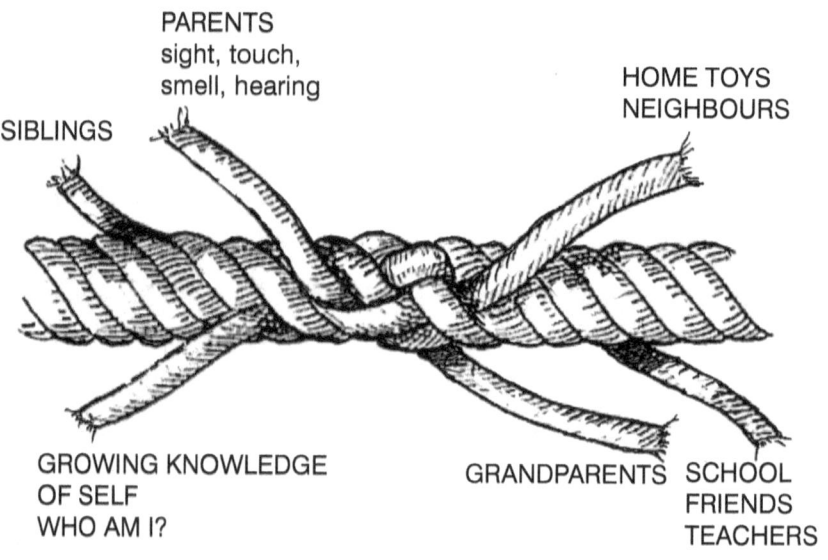

Affectionate bonds of attachment

As we mature, we extend our repertoire of activities and experiences within the limits of our capacities and aversions to danger and risk.

Gradually we become more effective and refined in increasingly more complex and varied activities. We choose our own pathways and begin to formulate our own history and identity. In other words we are becoming independent from our caregivers.

Now our social contacts expand as we meet and interact with others. We assume new roles in relationships with them. We learn to act within these roles. We learn to know what it is to be a child, grandchild, friend, pupil, and even a stranger.

In this journey we form all sorts of different types of bonds. So we formulate a range of bond relationships with their own particular strengths and peculiarities. Some of the bonds that we formulate are time limited, while others are far longer lasting.

> *Attachment Bonds* This is a deep survival bond that we acquire both in the womb and soon after birth. It enables us to find warmth, protection, food, cleansing, touch and love.
>
> *Contractual Bonds* It could be said that marriage is a contractual bond between two people where they make an agreement of what is expected from each other. Some may see it as a sacred bond that can't be broken.
>
> *Sacred Bonds* Perhaps a parent-child bond fits this description. When you have a child, you become a parent for life. This is a bond that seems impossible to break from the parent's point of view.

These bonds come with differing degrees of strength. Some bonds are time-related while others last a lifetime.

> *Identity Bonds* are where a person assimilates the quality perceived in another person's identity. They only persist as long as there is some benefit gained from it. If the benefit from the bond decreases, then the bond diminishes. As a child, I gained a great deal of benefit in

associating with my much older brother who was a footballer. Through this association I gained free football tickets to matches and made friends because of my brother's name in football. The link diminished when I became an adult and had little interest in football.

Crescive Bonds This is an unusual word but means something that grows with time; some marriages would fit this bill. Over the years you reach a point with your partner where you are both thinking in similar ways and will often say the very same sentence at the same time. So a parent bond to a child might be sacred and crescive, but the child might see the bond as more contractual and as an identity bond. The parent wants and expects the child to remain close throughout their lives. However the child seeks independence. Once the parent ends paying for university fees, etc. the child might well think they have little use of a parent. It is not surprising therefore that there is often friction between parents and their adult children due to their very different expectations.

As we form new relationships and gain experience, we develop abilities and sensibilities of our own that enable us to offer others something in turn. Our learning how to live in the world takes root in our capacities to both retain what we have learned from past experience and to anticipate the future. Here, we always carry our fundamental needs with us.

We find ourselves on a steep learning curve:

- We learn what works and what doesn't.
- We grow accustomed to how to do things and we make assumptions accordingly.
- We learn how to rely on the stability of the world and regularity of others' behaviours and responses. We learn how to anticipate what will happen next and what will result from our actions.

Our expectations rest on the sense of what is probable or likely, given our past experience. We use the stability and regularity in the world that we have encountered along with the confidence we have gained to make decisions in the present.

So we take our place in the world, we orientate ourselves in our physical surroundings and social surroundings. We become who we are, with established patterns, habits and routines. We learn to rely upon our experiences and begin to feel at home.

Along with this we formulate beliefs about the nature of the world around us, and the life we live within it. We adopt beliefs and theories often without realising or without careful critical examination. It is not only Christians who have belief systems, everyone formulates a framework for their lives, which allows them to plan and have goals.

We live our lives using our cognitive powers often unaware that these are secondary influences to the many non-cognitive assumptions we live our lives by. We wouldn't get far without them. If we had to analyse everything we did each day we wouldn't get far. Just for a moment think about why you got out of bed this morning? There were actually thousands of reasons ranging from deciding that:

World War 3 hadn't started.
You were well and healthy.
That there were no dangers downstairs waiting for you.
That you still had a job to go to or work to do.
That your legs still worked and your heart is still pumping!

All of these things, along with many, many more, have been unconsciously assumed as being safe and this allows us to get out of bed without too much worrying or anxiety.

We tend to make a few very large assumptions in life:

- In the western world we tend to assume that the world is benevolent along with the people around us. Otherwise we wouldn't venture far.

- That there is meaningfulness and justice and control in the world. This gives us a sense of purpose.
- That the world is not random, but that there is some kind of order to it.
- That we have our self-worth, our own goodness; we are under control and have our own luck in life.

All of these assumptions give us the freedom to do three important things:

> First, we organise our past events. This helps us to recognise what's familiar.
>
> Secondly, we can direct our choices for the present, so that we can control our environment.
>
> Thirdly, this enables us to anticipate intelligibly about the future. We develop an ability to predict what will happen in the future and therefore act accordingly.

So the bonds of attachment and self-awareness are developing like a spider's web. We have formulated, often unconsciously, a complex number of bonds, with people, with ideologies, beliefs. All of these formulate a kind of scaffold around our lives, which give us stability and a framework to explore further in life with a degree of confidence. If you watch houses or offices being built you will see the importance of the metal scaffold as the building takes form and shape. However, no scaffold is perfect or permanent as we will soon see.

WHY IS GRIEF SO IMPORTANT?

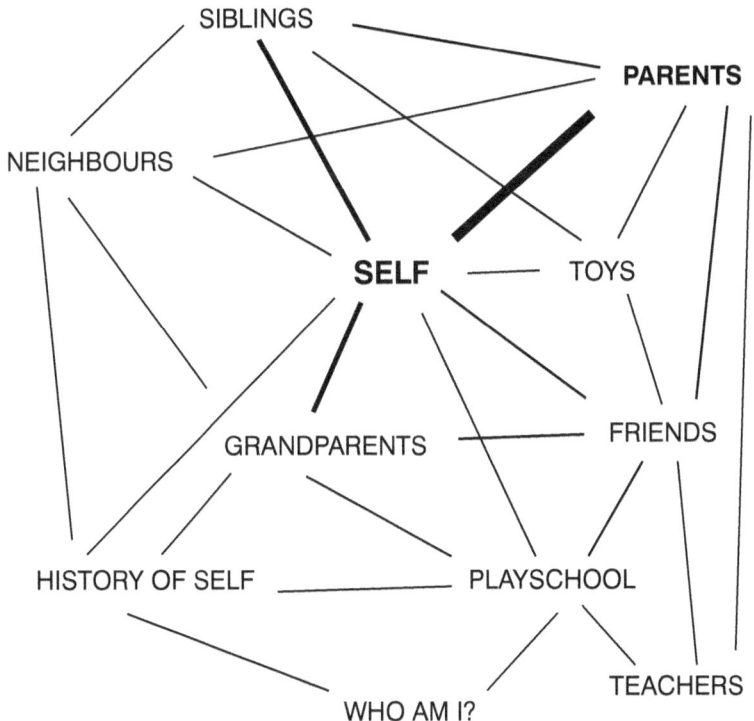

A spider's web of attachments

- Can you draw a spider's web containing your unique features of relationships, experiences and beliefs?
- Draw a picture of your bonds in life. Which ones are growing? Diminishing? Sacred? Identity bonds? How would you feel if we took some scissors and cut each bond?

THREE

When loss occurs

Back to my daughter. Let's imagine I have placed her in a room with strangers, her toys and myself. While I am present with her, she is content to feel secure and relaxed to play with her toys. But if I begin to move to the exit door my daughter will be showing an alarm reaction.[2] She will begin to watch me more closely, concentrating less upon her toys. In a sense the elastic band is being stretched. Even though she is with other people, she will be showing some signs of anxiety. And if I leave the room altogether? She will, without doubt, be either crying or shuffling towards the door. John Bowlby called this an 'alarm reaction'.

If I quickly return to the room, hopefully she will calm down and once again feel secure and soon become relaxed enough to begin to play again.

But what happens if I never return back into the room? The elastic band snaps! The bond has been severed with painful and long-lasting consequences. This is what bereavement is all about, it's when the elastic band, this affectionate bond, snaps. And when it does three things occur:

We try and escape the pain.
We try and mend the bond.
We try and make sense of it all.

For my daughter it would mean she would try and escape the pain probably by crying. She may be unaware of what has happened but

---

2. Bowlby, J. (1969). *Attachment & Loss, Vol.1, Attachment.* New York: Basic Books.

she would still have an emotional reaction. She may begin to throw her toys or resist any comfort from others. She would try and mend the bond by constantly looking at the door or bottom shuffling out of the door to find me. She will now find herself constantly thinking about her daddy. Gradually she will adjust to the change but it could take her the rest of her life to make sense of what has happened. In fact, she may never come to a satisfactory reason why her father left her with strangers and never returned.

All the old information that we have so far processed about life has given us a model of how to cope in the world. But when the bond shatters, we have to adjust. This new information creates emotion within us such that it either validates our belief system or invalidates it; either reforms it or affirms our beliefs. This is what grief is, *the art of relearning the world.* Loss disrupts the flow of our self-narrative such that we find ourselves on a long journey.

> We journey in a land called, 'the absence of meaning' through a terrain that finally arrives in a valley called 'meaning of absence'.

This journey, we will see, brings considerable changes to our lives and often leads to a new perspective on life, with modified beliefs and new goals to achieve.

Everyone's journey of loss is unique. It's one of the reasons why bereaved people feel very cross when people say that 'they know how they are feeling'. They may have an idea, and have had their own experiences of loss, but they can't truly know how a person feels in loss. This is because a range of factors affects a loss experience. This makes a person's experience a very personal one. Factors affecting us include:

The Bereaved
    Early childhood experiences
    The type of bond relationship

    How we coped with little losses
    Our age and gender

The Death Event
    Sudden or gradual
    Preventable?
    Type of death

The Environment We Live In
    The cultural background
    Whether we are in a rural or urban situation
    The support structure around us

Miscellaneous Factors
    Ambiguous losses
    Multiple losses
    Disenfranchised losses, etc.

This is why when we come to looking at a person's grief trajectory we need to be asking wider questions including:

- How does the person tend to cope with life in general?
- What previous losses have they encountered?
- How did the mourner deal with these losses?
- What is his/her personality type?
- What are the individual's social, cultural, ethnic, and spiritual backgrounds?
- What has their gender socialisation been like?
- What family and community support do they have around them?

In fact there are over 30 sets of factors that a grief counsellor could look at if they had the inclination. All of this raises our awareness of the dangers of over-generalisation when it comes to people's loss reactions. It places the focus in our care squarely upon the individual rather than in models or formulas.

Let us briefly look at some few key components.

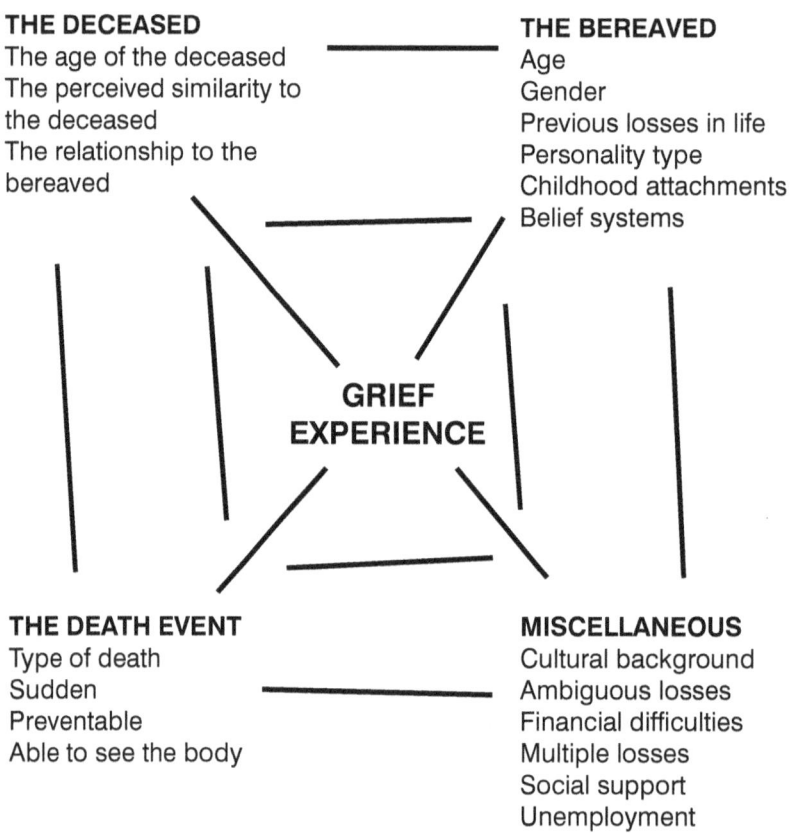

The Grief Experience Trajectory

The bereaved

The first is how we learned to react to our earliest experiences of loss. We know that not all attachments are healthy. A child's brain patterns will be different depending upon whether she has been loved and cared for. Her experience of security with her chief caregiver is not just psychological but forms physiological patterns within her.[3] Gerhardt found that brain scans of babies were different depending upon the care and love they had been given. If the bond is secure, there is joy and security and comfort, if it's not secure, there is confusion, anxiety, anger and jealousy. John Bowlby (1969) calls this an internal working model that we carry in our lives. He saw attachment as as important to a baby as food and drink. This is a blueprint hard-wired in us. A core belief internalised with these anticipatory images influencing our perception, emotions, and reactions to others. It's like a road map that we use subconsciously.

If there is close proximity then it leads to security. The child still wants to be close to the caregiver even if it results in rejection, pain and unhappiness.

In an experiment called the 'strange situation', Mary Ainsworth tested the reactions of children when they were separated from their mother and watched how they reacted when reunited.[4] She found four types of attachments.

Securely attached – child shows moderate level of proximity-seeking to the mother; is upset by her departure, but greets her positively on reunion. Here a securely attached child tends to develop working models of relationships in which others are viewed as available and dependable, and the self as viewed as resourceful and resilient. Such individuals are more likely to grow up able to adjust to loss issues and able to adapt to changes in their lives.

Insecurely attached: avoidant – child shows a weak desire to make contact with mother especially at reunion after separation and is not greatly upset when left with a stranger. This is often as a result

---

3. Gerhardt, S. (2004). *Why Love Matters*. London: Routledge.
4. Ainsworth, M. (1968). Object relations, dependency & attachment: A theoretical review of infant-mother relationship. *Child Development*. Vol. 40, pp.969–1025.

of a parent's undependability or neglect, simply not being available physically or emotionally for the child. This insecure attachment tends to encourage a child to develop a working model of relationships where the person sees relationships as dangerous and so learns to be independent of others, almost with a sense of compulsive self-reliance. When loss issues occur in later life, the individual tends to absorb the loss internally. This can lead to a higher degree of social isolation.

Insecurely attached: resistant – child is greatly upset by separation from the mother; on her return, difficult to console, the child both seeks comfort and resists it. Here with this confused pattern of behaviour the child is learning a working model of relationships, which are precarious and unpredictable. An example of this might be where a parent has an alcohol or a drug problem. The parent has times when they are caring and loving to the child but at other times might neglect or even be verbally or physically violent. When loss occurs later in life, the individual may revert back to their earlier hard-wired behaviour and exhibit high level of grief reaction, which is hard to console.

Disorganised – child manifests no coherent system of coping with the stress, shows contradictory behaviour to mother such as proximity-seeking followed by avoidance, indicating confusion and fear about the relationship. This leaves the child with a complex working model of relationships, which could greatly influence future relationships and reactions to loss in adulthood.

The key thing is that it tells us that the bond between the caregiver and the child has strong biological roots and is imbued with very strong emotion. The bond is deeply influenced by experimental learning; in particular, the mother's own experience of being parented. This in turn means that we tend to react to difficulties in life according to our previous attachment experiences. This is not saying it can't be changed. At the heart of the Gospel, I believe that Christ can bring deep psychological changes to people's lives. However, if we are unaware, we do tend to revert back to a formal default model of behaviour. Our earliest key relationships will therefore influence both our belief system and how we choose to react when loss and pain occur. Generally, those who have had stable secure attachments early in life have formulated a healthy way of dealing when loss occurs. Other forms of attachments tend to lead to more complex grief reactions later in life.

A way of thinking about this is to reflect upon whom you were closely attached to as a baby? Who was it that fed, clothed, protected and came to you when you cried? Once decided, think how far back you can go in recalling the first time you were separated from your chief caregiver? How did you react? Why do you still recall this, compared to so many other events that you can't recall? Key memories are often embedded with emotion, which is why we can recall them. For many, the first memory of separation will be going to school. Others recall getting lost in a supermarket or can't recall anything before being left at a boarding school. One person told me that she got separated in a lift only for a few minutes, but it took many years before she could venture into a lift again.

The type of bond

Secondly, there is the issue of what type of bond relationship and how strong or deep the relationship of the bond has become. If the bond (elastic band concept) is crescive or sacred or has a strong self-identity attached to it, then one would expect a more pronounced grief reaction. However if one has had little contact with a person who does not closely relate to your life, then the impact of the loss will be relatively small.

Let's imagine I get an email from Australia from a solicitor saying I've been named in a legal will. A very distant half aunt I didn't know existed has named me as her main recipient of her belongings. Five million pounds no less! Oh dear, I am sad she has died, but I'm rather pleased she left me so much. The strength of the bond I had with her has only just formed; it is a thin elastic band, which is extremely weak and will therefore cause a small grief reaction. The attachment with this deceased person may of course gradually increase as I venture into finding out more about the lady. In time, I might well begin to grieve over the loss of what could have been a healthy relationship. However, compare this to the death of your only teenage child when you are in mid-life. Here, there has been considerable input into the relationship over many years. Now the elastic band is thick and complex. It will include good and painful memories as well as considerable time, motivation and commitment to the relationship. The loss of such a key part of one's life will disturb one's life equilibrium considerably.

> Reflect upon your losses in life. What loss/gain factors have been involved?

Thirdly, our experience of small losses early in life and how we coped will influence how we react to greater losses later in life. This becomes important when we think about how we help children cope with loss (see

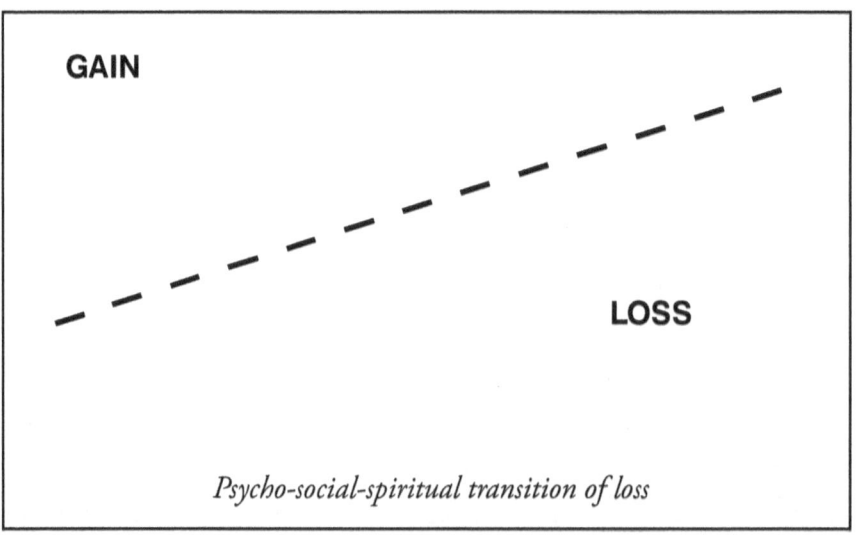

Psycho-social-spiritual transition of loss

Chapter 23). Many things make us secure: people, money, employment, prestige and home. And all of these can be lost.

> Growing up, going to school, changing school, siblings arriving, moving house, parents changing jobs, change in finances, divorce, educational problems, illnesses, child abuse, loss of parents through grief, disability, etc.

When we come to loving someone like a parent, sibling, family member, friend, spouse, teacher, colleague, they play a particular role and take up a particular place in our world. Each has a presence, a story, a unique, irreplaceable, complex and multi-dimensional location in our lives. Many of our hopes, emotions, needs, desires, motivations, habits and expectations are targeted in these individuals. So when they die, we lose their continuing presence. The way young people deal with any of these losses or 'little deaths' will affect the way they deal with the ultimate one of their own death or someone close to them. The intensity of the grief reaction will depend on how they have experienced the other losses, their personal characteristics, their religious and cultural background and the support available. If when we are young, we develop a healthy coping mechanism to handle losses, clearly it will stand us in good stead later in life.

This leads us to acknowledge that our age will influence our grief reaction. We know that it is not only adults who experience the pain of loss; babies along with young children show signs of grief. At each age, we deal with grief in a way that is appropriate for our life skills and experience.

- When you were a child, which person did you feel closest to and why? When was the first time you can remember being separated from your caregiver? How did you react?
- Draw a time line of your losses. How many loss experiences can you identify? Can you grade them in levels of significance?

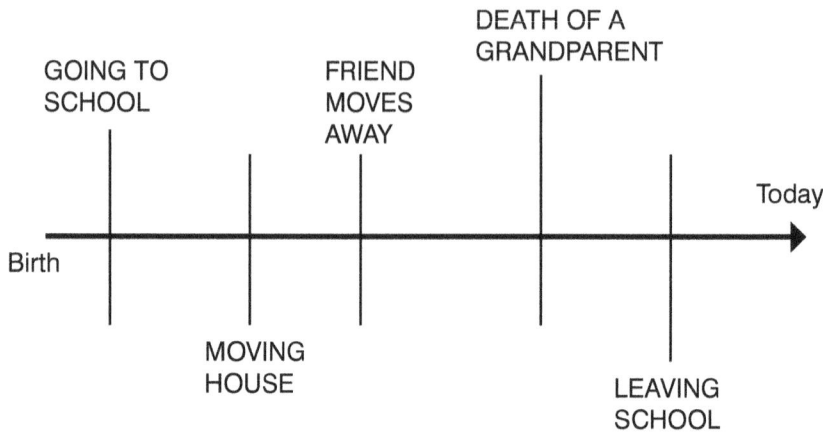

Example of a time line of losses

- How did others react to you?
- What kind of coping skills did you use?
- How did the loss affect your life at the time?
- How has it affected how you react to losses today?

Previous losses

There are different types of losses in life. Physical losses relate to something tangible that is no longer present. Relational loss relates to losing a relationship with someone to whom one has had an affectional bond. This could be a person or animal. Ties between individuals can be severed for many reasons, be it divorce, moving jobs or location. There are also symbolic losses such as the loss of dreams, hope and faith. Often a primary loss such as a death can trigger various secondary losses such as the loss of one's self-esteem, income, friends, and status in the community. All of these different levels of losses need to be recognised in a person's life, mourned and worked through.

How a person has dealt with these various losses will clearly affect how they subsequently deal with major losses later in their lives. If one has formulated a way of facing issues, working through them with the support of others, then one has a working model of how to react, adjust, cope and move forward in a healthy way. If, however, one has tended to shelve such issues earlier in life, then when a major loss occurs, one can find that there is not a coping mechanism to rely on that is healthy and productive. The person can find himself or herself not only dealing with a major loss but multiple other losses all cumulating into one overwhelming grief reaction.

Age

Some look at the role of age in grief from an evolutionary perspective.[5] However, the role of the age of the bereaved is very complex. We will discuss later particular losses for parents and for children (Chapters 19–20). One might think that the older a person becomes, the more experience they will have gained in terms of dealing with losses. This is not always the case, with many people going through life not really dealing with their losses. For the very young, one would expect a greater grief reaction depending upon an increased attachment to the deceased. But this will also depend upon other attached figures making the person still relatively secure. Daly and Wilson suggest that as offspring get older, parents will value them more, but as the parents get older, they will be valued less by their offspring.[6] I'm not sure it is that simple. We need to consider all the other factors mentioned within this chapter.

---

5. Archer, A. (1999). *The Nature of Grief: The Evolution and Psychology of Reaction to Loss.* London: Brunner-Routledge.
6. Daly, M. and Wilson, M. (1988). *Homicide.* New York: Aldine de Gryter.

Gender

> Gender may influence patterns of grief but,
> Gender does not determine patterns of grief
>
> *Martin, T., 2000*

It is clear that gender can influence grief patterns. The fact that men and women exhibit differences in the way they grieve has been recognised for some time.[7] The key is that while patterns of grieving are certainly influenced by gender, they are not determined by gender. Men have often been viewed as hiding their grief in work, alcohol, sport, etc., but may express it in the form of anger. They are able to handle their emotions in social situations and are generally harder to comfort. It has been thought that men process grief more cognitively (instrumental grievers) and require less time to grieve. Women on the other hand would be more willing to seek out help and support, and be able to express their grief on an affectional level. They are more intuitive grievers.[8]

This, however, does not stop women from being more socially at risk. Men are seen as being more at risk of a complicated grief reaction, while women are more vulnerable to depression and chronic mourning.

Generally, men use self-help groups less often than women. This may be due to the perceived role of the man as a provider, protector and problem-solver. This makes it more difficult to seek help and support. They are more likely to use a more private, intellectual, introspective coping mechanism. This particularly might involve activity as a way of handling unpleasant feelings, which results in going back to work earlier than women. There is nothing to say that this is a less appropriate coping mechanism than a more expressional

---

7. Stillion, J. & McDowell, G. (1997). *Women's Issues in Grief.* Washington, DC: Association for Death Education.
8. Martin, T. and Doka, K. (2000). *Men Don't Cry... Women Do.* London: Routledge.

response. Although there seems to be evidence that men are more likely to use substance abuse such as alcohol and drugs to cope with their pain.

The type of loss will clearly affect the genders differently. For example, widows often have to face more financial worries while men are more likely to return to work early, date and remarry. More will be said about the loss of children, but generally women show a more intense grief reaction needing to seek out more support and be more expressive about their loss. Both genders seem to be bewildered at how the other reacts.

Even at childhood levels there can be seen slight differences in the gender reaction. Girls are more likely to exhibit anxiety, idealise the deceased and cope with change in family circumstances less well than boys.

All of these variations should not surprise us. There is a masculine-feminine continuum that exists within a person as well as between individuals. Gender clearly plays a role in so many aspects of life, that it will also be relevant when it comes to a loss reaction. But we need to be careful we don't overplay the gender aspect. What if a client/parishioner exhibits a behaviour that doesn't fit the masculine-feminine style? It can be discomforting to be told you are not behaving in an appropriate way or if a counsellor encourages you to express your grief in a way that is inappropriate for you. When males express their grief in an emotive way that has in the past been called a 'feminine form', or females have addressed their loss in a solitary, active cogitative response often called a masculine form, they both may well resent the assertion.

It is more appropriate to think more in terms of an 'instrumental' or 'intuitive' response that allows an individual to relate to their loss in the sexual expression that is appropriate for them.[9]

---

9. Martin, T. and Doka, K. (2000). *Men Don't Cry... Women Do*. London: Routledge.

An 'instrumental' griever tends to temper their emotional response to loss; they are more likely to talk of their loss in physical and cognitive terms. They tend to attempt to validate their loss cognitively rather than express it emotionally. Cognitive here is referring to the conscious and subconscious mental activities that involve thinking, remembering, evaluating and planning. The behavioural expression of their grief can often take its form in some activity. This may be generally expressed in work or more focused upon the loss perhaps with legal action or promoting social change or setting up charities, etc. They will more likely want to explain their circumstances around their loss rather than express their feelings to others. Their thinking revolves around an assumptive worldview that they will control and eventually master the circumstances of their lives. They find themselves less in a state of panic, more in a state of challenge. This means that they are less likely to cry or may even have no desire to. They in fact may have no understanding of the benefit of crying. All of this does not mean that instrumental grievers do not have feelings of pain, loneliness, anxiety, etc. The difference is that the strength of such feelings is simply not as strong. You might like to think of it in terms of shades of colour. Instrumental grievers have feelings of pastel colours while intuitive grievers have feelings of strong vibrant colours. Thoughts and feelings merge for intuitive grievers while instrumental grievers seem to be able to think about their experience and feelings in an objective, rational way.

'Intuitive' grievers may express their grief in a more emotive form, seeking to express their feelings with the desire of support from others. Here, a grief expressed is a grief experienced. The intuitive griever gains strength and solace from sharing their inner experience. Some suggest that male intuitive grievers tend to seek out counselling to validate their grief, as their feelings may seem to run counter to the normal male role expectations. They may need someone to reassure them that this way of grieving is normal for a male.

Give sorrow words, the grief that does not speak knits the o'er wrought heart and bids it break.

Macbeth, Act IV, Scene iii

The retelling and re-enacting of the pain of loss is paramount in this style of grief.

So in one family, when a prominent member of that family unexpectedly dies, the grieving members may well express their grief in various forms. One might turn inwards and withdraw from family and friends; they might seek comfort from drink and drugs. While another may be inconsolable and end up seeking a self-help support group where they find some solace. Another member might show little emotion but work through their grief by thinking through what has happened in a constructive way, which leads to a new career direction. Here we see a blend of reactions between instrumental throwing of oneself into activity, to intuitive grieving with clear expression of emotion, to a blend of both. For an intuitive griever their energy is taken up with their feelings. This leaves less time for cognitive and physical expression. This leaves them in a state of prolonged confusion and disorientation. This clearly affects how they work and concentrate. It can be a real battle to complete important tasks as well as the smaller daily routines of life. A feeling of exhaustion results from expressing the feelings of pain (crying), anger and despair along with poor sleeping and a change of eating pattern. One reason for the lack of sleep is an intense arousal feeling of anxiety. Here, it helps if intuitive grievers find a channel for their energy.

One area where there is a difference in gender is in how society assumes men cope less well than women domestically. It is interesting to note that older widowed men seem to receive more formal support than women. This may be a cultural reaction as many of these men had been coping well caring for their seriously ill wives before death.

We may just make the assumption that men can't cope domestically in loss as well as women with little evidence to back it up. Men may have just not had the opportunity to adapt and to cope.[10]

One final point about gender is the tension it can cause in relationships when one person grieves in a different way than another. If one does not recognise different coping mechanisms, people can very quickly blame one another for not appearing to have any feelings about the loss. One can seem to be indulging in their feelings while another appears cold and mechanical with no outward sign of change. More well be said about this later (Chapter 22).

Generally, a person who draws from a broad range of adaptive strategies is likely to do better. Persons with a wide range of responses, who effectively integrate all aspects of self, seem to be able to respond to crisis. From a counselling perspective, we need to recognise that counselling is a channel often for those who are grieving 'affectively' rather an 'instrumentally'. This means that counsellors will more often encounter the expression of grief in a particular format. However, counsellors need particularly to be able to recognise and to adapt their approach to accommodate people's own style of grief expression. Otherwise, those who are instrumental grievers will find the emphasis on 'feeling' in the counselling room very off-putting and will vote with their feet.

Pastors and care-workers will more likely encounter a broader range of grief reactions as they visit within a particular community. This raises the importance of the role to affirm what might be a very normal natural way to grieve even when others in the community fail to understand. We are also more likely to come across 'dissonant' grievers. These are people who experience grief one way, but because of constraints, fail to find compatible ways to express and adapt to their loss. These are often

---

10. Bennett, K. M. (2009) 'Can't do enough for you.' Why do older men get more social support than women following bereavement? *Bereavement Care Journal*, 28(3), pp.5–9.

intuitive grievers but because of perhaps gender, or cultural or social constraints, end up hiding and containing their emotions.

If 'dissonant' grievers are often unlikely to go for counselling, the pastoral care worker has an important role in providing additional support for such people, thus allowing the bereaved to acknowledge their experience, consider the factors that might be blocking their expression of their feelings, and identify adaptive strategies for dealing with their feelings. This is especially important when in a family two members are expressing their grief in different ways. Our role can be assisting each person in understanding how the other people in the family context experience, express and adapt to their loss. This can help a person to realise that they are not the only one who is hurting deeply. Others may be just as deeply affected by the loss but are just expressing it in a different form.

Pastoral workers can also assist in helping an instrumental griever assess whether their own coping strategies are working and are effective for themselves and their surrounding family and friends. For example we may detect that the bereaved is using alcohol as a coping mechanism, which will ultimately compound the problem, or they are looking for a quick substitute to replace the role of the deceased.

Personality type

Every person has his or her own unique personality. This reflects the sum of the individual distinguishing qualities that the person expresses over a long period of time and across various situations. We tend to assume that a personality type is fixed and stable over their life course. Jung saw the personality functioning through how we think, feel, sense and through intuition.[11] While there are those who see clear flaws in Jung's approach (particularly how it is expressed in the Myers-Briggs type indicator), it can be a helpful way of reflecting

---

11. Jung, C. (1920) *Personality Types*. London: Routledge & Kegan.

upon how people grieve. When death has taken place, the bereaved has to process the event. They may either do this in a thinking way or in a feeling way. So the thinking-feeling functions will dictate a person will grieve either instrumentally or intuitively. This is not to say that a person doesn't have their shadow side of their personality that might well be well used in grief. Indeed it is important that both thinking and feeling find ways of expression. We all have a tendency to prefer to express things in a particular way. So for an instrumental griever, their energy is channelled into thinking and finds expression in planned activities. However, an intuitive griever may discharge their energy by venting their feelings. These are important factors when it comes to a couple having to cope with how they grieve. One partner may be expressing their grief in a way that the other partner just doesn't understand or value. This is where the work of a pastor or care worker can be invaluable in helping couples to appreciate their differences and giving room and recognition that they are indeed grieving, it just manifests itself in a different form.

Another aspect of personality is the degree or strength to which an individual expresses their emotions. Some people feel emotion very intensely, regardless of whether it is a positive or negative emotion. Those who experience intense positive emotions are equally likely over time to experience more intense negative emotions. This increased intensity manifests itself not just emotionally but also somatically with increased heart rate, arousal, poor concentration, etc.

It seems common, that when people experience such high intense reactions that they assume others will experience the same intensity. However, this intensity seems generally to diminish with age.[12]

---

12. Larsen, R. J. and Diener, E. (1987). Affect intensity as an individual difference characteristic: A review. *Journal of Research in Personality*, 21, 1–39.

Complicated grief

> Expression of feelings lead to momentary pain and long-term relief,
> Suppression of feelings leads to momentary relief and long-term pain.
>
> *Chinese Proverb*

In the early stages of grief it can be very difficult to categorise an individual's grieving pattern. There is a generally recognised pattern of disorganisation with grief. When someone is exhibiting shock, numbness, hysteria and confusion, it is hard to say to what extent this is abnormal compared to most people in grief. Intuitive grievers may initially suppress their emotions, which might be a very normal way of dealing with their loss in the first few days. This, however, is very demanding on someone who would more naturally just express his or her emotion. It is as if they have simply turned the volume of their emotions right down for a short period. Sometimes sleep becomes a way of handling this. Generally intuitive grievers will revert to their customary pattern of expressing their feelings through crying, etc. An instrumental griever will probably also use a similar strategy in the first few days, although they will do so more naturally.

For some grievers, they find themselves stuck in their initial strategy. For an example, a man who is an intuitive griever wanting to express his emotions may feel trapped in our present-day culture in suppressing the tears to follow a manly norm of behaviour. This is called 'dissonant', where a person is expressing grief in a way that is at odds with their more natural way of expression. It is a very difficult place to be for the bereaved. At first, suppressing emotions is a valid way of coping but if it becomes a long-term strategy then it turns into repression. This is particularly risky for an intuitive griever. In this state, the person is avoiding the reality and the pain of the situation. This self-deception can have damaging affects upon a person's long-term well-being.

Some people choose to behave in a way that matches those around them, to conform and make their lives easier. This may be an appropriate initial reaction, but if it is at conflict with their deeper feelings, then internal dissonance will result. An example of this might be when one's elderly parent dies. There can be an assumption in the community that such a death will not be too upsetting. This ignores the depth of the bond with the parent with all its complexity over the years.

Just because an instrumental griever is not expressing their grief through crying, emotional expression and seeking help, it doesn't mean that they are not handling the situation or facing it. They may be exhibiting a reaction in a different form. For example, they may show a higher degree of restlessness, pacing, insomnia and muscular tension. They may be visiting the doctor with very real somatic issues. Anger may become a valid secondary form of coping. It can become a way of solving problems and achieving goals that fits more comfortably with them as compared to an intuitive griever for whom anger may feel far too emotive to let loose. Using their cognitive abilities, the instrumental griever, male or female, may use anger as a way of mastering their environment.

Complicated grief is often referred to as prolonged grief disorder. This has been characterised by intense longing and yearning for the person who has died. Along with this are recurring intrusive and distressing thoughts about the person's absence. This seems to prevent a bereaved person from moving forward. Issues associated with this type of behaviour include:

- Trouble accepting the death.
- Inability to trust others since the death.
- Excessive bitterness.
- Feeling uneasy about moving on.
- Detachment from former close friends.

- Feeling that life is meaningless.
- Feeling that the future holds fulfilment.
- Feeling agitated since the death.

These need to persist for at least six months to result in significant impairment in the person's functioning. Alas, these days our society expects a quick fix, which results in people wanting the bereaved to receive counselling days and weeks after the death.

There are certain factors which raise the risk of complication. These include:

- Poor childhood attachments.
- Previous mental distress or depression.
- High levels of care-giving, be it a positive or negative experience.
- Feeling exhausted, overloaded.
- Lack of support.
- Low income.
- Debt.

A combination of these factors will increase a person's vulnerability in having a complicated grief reaction.

The deceased

The type of relationship we had with the deceased will clearly influence how we react to a loss. The complexity of the baggage we carry in a relationship will overshadow how we feel and handle a loss. The age of the deceased will also influence how we behave. There is a considerable difference between the death of a 90-year-old as compared to that of a 21-year-old.

The type of death is also significant. Whether the death is sudden and unexpected as compared to a person dying through a long illness will cause a different grief reaction. How preventable the death might have been will alter the degrees of emotion produced. We see this often when a family believes that the medical profession could have prevented their relative from dying. Alas, sooner or later, the NHS has an impossible task!

Death arrives in differing packages:

- Certain death and known time – e.g. liver cancer. Here the prognosis is poor and the likelihood of surviving long with this type of cancer is low.
- Certain death but unknown time – e.g. cystic fibrosis. Here there is a prolonged illness and the length of a person's life will vary.
- Uncertain death but known time of resolution – e.g. heart surgery. With an operation, one knows the risk that death may take place but the risk diminishes if the operation is successful.
- Uncertain death and unknown time of resolution – e.g. multiple sclerosis (MS). Here a person is ill but the illness may not kill the person, in fact it is more likely that the person will die from other factors.

There are also the individual complex situations such as when the person is only alive because of the medical machinery. How do you cope in such a dilemma? What about when the machine is switched off but the organ transplant might mean that the person is perceived as alive, only in a different form?

Also, how closely we perceive ourselves to be similar to the deceased will influence us. In reality, the closer the person is perceived to be like ourselves, the more we are in a process of reflecting upon our own potential death. We see this in schools where perhaps a teenager is killed in a car crash, soon after he passes his driving test. Listening to fellow classmates, one can perceive how they are not just grieving the loss of a school friend, but also the loss of their innocence. If you suddenly discover that you can die at 17 years of age, it has a profound impact upon how relevant you think A-level exams are in your life. A friend has died who sits next to you, is the same age, doing the same subjects and supports the same football team. It is understandable that this loss will have a big impact upon the deceased's friends.

The culture and environment

Culture encompasses both the material and the non-material aspects of life. While the material aspects of culture, be it clothes, food and technology, are very visible to the eye, it is the non-material aspects such as beliefs, norms and values that are important when it comes to grief. This involves the way we think, believe, behave and relate to others. In a modern world this is becoming increasingly difficult to categorise. In Britain we are increasingly living in a country that is surrounded by many sub-cultural groups within a large culture. People are now living in their own social enclaves, which might be determined by work, class, age, religion, shared behaviours and lifestyles. Most of us are born into a culture that we adopt and acquire. This becomes the way of life for us as if it is the 'only way of life'.

These cultural norms affect the attachment people make to their partners and children. For example, in parts of Brazil where the survival rate of babies is small, mothers protect themselves from becoming too closely attached and naming the child till it is clear that it will survive long term.[13] In other cultures, children are reared not only by the mother but by all the mothers within the community setting. It is then suggested that the loss of a parental figure is less traumatic in this context than in other cultures.[14]

Some suggest that the grief pattern, the emotions felt and how they are expressed and understood, is determined by the cultural

---

13. Rosenblatt, P. C. (1993). Cross-cultural variations in the experience, expression and understanding of grief. In D. Irish (ed.), *Ethnic Variations in Dying, Death & Grief: Diversity in Universality.* Washington, DC: Taylor & Francis.
14. Parkes, C. M., Laungani, P. and Young, B. (1997). *Death and Bereavement Across Cultures.* London: Routledge.

setting. There may be some truth here, but we must remember that culture is not the only influencing factor. Also, if the culture were one that was diverse and complex, then one would expect to see this diversity and complexity mirrored in the community. This diversity can be expressed in the different ways that a community expects a person's grief to be manifested over time. For many in Britain, it seems that there is an underlying expectation that one will grieve in a controlled and almost dignified way. There is an acceptance that at the funeral people can be free to weep or be in fact very calm during the ceremony. Afterwards, again the calm resolute expression is taken up. This does not mean that the community does not recognise that you might be feeling deep pain and heartache but just that it is not over-expressed in public. This is a contrast with other cultures, for example in Uganda or Tanzania where there will be an outpouring of weeping and tears in the first few days, or in Lebanon where there are set times over the months after death to publicly express grief. In Poland on 'All Souls Day', there is a national expression of grief with a mass exodus of people attending the cemetries with candles and flowers. This is the time when there are more accidents on the road all year due to people travelling to get back to their families for the occasion. It has the feeling of going to a football match in Britain, being carried along with the crowd. This might make Britain's Remembrance Day look rather tame in comparison. It just goes to show that you cannot judge a community's reaction purely upon how people express their grief culturally.

The environment we live in brings its own unique reactions. This might involve very local community ways of conducting oneself to profound behaviour and actions in other cultures. Locally, there is a difference between experiencing a significant loss in a rural community where you are more likely to be well known as compared to living in a busy city surrounded by strangers unaware of your experience. Compare, then, how people grieve from different religious communities in Britain and you will observe very specific types of reactions. Take this a stage further and compare people's reactions from different continents; you will see extreme reactions that might be considered abnormal in one continent only to be seen as very normal in another. History has shown that what was once a normal reaction in loss can very soon seem strange to a community.

We need to recognise that terminologies often get confused here, which doesn't help. For the rest of this book we will take the stance that Bereavement is the overall term referring to how people behave when a loss occurs. This can be broken down into two areas, Grief and Mourning. Grief is seen as the psychological reaction to loss. Some see this as a universal reaction hard-wired into us. Whereas Mourning is the external, cultural, environmental reaction, which will vary considerably.

Every society has its own prescribed 'grieving rules' that dictate what ought to be expressed in a certain situation and what kind of sympathy and support should be offered.

There is a Russian folklore that tells of how men make caskets and tell stories while the women weep and wail. It is interesting that the monument put up after the Lockerbie aeroplane crash in which 33 children were killed consists of 103 women weeping with not a man in site. The stereotypical assumption is still alive and well in our modern western society.

It is important to recognise the role that social class also plays in our 'grieving rules'. In the past men were costumed to live their lives out in the social public world with their involvement in work, community and the home. While women have traditionally lived their lives in a more private world of the family and home. There is a kind of assumption here, that women will be more committed to the family role and so when loss occurs, it will have a larger disruptive effect upon the women. However, with couples having to share roles more equally with both playing a more public role, one might expect to see a blurring of the grief reaction between the sexes, at least from the perspective of the roles we play. Whatever the cultural role of a given community, there is still considerable room in more open societies for the family to find their own unique way of functioning. So one family may follow a very traditional route of behaviour using stoicism, self-reliance and a stiff upper lip while, next door, a family may value the importance of expressing their feelings and sharing their own inner thoughts and concerns. This is in contrast with many cultures where there are clear rituals to remember the dead. The western world leaves people more in a position of inventing their own way of remembering.

Miscellaneous factors

I hope by now you are beginning to get a picture of the complexity of grief. It is like entering a spider's web, where the breaking of one relationship has significance upon all the other bonds of the web of life. All of this is without including the more complex grief situations that result from ambiguous losses, multiple losses, disenfranchised losses, etc.

Now you might be thinking how on earth am I, as a pastor, going to be able to engage when you are painting such a complex and varied grief experience. I am not expecting you to suddenly become a bereavement counsellor. The key is to just be aware of the issues involved. Pastors do more damage by diving in with platitudes and quick-fix answers rather than simply empathising with individuals and knowing when and how to refer on to others. The beauty of the body of Christ is that we don't have to be skilled to handle all the pastoral situations that befall us; but we do have to be responsible to know when we are out of our depth and to use others with the skills necessary to bring the healing that is required. We will think about strategy and team work in Chapter 40.

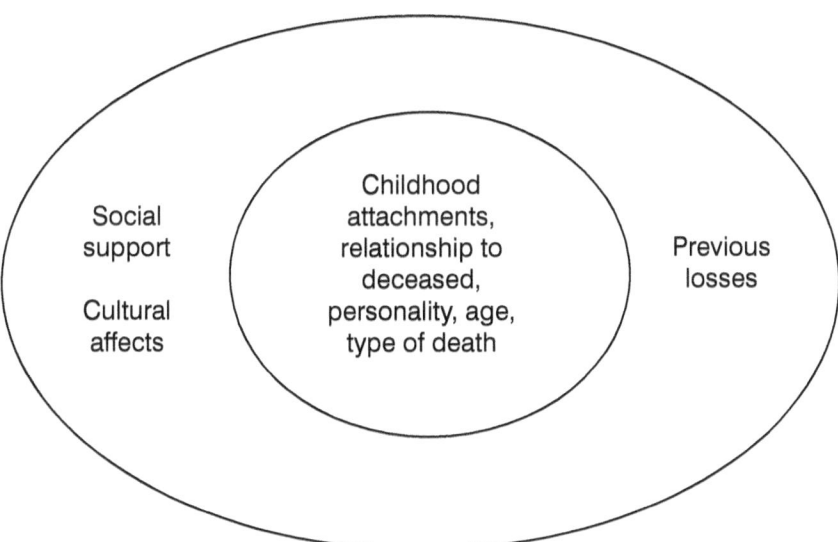

Issues affecting the grief experience

FOUR

Making the issue real

How many times have I heard it said, 'I never thought about death and its impact until it knocked on my door.' It's strange that the statistics are very clear and unambiguous, 100 per cent of people die. It reveals the degree of denial that we create to allow ourselves to function daily and plan for the future. This is a good thing provided we are not so deluded that when loss does occur in our lives we fail to have a coping mechanism to adapt. So let me take you on a journey that allows you to perceive it as it really is. We are going to imagine you had an accident this morning, which resulted in your death, and reflect upon the outcome for those around you. If this seems a bit too much to bear, please feel free to skip this chapter.

Let's begin by finding a relaxing place to sit where we won't be interrupted for 30 minutes. So pull out the telephone and switch off the mobile and close the door. Begin by sitting in a relaxed position, with feet on the ground and arms resting on your uncrossed legs. Close your eyes and breathe in deeply through the nose and breathe out slowly through the mouth. Do this for a few times before we begin to relax the muscles. Now tense your forehead and eyebrows and then relax them. Tense your neck and shoulders and then relax them. Keep breathing slowly and regularly as you work through your body, tensing and relaxing. Work down the body to the arms and hands, legs and toes. Once the body is relaxed, now let's relax the mind.

Take your imagination to somewhere special that has fond and special memories for you. I imagine a little beach I know well in Spain, where the sand is always hot and the sea is a deep blue colour. When you have decided a place, it could be a home you lived in or a favourite country spot; then paint a picture of it in your mind. See the colours, the smells and sounds. This exercise is a safe way of relaxing body and mind at any point in the day when stress levels get high. The place you have thought of is somewhere you can go at any time to induce a sense of safety and calm in one's inner being.

Now let's take the mind somewhere else. Let's imagine you popped out from your home this morning to get something from the shops. On the way you crossed the road only to be distracted and knocked down by a car. This resulted in your death. Come away from your body and imagine what happens around you. Who comes to your aid? How long does the ambulance take? How is it affecting people around you? When you are finally taken to hospital, how does the staff need to find out who you are? What identification did you have on you this morning? How long will it take before they contact a relative?

Now imagine a few hours have passed and a police officer is coming to your next of kin's door. Will they be in? Will it be a convenient time to call? How will your relatives react? Will they invite them in and make them tea or will they go into shock and panic? Who will they contact and who will gather at the home to bring support?

A day has passed since you were killed in a road accident. The family are having to develop new skills, organising a funeral, registering a death, communicating to many people – how will they fare? The funeral takes place; will it be where you would have wanted it to be? Who led the service? Was the service the way you would have wanted? Did the family know whether you wanted burial or cremation? What did your family find the most comforting within the service?

A few weeks have now passed, how do you think your closest relatives are coping? Who will be offering any support? How will they survive financially? Will they have to move house or make other big changes?

Six months have now passed, who will still be offering support and friendship?

Let's now leave this scene and return to imagining your special place. See it, hear it, smell it, enjoy it, knowing that you can return here at any time of the day. Continue to breathe deeply and slowly. Go through the relaxing exercise again, tensing and relaxing your muscles. Don't rush it; take your time. Finally open your eyes and take in where you are.

If you were able to engage in this exercise, you will have found that all sorts of questions and realisations will have come to your mind. There may have been surprises for you, things you wished you had pre-organised such as a will and funeral instructions. Perhaps it dawned upon you the extent of the pain and anguish that would be created by your death. There would have been many negative things resulting in their lives that would have a long-lasting effect upon their lives. There are also a few positive things psychologically and socially resulting. Learning to cope with change, discovering new skills and perhaps formulating a new perspective of life. These things do not outweigh the loss, but they do allow bereaved people to move on in their lives.

The one thing this exercise makes one reflect upon is how we can make our loved ones' lives much easier if we are willing to do a small amount of preparation. Making a will and leaving a letter with your views about funeral arrangements can assist the bereaved. They don't have to follow your wishes, but at a time when there are many questions and things to arrange and when they are in deep shock, it can certainly take away some of the strain to at least know your wishes. Ministers spend so much time caring for others; we need to make sure it is not at the expense of our own family.

- Is there anything I need to organise now to help my family?
- Do I know the wishes of other members of my family?
- Do I need to reflect upon the priorities of my life?
- If a Church leader/pastor, do I need to inform someone with my permission to destroy any confidential notes I may keep?

FIVE

Anticipatory grief

Sue was a 17-year-old girl in the prime of her life, except that she was about to die of leukaemia. It all started when she became a teenager. Sue was a keen horse rider when she began to have severe pains in her shoulder blade. Naturally the family thought she had just strained a muscle, riding the horse, but after the problem persisted and various visits to different doctors and hospitals, she was diagnosed with cancer. A long battle proceeded with the family doing everything possible to get their daughter better. After some highs and lows, Sue had an operation to remove the collarbone, and there followed a period of remission in which she was able to go back to school. However, sick children tend to attract bullies and it wasn't long before she had to change school and make new friends who could cope with her illness. Chemotherapy brought on a headscarf and finally a bone marrow transplant meant Sue had to be isolated for a period of time. Three years had passed with the family adjusting to the changing circumstances of their lives. The family had made many changes to their lives. The mother had given up her job to look after her daughter. She had spent weeks and weeks sitting and at times sleeping in hospitals. The father took early retirement and re-arranged the house to allow a bed to be placed in the living room. It became clear to all that by now Sue had only months, perhaps weeks to live. Sue was herself aware of this when she asked me to visit her to begin to prepare her funeral arrangements. Sue had already been through the emotional roller coaster of emotions of feeling angry, guilty, fearful and overwhelmed with despair. She was beginning to protect her parents by preparing for her departure. We had many sessions talking about her feelings, disappointments, worries for her family and boyfriend. She kept a small book in which she kept her notes about her thoughts and requests. She discussed with her parents where she wanted her belongings and finance to go after her death. At times dad was unable to sit through these conversations, they were just too painful. By the time of Sue's death, much was in place for what had to follow. The will, funeral arrangements, belongings and letters had all been prepared before-hand. Whether the parents liked it or not, their daughter had been preparing them to release her and to be ready for what lay ahead. Just by letting me as their minister into their home was a sign of acknowledging that their only daughter was about to die.

Anticipatory grief is when a person is aware that death is going to take place in a relatively short time and therefore they begin to grieve the death. This can occur for the dying person, the supporting relatives, friends and care professionals involved. We see this more obviously in the hospice movement. Here, there is the recognition that someone has a terminal illness and a support structure is put into place to allow the people involved to begin to work through their emotions.

We will look at the general emotional reactions that people experience when a death or major loss occurs in Chapter 6. What we need to be aware of is that these emotions of shock, numbness, denial, anger, guilt, fear, despair and searching for answers can all occur well before the death takes place. There are occasions with people when they are even in a hospice; that they are in such denial that they refuse to recognise what is happening to them. You might see this as the beginning of a grief reaction that has got stuck at the denial stage. We will hear more about this later.

What is clear is that when people are aware that they are dying, there is a change of perspective and outlook by both the dying

ANTICIPATORY GRIEF

person and the people supporting them. All of this reveals that death is not just an event, but more of a process. It can be seen as a journey or a movement that begins to separate the dying from the living.

For the dying, perhaps the obvious change is their physical appearance. Unless it is a sudden death, most illnesses leave their mark well before death occurs. This has an impact both on the dying and the carer. As one ill patent said,

> 'I don't look in the mirror any more.'

The dying find themselves in a limbo land, where they don't seem to belong anywhere.

> 'It's all of a muddle now; I don't belong at home any more but am not ready to move on. There are things I'm just not interested in. I'm writing some Christmas cards but I don't know if I'll be around to celebrate it. I don't think about the future. I read the newspaper but it's just not relevant to me any more. When you give up expecting the miracle to happen, there is nothing worth bothering about, I just go back to sleep.'

For the carer there are also issues. When do you begin to prepare for the end? Does that make you feel guilty that you have given up or are you being realistic in preparing for the future?

> 'I went out and bought a hat the other day. My husband hates hats. I guess I'm getting ready for when he's not around, getting ready to be an individual again.'

The carer has to both live in the world of the dying with all of their personal needs, while at the same time begin to live as if they are not around any more. They are aware of the tasks and the issues they will have to face after death and it is natural to begin to think about them before death has taken place. This creates a grey area where the dying and the carer never venture.

> 'I don't know how my partner is coping, I never ask him; perhaps I don't need to know.'

There seems to be a hidden agenda where both sides silently agree not to meddle. It is very natural as we look at a dying person to see ourselves, and our own fears about death. We therefore understandably pull back from our fears and tend not to ask too many questions. We might not like the answers. It is not uncommon for the carer to begin to speak for the dying in their presence. This is all part of the carer having to take more and more decisions and thus taking control of the situation. This creates loneliness on both sides. It can be why some people prefer to die in hospital or in a hospice rather than at home. The institution can protect us from our relatives and all those difficult moments when we don't know how to behave or what to say.

Supporting people before death

Supporting people through the final stages of life is both a demanding role and challenging to one's belief system. And this is how it should be, after all the dying are well ahead of us in our understanding. We will meet people who didn't believe in God and with the 'cards' that they have been dealt, they are even more convinced that there is no God. Others hold onto their faith in a dogged and determined way that is a witness to those around. Atheists can die as peacefully as religious people. The harder place to care is when those with faith begin to struggle with doubt and uncertainty. This can be challenging to the carer as it raises issues for ourselves of how we will be when the time approaches. We mustn't shy away from issues of faith and doubt; it is here that faith is tested and made real, however small it might become. The role of a pastor here is surely to journey with the dying. If they feel secure enough in our presence they will share their grappling issues with us; it is not for us to burden them with our beliefs, for this would be inappropriate (we are not where they are, how can we be so arrogant to assume our belief fits where they are sitting) but to enter into dialogue as a friend enabling the dying to find their way in a dark place. We will discuss this further but for now let us ask the question 'whether one should persist in visiting people who show little religious belief or may be anti-religious'. This is a hard question when one might be busy enough caring for those within your church. However, in terms of outreach and Christian example, I would like to suggest we should persist with our contact and offer of support. We may feel the brunt of someone's anger and it may seem that we spend out time talking about other things than religious belief. However, that doesn't mean the person doesn't want to talk about faith, it may be just too painful and they haven't gained the trust to venture there with you. Journeying with the everyday events of life can assist in helping a person finally reach a point to talk more deeply with you. I appreciate this is time-consuming and a hard place to be. However, it can take time for a person to work through their years of pain, anger and frustration before they are able to share their inner fears. I think of the woman with the flow of blood, where although Jesus had healed the woman with a physical touch and despite the fact that he was rushing on to heal a dying child, he paused and listened to her story. Would she have been fully healed without the emotional outpouring? We have to hold in, if we want to reach that point.

To do this we have to handle the everyday events of a person's life ranging from burning the toast to talking about sport or the mundane issues of the weather or what we have eaten that day. Remember whatever becomes important to a dying person simply is important. Journeying in this way might seem trivial but it is also very draining. We need to be aware of the toll it takes upon ourselves and have a support structure in place to aid us (see Chapter 38).

One area we can help a dying person is where they are particularly clinging on to life in fear and dread. This is something that is observed by the family and friends and creates a very difficult and tense place to be. If we have developed a 'good enough' relationship, we may be able to approach issues about fears and worries that relatives find hard to raise themselves. It may be a faith issue or it might be a simple issue that we can address with the family, which puts the dying person at ease. When the dying person feels reassured about the aftercare of their family, I have seen a person simply let go and die very quickly and peacefully. However, we have to be aware of the impact upon our own faith when handling and supporting seriously ill people. It can be worrying for ourselves when we see a person struggling to hold onto their faith. It also raises the issue of whether we engage with people who are either struggling or have no faith. How much time do you give if someone is not responding to our visits? Scripture may seem to encourage shaking the dust off your feet and moving on; but in some cases, because a pastor has persisted and been willing to build a relationship, they have been able to see an individual open up and begin to share at a much deeper level. We need to recognise that often night times are the worst for a terminally ill patient. Hence it can be a rewarding time to sit with them. Although we have to recognise the difficult tension between allowing a patient to talk perhaps with pain or increasing the painkillers such that the patient finds themselves sleeping. Although many people will say that they would want to die quickly, the reality is that a terminally ill individual has the opportunity to say their farewells if they are given the support and encouragement they need. It is also a unique opportunity for the pastor to sensitively support and engage with the person on issues that perhaps they will speak about with no one else.

Reflections

- Read 'Tuesdays with Morrie' by Mitch Albom. An account of a dying professor preparing to die and giving instructions to a former student on how to live.

SIX

The journey of grief

Over the next two chapters we will look at a typical journey of grief. This chapter will look at a traditional model of what occurs. In the next chapter we will outline some of the more modern approaches to grief, which will allow you to reflect upon which feels more appropriate to your experience.

When death occurs it leaves the bereaved with two aspects to deal with, the physical, practical aspects and the emotional aspects of loss. The practical aspects are more obvious and clear-cut whereas the emotional aspects are far more complex and varied.

Practical aspects

It is surprising how many practical things there are to do when someone dies. The tasks are often new things to the bereaved and may result in new skills acquired because of the loss. You will see from the flow diagram how the tasks vary according to whether the death is unexpected or anticipated.

Sudden in hospital	• Next of kin/police — Relative identifies the body
Sudden at home	• Police/doctor — Contacts undertakers for removal of body
	• Coroner — Orders post mortem — Holds inquest — Issues disposal certificate — Gives undertakers a disposal certificate
Expected at home	• Inform doctor — Decide between burial or cremation — Obtain medical certificate of cause of death — If cremation complete forms B & C — Contact registrar — Registrar issues death certificate and disposal certificate
Expected in hospital	• Hospital informs next of kin — Decide between burial or cremation — Relative collects medical certificate, and B/C form if cremation, takes away belongings — Contacts undertaker for removal of body
Cremation	• Crematorium require forms A,B, C — Book day & time — Decide about ashes — Pay undertakers — Claim national insurance benefits — Order memorial stone
Burial	• Churchyard or cemetery — Book time, choose coffin, etc — Newspaper, flowers, cars, refreshments — Memorial? — Reply to letters

When someone dies

Just over 60 per cent of deaths do not require the involvement of a coroner. There are also tasks to be done immediately and within a short period of time as compared to those which can be dealt with in the weeks and months ahead. If you have never dealt with a coroner or funeral director or registered a death before, then it is a challenging encounter when you are also dealing with your own emotional trauma as well as that of close relatives and friends. You then have to organise a funeral with all the important decisions to be made. This is where a will can be helpful, especially if the deceased has left instructions as to what they would prefer in regards to burial or cremation and what they would like within the funeral service. We will see when we look at grief theories how important the practical aspects of loss can be with the grieving event. Doing tasks provides an emotional break from the intensity of the loss.

There is in fact a range of aspects to address when loss takes place.

- Emotionally, we have to express the pain within and learn how to handle this pain in the future. This might be being aware that our emotions are very close to the surface. It might also involve talking to someone such as a counsellor to whom we feel safe expressing our feelings.
- Physically, we have to adjust to new patterns of how we meet our basic needs. This might affect where we live, how we earn a living and pay our bills.
- Cognitively, we have to discover who we are afresh which will affect our self-confidence, self-esteem and self-identity. This might mean we will withdraw within ourselves to process this for a while.
- Behaviourally, we have to adapt to doing things differently and come to terms with the fact that this will be long term. This might be simply putting out one set of knives and forks instead of two or adjusting to buying and cooking less food each day.
- Socially, we have to find our way in changing patterns of give-and-take with others. Often this can mean we find new friends who can accept us as we are. We might find ourselves sitting in rooms near the exit so that we can leave if we feel uncomfortable. We might also join charities that provide friendship and a sense of purpose.

- Intellectually, we find ourselves on a journey to seek answers to the questions that trouble us and pursue them till we find a satisfactory answer. This might involve joining a support group where you are all asking similar questions or reading extensively about grief and loss.
- Spiritually, we grapple with the big questions of life and death as we wonder 'who am I and who are you and what am I doing here?' This takes courage to be open to our own stories, being willing to adjust our belief system and seek to find some peace and hope.
- Philosophically, we have to learn to live with the 'unknown' and know that it is okay.

Let's go on a journey of some of the emotions that are involved in grief.

Emotional reactions

This is how grief is commonly expressed, with a range of emotional reactions including anger, guilt, anxiety, fear, shame, hopelessness and relief. Such feelings do not occur sequentially but can arrive at your door all at once, often with contradictory emotions competing for your attention. For those who have never experienced such a wave of emotion, it can be a frightening situation in which you feel your whole being is out of control.

In our brains we have a section that contains our emotions, it's like a small thimble cup waiting to fill up with a mixture of chemical feelings. Just imagine for a moment that someone accidentally dropped a brick on your toe. What would you instantly feel? Hurt, shock and surprise I guess. Think of it as a chemical of hurt going into the cup. Within a millisecond you probably will feel a second emotion, anger. This emotion always follows on from hurt. You never feel angry without first feeling a sense of hurt. However, for some people, the chemical of anger gushes into the cup so quickly, a person doesn't realise that they are hurt, they just feel angry. Anger often shows on our face or in our words or behaviour. Perhaps you shout out at the person who has dropped the brick. Now everyone is looking at you and a sense of embarrassment shows on your face. Suddenly guilt pours into the cup. Now the cup is filling with hurt, anger and guilt, which creates an uncomfortable feeling in itself. What if the person picks up a second brick and heads in your direction? You are quickly moving your feet and feeling a sense of fear and alarm. Now your cup is getting very full, in fact putting all these emotions together is creating a mixture of anxiety and if it continues, stress. If someone bumps into you, some of this emotion is likely to spill out in one form or another. It's like having a can of fizzy pop that has been shaken up. When you open it, you are likely to get the contents spilling all over you and others. All of this results in physical symptoms, which manifest themselves because of the emotional turmoil. We will hear in a moment how these physical symptoms often leaf a person to the doctor.

Disbelief and Numbness

We live in an assumptive world. We make many assumptions about life every minute of the day. This allows use to be relaxed enough to get on with life without worries about a million possibilities that might affect our lives. Take for example the roofs over our heads. Unless we live in a part of the world where earthquakes take place, we assume that our ceilings are secure and safe. I recall one day discovering that the ceiling in our vicarage lounge was collapsing. As I moved to the door, the whole ceiling, lath, plaster and horse hair demolished the living room along with our possessions. For the next few months, wherever I went, I would pay particular attention to the ceilings in rooms. My assumption that ceilings were safe had been shattered.

You might have had a similar experience if you have been burgled. Suddenly your home is not safe any more. It's rather like being thrown into a turbulent waterfall. We go from being organised, everything in its place, to a state of chaos in thoughts, values, beliefs.

Sigmund Freud wrote to a friend after the death of his son,

> 'Although we know that after such a loss, the acute stage of mourning will subside, we also know that we shall remain inconsolable and will never find a substitute. No matter what may fill the gap, even if it be filled completely, it nevertheless remains something else.'

When our assumptions have been shattered, it is understandable that we will go into shock, disbelief and numbness. It's why many will say that the funeral was a blur. This of course has implications in how you conduct funerals (see Chapter 16).

It is as if we are saying, 'if I don't see, hear taste, touch, then it can't be happening'. It is as if you choose to be unaware, dissociating yourself from the situation. Here you are deadening yourself physically and mentally to avoid the emotion of death. Part of this is a self-protection mechanism, which protects us from experiencing an event too painful to handle. There will also be a small part of us in which we are protecting ourselves from admitting to our own mortality.

So in the first few hours and days people will be experiencing a sense of haziness and unreality. The days will pass like a blur with people they meet being faceless, without identity. Everything has become numb which creates a 'sameness' to everything where comfort and discomfort, heat and cold, noise and silence all merge into one. Suddenly, all the things that were so important a day before have now disintegrated because now, nothing really matters.

Anger

The word 'anger' appears in the Bible 228 times and is sometimes associated with grief.

> And when he had looked round about on them with anger, being grieved for the hardness of their hearts. (Mark 3:5)

When it dawns that the person is dead it is inevitable there should be a reaction of anger,

'My God, my God why' is a natural response. Our belief system has been radically challenged; it appears that there has been an error of magnitude. If something happens that challenges our beliefs, it is understandable we will feel angry at some point.

I recall being called out on a Saturday afternoon to the children's hospital. I strolled in only to find a mum who picked up her dead, seven-year-old daughter and thrust her into my arms and demanded 'Why?'. I've often been asked, 'what was my reply?'. In such an early context of a relationship, all one can do is to echo their call and, like the Psalmist, cry out with the people.

In the past the American Indians would shoot arrows into the air as a way of expressing their anger. Today we thrust our anger to the doctor, the hospital, the clergyperson and to God. God is fortunately big enough to take it. For ourselves in ministry, often we have to take it in silence.

For some people, life is just not fair.

I think of a friend whose first wife was dying with cancer. They had two small children at the time. As a church, we would carry out door-to-door visiting with a questionnaire This led the couple to join the church and become Christians. After the death of the wife, the father gradually grew in faith and about 10 years later he remarried a divorced woman in the church. After about 10 months, on a Sunday morning, the new wife was getting ready for church, then collapsed with a brain stem injury. Hours later I was with the husband, discussing whether the life support machine should be switched off. I still remember having to explain to the two teenagers what had happened. Words were just inadequate. Whatever I did say, it was simply not good enough.

Lightning does strike more than once and it is understandable that anger is a natural and right form of emotion to be expressed. It comes in many forms, anger at God, at yourself, at the deceased, at others who avoid you. This emotion can be hard to handle and can have a mind of its own as it bursts out unexpectedly.

> 'I know it's irrational but I'm so angry with my husband because he abandoned us'.

There are two states of anger. One is a brief, acute, situational, specific response. The other is more of an angry trait within a person that forms part of their personality. This means that some people are prone to focus upon it more than others. When it comes to grief, therefore, anger might be observed in two ways. One is an emotional response that hopefully is short lived. Another is where the anger becomes an adaptive coping strategy. In both cases the emotional reaction can erupt at any time. A person might find themselves shopping in a supermarket or just driving the car by themselves and sense an overwhelming rage within at the injustice of it all.

> 'I went to pick up the ashes at the funeral directors and just didn't know what to expect or what to say. What do you ask for? So I stood outside practising what to say. When I got them I was so surprised at the weight of the container, it was like a heavy brick the size of an old fashioned large sweet jar. I wondered if they were the right ones. It was suddenly on the way home that I felt so angry. I started shouting, screaming and swearing and crying. I was alone with no one to help me. I called her all the names under the sun, "Why have you left me to deal with all of this mess?"'

Guilt

Guilt seems to always follow anger in some form or another. Both emotions can seem so primeval and raw. It is as if you are looking for a target to hit and you choose yourself. And there can be a new reason for feeling guilty every morning. There's parental guilt, children's guilt, survivors' guilt; one can even feel guilty for planning your partner's funeral ahead of time. As beneficial as this often is, it can leave the bereaved feeling guilty, as if they wished the person dead.

The mind manifests guilt in different ways. You may survive a car crash while your partner is killed. A person's subconscious can think that by not sitting where the partner sat they were condemning them to death. Here the person is taking responsibility for the death. Others might feel they have been especially chosen somehow to live while another dies. When your best friend is killed in a war context and you survive, one has to ask, why me and not them? Others can think that life is a kind of competition in which we all compete for survival.

Guilt often has an element of exchange about it, as 'if I had done this or that, it would have been different'. What we are saying is that we are taking responsibility for the terrible loss.

Other aspects of guilt might include feeling guilty that you are euphoric, on a high, or just relieved that the person has died. Inherited guilt occurs when someone gains by the death. I think of a lady in a church who had cared for an elderly gentleman in the church. She felt she hadn't done a great deal for the man but on his death he left a considerable sum of money to her. The lady found it very hard to accept, she was anxious that others might think she had been after his money.

What is hard to handle is that you can have a different form of regret every day. It is as if you are on a roller-coaster of emotions, being tossed about with a swirl of emotions.

C. S. Lewis put it this way,

> 'No one ever told me that guilt felt so like fear. I am not afraid but the same sensation is like being afraid. The same fluttering in the stomach, the same restlessness, the yawning. I keep on swallowing'.[15]

Fear and Anxiety

By now the part of the brain that houses our emotions is getting rather full. It is filling up with pain or hurt, anger and guilt. It is understandable that what follows is a high degree of fear. In Britain we have the saying 'once bitten, twice shy'. How true this is in regards to grief. If you can be so unfortunate that someone close to you dies, what is there to say that it won't happen again?

This fear and anxiety comes from the fact that you are in a new situation where you have not been before. It is an uncomfortable place to be and is very disorientating.

Eventually people are left with a kind of sadness or solace, dullness to daily life. It's as if the colourful world has become grey.

The Anguish

The anguish…is here now…choking, physical pain, verging on hysteria, the mind racing, jumping, crying, 'no, no,no.'

The anguish…has slowed down, is taking deep breaths, breath, breathe. The mind slows, the face relaxes. The tears start again, this time slowly rocking, the violence subsiding.

The anguish…is sleeping, exhausted, functioning on reserve energy. The body has taken over calmly, working methodically.

The anguish…is awakening, a few seconds of nothingness, normality, and then flash, the realisation of what has occurred.

The anguish…is no longer alone, but being shared with others. The pain is spreading out, the grief is paired together.

---

15. Lewis, C. S. (1966). *A Grief Observed*. London: Faber & Faber.

The anguish…smiles today, once, twice. The body still functions methodically. The mind thinks a little of other things today – former things before.
The anguish…tasted food today. Talked matter-of-factly today, noticed the outside today, and the sun.
The anguish…went back to life today, normally. Thought of pain at brief, alone moments. The mind had room for other functions, ideas.
The anguish…is under the surface, of the past, something in quiet moments, alone, in silence.
The anguish…moves on.[16]

You can see that people are on a journey that is very fluid. So a person might go back to work and find that they handle situations each day very differently. One day the person might hear someone say that they are 'sorry for their loss', which results in the bereaved breaking down in tears and having to go home. Another day when they encounter someone, they might get tears in the eyes and need to withdraw to their office for a short period, or they might just get butterflies in the stomach that unsettles them for the rest of the day. Another day they may feel perfectly calm. There seems to be no rhyme or reason why each day is different, it just is that way. It is as variable as the weather. It is helpful to inform people of this fluidity as it enables them to be prepared for the ever-changing 'weather of feelings' of their grief and behaviour.

> 'I have forgotten the reason; there is a spread over everything a vague sense of wrongness, of something amiss. Like in those dreams where nothing terrible occurs – nothing that would sound even remarkable if you told it at breakfast time – but the atmosphere, the taste, of the thing is deadly. So with this. I see the rowan berries reddening and don't know for a moment why they, of all things, should be depressing. I hear a clock strike and some quality it always had before has gone out of the sound. What's wrong to make it so flat, shabby, worn-out looking? Then I remember…'.[17]

16. Harvey, A. (1996). The Anguish. *Bereavement*. Mar./Apr.
17. Lewis, C. S. (1966). *A Grief Observed*. London: Faber & Faber.

All of these feelings can lead to a sense of simply being overwhelmed, which brings a desire to escape it all and join the deceased.

> 'You can't understand it unless you experience it. You can talk about death and dying, but from the moment my partner died, I knew I was different. Something had changed within me. In a way I died within, I had this deep, deep ache to pass away as well.'

The Bible has given us an insight to the many emotions that engulf a bereaved person.

HURT needs to be listened to as the beatitudes tell us. It is only as we mourn and express these feelings to others that we are comforted (Matthew Ch 5:v4).

ANGER needs to be dealt with. Scripture tells us not to let the sun go down on our anger (Ephesians Ch 4:26). In other words we mustn't keep it inside, lingering. This will only do us long-term harm. However, we are also told to be careful otherwise the anger will lash out to others and might do them harm (Psalm 4:4). We have several examples of angry people in the Bible (Moses, Exodus Ch 32:15-35, Jonah Ch 3–4. David was averted from anger by the help of others (1 Samuel 25:32). Anger therefore needs to be constructively released without it leading to sin and further harm of self or others. We are told to seek help in others who can help us to manage these feelings.

GUILT is a subject that is well covered both in the Old Testament and in the New Testament. In the Old Testament we are told that we can indeed be engulfed with guilt (Psalm 38). We are to acknowledge guilt but also to do something with the guilt. Guilt offerings were made as a way of moving forward (Leviticus Ch 5:14–Ch 6:7). In the New Testament there is a clear message that God wants to forgive and wipe away all guilt from our eyes. 1 John Ch 1:5–Ch 2:2 is a positive statement that God wants no one to feel guilty or trapped in real or false guilt.

FEAR is something we are told that is cast out when we experience perfect love (1 John Ch 4:18). This kind of love needs to be manifested through the church in its care of others as we seek to bring security to people's lives at an insecure time of life.

ANXIETY seems to be calmed in the Scripture with the knowledge of a God who cares for us even through stormy times (Psalm 23 and Matthew Ch 6:25-34). Prayer here plays an important part of bringing a release from anxiety (Philippians Ch 4: 4-9).

Physical reactions

Physical reactions involve a range of somatic complaints that the bereaved take to the doctor, resulting from their anxiety. They include:

- Headaches
- Muscular pains
- Nausea
- Tiredness
- Exhaustion
- Loss of appetite
- Insomnia
- Heart palpitations
- Digestive problems
- Dizziness
- Nightmares
- Constriction of throat
- Impeded concentration
- Poor memory
- Damp hands and dry mouth

For some, elucidating care for such physical ailments allows them to receive support that is not threatening. It is a very valued form of expressing grief in a physical way. Particularly with young people, this physical expression can be released through sport and outdoor activities. For others, it comes through their work environment or sorting out property and belongings of the deceased. It is common to see the bereaved in a very disorganised state at first. The jigsaw of life has been thrown up into the air and the pieces are scattered all over the floor. Some are turned over while others seem to be missing and some pieces just don't seem to fit together any more. Eventually some order returns to their lives although for some a deep physical ache remains. Alongside these reactions is often the deadening of any sexual desire. Sometimes this is the last issue to be resolved for a person, especially with the death of a partner. However, some may find that the death of a partner heightens their sexual need. This can be an uncomfortable feeling and one that is difficult to talk about with others. If pastoral carers are aware of these potential feelings, we can be brave enough to raise the subject. A bereaved person may be embarrassed or they may be relieved at having the chance to talk about it. No harm is done if someone doesn't want to engage with the subject whereas if no one talks about it the person could feel very trapped with their feelings, which only isolates them further.

Cognitive reactions

Cognitive reactions manifest themselves in various forms:

- Sensing the deceased's presence
- Dreaming
- Fantasising
- Obsessive thinking
- Inability to concentrate
- Apathy
- Replaying the story of the loss over and over in the mind
- Disorientation and confusion

All of this clearly has impact upon how a person functions out in the world, particularly at school or work. We need to see that this reaction is not about denial of the loss but a valued way of both holding on to the deceased as well as trying to make sense of what has happened.

In the early stages, belief and disbelief frequently operate simultaneously. Looking for the loved one is very common. It has been commonly correlated to the reaction when people experience the removal of a limb. The limb feels as if it is still there even though you know it isn't.

People sense an invisible presence of the deceased. They smell, hear and sense the deceased; it brings doubt that they are really dead. 'Perhaps they are still alive' – this brings a temporary comfort.

Dreaming of the deceased is also common with very vivid, often comforting dreams. This can be an issue with those who don't dream, as they feel robbed, or a sense of sadness when the dreams cease to occur, creating an additional loss.

There is the hope, however irrational, that perhaps God (even if you don't believe in him) will change his mind, 'if only'. Part of this manifests itself in the way people hold on to belongings as a temporary comfort as though holding on to the deceased's presence. My elderly aunty, whose husband died 30 years ago, still has his trilby hat sitting on the chair in the hallway of the bungalow. Others can suddenly think they have seen the deceased alive, perhaps in a supermarket or busy shopping complex.

> 'I recall visiting my father each weekend after my mother's death. My mother had been treated for cancer and the chemotherapy had caused her to lose her hair and so wear a wig. After mum's death, the one thing dad did not change in the house was the wig sitting on a polystyrene bust in the window. I would find myself walking through the back door, seeing the wig and about to say, "where's mum?".'

It can feel rather like going to work via a particular route for many years only to find that there has been some roadworks and a detour. Alas, no matter which way you turn, the road will not allow you to get to the old destination. But old habits die hard and you find yourself keeping on driving down familiar roads, hoping it will lead to the deceased.

At first it can be hard to picture the deceased. The more you try the harder it seems to get. This can seem very strange; here you are thinking constantly about them yet somehow their visual presence eludes you. It seems only as you ease up on the trying to hold and remember that their face comes back to you crystal clear.

Behavioural encounters

However the bereaved react emotionally, it eventually manifests itself through some kind of behavioural response. This might be through:

- Regular crying
- Ongoing illnesses
- A change of belief system, e.g. change of religious views
- Ongoing searching
- Obsessive behaviour
- More accident prone
- Social withdrawal
- Increased use of drugs such as smoking and alcohol
- The need for a ritual related to the loss

In order to fully realise a death, it is imperative that the bereaved see some evidence of it. I think of a family whose son was believed to have drowned but the body wasn't found. Part of them believed he was dead but, as I interviewed them, there was a clear hope that it was all a mistake, one day he would walk into the house and say 'hi'.

Often people will say, ' I want to remember her as she was; at work, in the house or garden'. The problem is that 'the way she was' or 'as he used to be' is about how the person was when alive but the person is not living, the person is dead. That's why memorial or funeral services are helpful as you are less likely to subconsciously deny the death if you have taken part in a final service. This also raises issues for us in these services in not colluding with people that the person is not dead. Increasingly today, people seem to want a funeral service that gives the impression that the person hasn't died.

With traumatic or sudden loss, the bereaved can have a very clear recall of the events just before, during and after the death.

> 'I still see him there dead, why couldn't I save him? I have to just hold myself together, I know its just how life is, but I feel abandoned.'

There is a kind of unreality of the reality. Each time a person tells the story of what has happened, they journey back into the experience. They find themselves on a roller-coast, where they can neither sit comfortably with the situation nor let go of it. The bereaved are in a time of re-aligning themselves, still emotionally engaged with the deceased despite the absence of the physical presence. They meander through each day fulfilling the basics with a sense of emptiness at heart.

> 'I feel I have a plate full of emotions on my hands. It's all so primitive, I just want to lash out at everyone and at myself.'

The bereaved now find themselves in a new situation, where their relationships both with themselves and others feel totally different. There is a heightened sense of awareness of nature, trees, flowers, a real need to get some fresh air and to get out and walk it off. Here there is a changed relationship with oneself, with others and even with the environment around you.

> 'You can't understand it unless you experience it. You can talk about it, but from the moment my husband died, I knew something had

changed within me. It felt as if something inside me had died forever. I longed to be with my husband.'

Social impact

There is often a change of perspective in how a bereaved person relates to the community and wider society. For some, they find their way of coping is to go on a crusade, they find a new career promoting some cause or another. This might be by starting a charity or writing a book about their experience. This kind of activity provides a link with the deceased. This is a valid way of manifesting grief that is often not recognised. This can in the long run have both positive and negative consequences. If it proves to be a way of adjusting to the loss, then it can be seen in a positive light; but if a person can't stop promoting their activities such that their whole identity is wrapped up in this action, then it can be detrimental to their long-term well-being.

Almost without exception, the bereaved person changes his or her priorities in regard to social participation and personal goals. What was once important may no longer have the same importance, in fact it may now have no value at all. So that the person has now gone from being disorganised to reorganising their life in a different way.

> 'What really matter is people, their relationships, love and caring, nothing else really matters, money, power and all that.'

> 'I'm not as social as I used to be, I don't like small talk,
> I was always a little that way but now more so.'

Grief is an overwhelming drive in people's lives when an attached figure is removed from them by death. But another strong drive in life is sexual desires. Sexuality is an important part of life for the formation of families and brings intimacy and companionship. What happens when one's partner dies and this intensity is removed? The sexual intimacy with a partner gives off deep psychological messages. It says that I am not alone, I am accepted, warts and all, I am wanted, needed and have something to offer. A bereaved widower has many needs with the death of a partner. He has to deal with work, financial issues, perhaps the children, transport problems to school as well as the cooking and house-keeping. In the midst of all this there is also the deep need for companionship and sexual fulfilment.

One might assume that people's sexual desire diminishes with bereavement but this is not always the case. Some can find sex a way of getting in touch with their deep feelings or seeing it as a safe way of releasing these feelings. It can certainly create a tension within couples after the death of a relative or friend. For the widower, he may have great responsibility suddenly but he will also have a new freedom to engage with other individuals. What can result is that another person is brought into the family to almost resolve the grief within the house. A widower may be trying to balance finding a helper who will handle his children's issues while also bringing a deeper physical fulfilment to himself. The reality is of course that one unique individual cannot possibly replace another human being. The danger is that a man's physical needs can sometimes outweigh the needs of the family as a whole, which inevitably results in a stepmother who might not come up to the standard required for grief-ridden children. It is not surprising why we have so many fairy tales and children's stories involving wicked stepmothers.

For a young widow, she has just as many issues to resolve socially, personally, economically and sexually. In her need she may well swing to being over-aggressive or too dependent upon her children to fill the gap. There may also be the need to downsize the family home which might take her and the children away from their local church and community where they have the potential for the most support through the difficult times ahead. Statistically, young men tend to remarry more quickly than women, especially when they have children.

For older widows and widowers the problem may seem less pressurised. There is no rush to provide that additional support for children. What becomes a bigger problem is that, as an older person, we are more settled in our ways of behaviour and expectations. Two people in mid life or older coming together on a twenty-four hour basis can create tensions.

In the midst of these complex situations, we have the influence of chemical hormones, which can be released in grief-stricken individuals and give them an extended drive that is not characteristic for the individual. All of this can lead to behaviour that seems irrational to friends and on lookers.

In all of these cases the church can play an important part. We can first understand and at least try and appreciate what is going in a bereaved widow or widower's life. Secondly, we can provide an anchor of contact and support. Thirdly, we can help to protect a vulnerable individual from the danger of entering unhealthy relationships before they are ready to re-engage in an intimate relationship. Lastly, we can begin dialogue with the individual about subjects that family and friends may well avoid talking about. Knowing that someone understands that there may be sexual, emotional issues flooding the mind can be reassuring and can provide a release just through talking therapy.

Intellectual adjustment

When the scaffold of our assumptive worldview has collapsed around us, sooner or later we will have to start to rebuild it such that it gives us a way of coping with the future. We soon begin to seek answers to the questions that trouble us and need to pursue them till we find satisfactory answers. Part of this is coming to terms with the fact that life is not about holding good cards but playing those you do hold well. Here there is a recognition that disasters and tragedy do happen, but that we mustn't allow them to pervade our own persona and view of life. We need to rationalise the fact that good and bad things happen in life and while recognising that disillusionment exists, there is also hope. Here we are developing a faith in ourselves to handle life. Faith in my ability to perceive potential dangers and an ability to handle whatever life throws at me. We are now reformulating new assumptions about life in such a way that enables us to re-engage with out lives back in the community.

'It has changed my relationship with myself, others and the environment I live in.'

Spiritual reflection

Part of our intellectual adjustment includes our spiritual awareness of life. Our spiritual awareness of how we find meaning and purpose in life is certainly reviewed if not shaken to the core. Our transcendent system of belief may centre previously upon religious grounds or more on a philosophical framework. Some losses are not significant enough to challenge our belief system while other losses are so deep that they lead us to reconstruct the meaning of life to take into account this traumatic event. Clearly, if the scaffold of your belief system incorporates the circumstances of your loss, then your belief will sustain you on your journey. However, many find, regardless of what their belief system might be based upon, that they need to re-evaluate afresh what they think spiritually.

- If your belief system holds that wrong behaviour leads to serious consequences and your son dies through an overdose, then you might find that your belief system doesn't change.
- Some might have believed that their God would not allow bad things to happen to them, so that when a close relative unexpectedly dies, it leaves them feeling confused with their belief system. They will have to adjust their understanding of God. They may either totally throw out their belief system and

stop believing in God or modify how they see Him. God may still be a reality but less relevant to their daily lives.
- Others will find that their faith is challenged but eventually their understanding is increased and faith deepened. A key issue in one's spirituality will be the perspective a person has in regards to heaven and life after death. More will be said about this in Chapter 15.

'You are still a fragment of who you were, it just becomes a part of your story.'

Reflections

Think about your or a friend's experience of bereavement. How have you seen changes in the following aspects?

- Emotional
- Physical
- Cognitive
- Behavioural
- Social
- Intellectual
- Spiritual

SEVEN

The history of grief theories

Let's now put all of this into a historical context of grief theories.

At the turn of the 20th century Freud was one of the first to begin to write about grief as a concept. That is not to say that there were no writings about bereavement before this. Indeed, many people wrote in stories or poems about their loss. But Freud was the first to introduce the term of 'object loss' in which he felt the aim of grief was to break the bond between the subject and the object.

Eric Lindemann in the 1940s observed war veterans and also saw how people reacted after a huge fire that killed 500 people.[18] He discovered that there was a uniform reaction that included:

- Somatic problems – heart palpitations, loss of appetite, digestive problems, dizziness, nightmares, constriction of throat, muscular pain, impeded concentration, poor memory, damp hands, dry mouth, insomnia
- Preoccupation with the deceased
- Guilt
- Hostile reaction
- Inability to be organised

If they reacted in this way, Lindemann called this 'normal grief'. Here, the bereaved would have dealt with three aspects of their lives:

---

18. Lindemann, E. (1944). Symptomatology and management of acute grief. *American Journal of Psychiatry*, 101, pp.141–8.

- Deliverance from the past by recognising the signs of loss
- Rebuilding their 'present' with what's left with all its changes
- Experiencing the future with new possibilities and new pathways

However, if they did not react in this way the bereaved would be called 'pathological' and would require professional help.

This led to a debate about whether grief was a disease.[19] John Bowlby in the meanwhile had been looking at the 'attachment theory' and observing children's reactions when separated from their chief caregiver.[20] Bowlby was key in changing the way we relate to patients in hospital by recognising that the patient (especially children) needs to feel safe in a new environment and therefore needs access to their relatives. Bowlby recognised an 'alarm reaction' occurring when a person is separated from their close attachments. This alarm reaction included:

1. Shock, numbness
2. Yearning
3. Disorganisation
4. Reorganisation

Colin Murray-Parkes took Bowlby's theories of attachment and observed widows' reactions.[21] He found that widows over 54 years of age had a 40 per cent increased chance of mortality in the six months after loss. You can see where we get the term of 'dying from a broken heart'. This break of a close bond leads to distrust in other relationships and can lead to isolation, hence the need for support. This led to the beginning of the charity Cruse, a bereavement support agency. Murray-Parkes observed the following reactions:

---

19. Engel, G. (1961). Is grief a disease? A challenge for medical research. *Psychosomatic Medicine*. 23, pp.18–22.
20. Bowlby, J. (1969). *Attachment & Loss, Vol.1, Attachment*. New York: Basic Books.
21. Parkes, C. M. (1972). *Bereavement Studies of Grief in Adult Life*. London: Tavistock.

1. Alarm
2. Search – Mitigation
3. Identity
4. Anger and guilt
5. New identity

Here, the grief reaction was seen very much as a natural process.

The American J. William Worden produced a different approach in the 1980s with his 'Tasks' model. Worden saw grief as something the bereaved has to work at in order to move on.[22] This will include:

1. Accepting the loss. This involves coming to terms with the finality and irreversibility of the loss.
2. Experiencing the pain.
3. Adjusting to the new environment. This might involve adjusting to a change of role in the home or acquiring new skills, e.g. going to a funeral director, organising a funeral or handling accounts for the first time.
4. Withdrawing emotional energy and reinvesting in new relationships. This can involve thinking about who the dead person is now in their lives? What significance do they now have to their daily life?

Grief is often a time in which people get in contact with their 'true selves'.

Irvin Yalom (1980) came up with four concepts which we have to come to terms with in life – death, freedom, isolation and meaninglessness.[23] When we enter grief, Yalom believed we have to deal with all four of these issues in some form to be able to move forward.

22. Worden, J. (1982). *Grief Counselling and Grief Therapy: A Handbook for the Mental Health Practitioners*. New York: Springer.
23. Yalam, I. (1980). *Existential Psychotherapy*. New York: Basic Books.

Grief theorists over the latter 20th century tried to express what was happening to the bereaved and kept adding minor additions to the earlier theories. Theresa Rando saw three distinct operations. First, there is a reorientation of one's relationship with the deceased.[24] This stimulates the acute period of grief as one acknowledges that the current ties can no longer be maintained. Secondly, the bereaved has to redefine their own identity after the loss. Thirdly, they need to modify how they see the world and adjust to the many changes necessitated by the loss. This is expressed in the 6 R's:

1. Recognising the loss: acknowledging and understanding the death (avoidance phase)
2. Reacting to separation: experiencing the pain (confrontation phase)
3. Recollecting and re-experiencing the deceased and their relationship
4. Relinquishing the old attachments to the deceased and the old assumptive worldview
5. Readjusting to move adaptively into the new world without forgetting the old (accommodation phase)
6. Reinvesting in new relationships

A very useful model is the Stroebe and Schut Dual Model.[25] Here we see grief as a pendulum that oscillates between focusing upon loss issues and moving forward with new initiatives. We see this in action when a bereaved person finds themselves engulfed in the pain of grief then goes and makes a cup of tea. Reaching for the cup, the person sees the deceased's mug and suddenly finds themselves swinging back into emotion and tears.

---

24. Rando, T. (1986) *Introduction in Parental Loss of a Child*. Illinios: Research Press.
25. Stroebe, M. and Schut, H. (1999). A model for coping with grief and its practical applications for the bereavement counsellor. In Payne, S., Horne, S. and Relf, M. *Loss and Bereavement*. Buckingham: Open University Press.

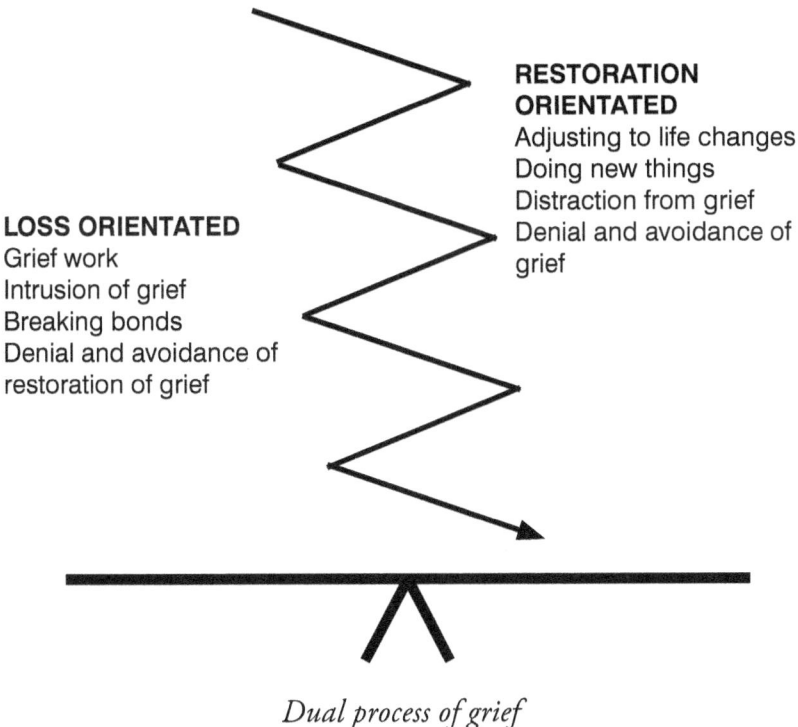

Dual process of grief

C. S. Lewis expresses this well when his wife Helen dies.

It feels like being mildly drunk, or concussed. There is a sort of invisible blanket between the world and me. I find it hard to take in what everyone says. Or perhaps, hard to want to take it in. It is so uninteresting…I dread the moment when the house is empty.

There are moments, most expectedly, when something inside me tries to assure me that I don't really mind so much, not very much at all… then comes a sudden jab of red-hot memory and all this 'common sense' vanishes like an ant in the mouth of the furnace.

No one ever told me about the laziness of grief. Not only writing but even reading a letter is too much.

In 1996, Dennis Klass, Phyllis Silverman and Steven Nickman coined the concept of the Continuous Bond theory.[26]

This model recognises that people do not seem to totally disengage from the deceased. Their emotional bond does not seem to sever totally. This can be seen particularly in parishes with graveyards. It is common to see people visiting the grave on a regular basis tending it with love and care. This shows that people may be getting their lives reorganised but are still very much thinking and relating in some capacity to the deceased. Here the loss is accommodated within the person. They carry it within themselves and don't fully de-attach from it. Ongoing relationship with the deceased can be a healthy part of reconstructing. It involves renegotiating the meaning of the loss rather than letting go of the deceased. This renegotiating becomes part of the person's ongoing life experience. Here, the bereaved needs to:

1. Make an effort to locate the deceased, e.g. religious beliefs play a part here helping to locate the deceased in an afterlife.
2. Experience the deceased, e.g. thinking or dreaming about the deceased.
3. Remembering the deceased. Having an opportunity of acknowledging the deceased and talking about them. Birthday and Christmas are all times to acknowledge one's loss.
4. Attaching to the deceased through transitional objects. Objects help here in connecting one realm of experience to another, visiting the grave can help or having photographs visible in the home.

We now might like to think about these different theories in a simplistic way, in the manner of a series of journeys.

---

26. Klass, D., Silverman, R. and Nickman, J. (1996). *Continuing Bonds*. Washington: Taylor & Francis.

There is a ***train journey*** (a process of grief). You get on the train when death occurs and venture through railway stations called shock, numb, disbelief, disorganisation, yearning and eventually reorganisation and re-engagement. This is seen as a natural process that you don't drive or control.

The bereaved only needs help if the train, for whatever reason, gets stuck in a railway station for a long period.

A ***car journey*** (grief work) that goes through the same towns; the only difference being that you are driving the car. The speed and pace are in your control. You can even vary which town you visit and how long you choose to stay there.

A ***long walk*** (continuous bond) that is a life-changing event and can take all of your life.

All of this only shows us that grief is not something we can explain through simple theories and expect the theory to sum up all of what is actually happening to an individual. People and their relationships are complex as has been earlier said. We also need to acknowledge there are other aspects to all of this.

Do grief theories work?

As helpful as different grief theories may be to give us a window on what is happening in an individual's loss experience, they also have their weaknesses.

- Death is mysterious and is beyond the concept of stages.

It's not just a matter of going from A to B but requires a time of reflection, wonder and searching to find your own answers. People may have to learn to live without answers.

- Grief can be cyclical not linear.

It's not a checklist. Many find themselves in cul-de-sacs of anger, self-pity or depression. Each day it can seem as if you are going around and around the same thoughts. It's no good saying, 'I've done anger so I'm now moving onto something else.' It's more one step forward and three steps back. It is more like a whirlpool experience in which you might feel angry, sad, lonely, experiencing longing, laughter, pain and calm all on the same day.

- Grief is more about an experience than just getting over the loss.

The theories too often have focused on how the bereaved survive. Theories tend to be about getting people back functioning into society rather than seeing how a person can encounter the experience of loss as fully and meaningfully as possible.

- Theories can give a false sense of security.

Human beings are very good at finding answers and categorising situations. It gives us understanding and a sense of control. We feel far more vulnerable when we don't understand something. The danger with theories is that they may be just giving us a false sense of security that we understand what is happening. The danger is that this diminishes the unique experience of the bereaved person. It also leaves those who never find satisfactory answers nowhere to turn.

- There is a sociological response to grief.

Some find themselves in new jobs, become pioneers of charities and causes. Who are we to tell them they are in denial or should move on?

- Grief counselling can make people victims, vulnerable and dependent upon so called experts.

This is not always enabling. This is where self-help support groups can be liberating. Here, each member of the group can understand each other and help to normalize their experience. The only proviso is that a person is allowed to feel able to leave the group without any member of the group feeling let down. The ground rules need to be clear that there is flexibility about being a part of such a group with no strings attached.

- There are more people involved than the chief mourner.

Too often theories have focused only on the chief mourner. Loss can only be understood in a broader social context. What about the community's reaction, the role of grandparents, neighbours, etc?

- Grief is more about 'meaning-making' rather than an emotional response.

We are more than emotional beings. People are on a pilgrimage of discovery and change, formulating their beliefs. Finding a way forward. A Pastor's role is to help a person not just deal with emotion but to help them search for meaning out of the experience of loss. Grief is a friend enabling you to reflect upon life.

Encountering people in grief is therefore an exceptional opportunity to help people into spiritual growth. With sensitive care, people can be nurtured in faith. However, if we mismanage it, we can cause them to stumble and fall away. We need to help the bereaved to create a loving, growing relationship with the dead that recognises the new psychological or spiritual dimensions of the relationship. Here we are recognising the importance of 'creating continuity' with the deceased. Robert Neimeyer defines mourning in this new approach where it is seen as,

> 'Involving the transformation of the meanings and affects associated with one's relationship to the lost person. The goal of which is to permit one's survival without the other, while at the same time ensuring a continuing experience of relationship with

the deceased. The work of mourning is rarely done in isolation and may involve active engagement with fellow mourners and other survivors...thus mourning involves a reorganization of the survivor's sense of self as a key function of the process.'[27]

This approach highlights the importance of treating each mourner as unique, exploring the value of the deceased within one's life and the importance of others in a person's recovery.

This is a process of psychological reintegration impelled by the contradictory desire to recover what has been lost and to escape from painful reminders. There are two important innate dispositions here: the need for attachment and the need to conceptualise. These combine to form habits of feelings, behaviours and perceptions which create structures of meaning enabling people to predict, interpret and assimilate their environment. So when loss occurs, it challenges the meaning of life.

This approach comes from the cognitive science that has shown that we organize our life events into stories with a plot structure with beginnings, middles and endings. Self-narrative is the way we think, feel and act. It is like something that we wear. These small micro-narratives of our lives lead to a macro-narrative of who we are. The fascination with soap stories on TV in a sense helps us here as we watch other lives (perhaps extremes) which give us time to reflect upon our own story. In ministry we meet all kinds of narratives in peoples lives. There are disorganised narratives, e.g. trauma; dissociated narratives, which often include silent stories such as incest, suicide; and dominant narratives that constrict, e.g. depression, where the self is problem-saturated, for instance through the loss of a child, which can become an all encompassing loss.

27. Neimeyer, R. (2001). *Meaning, Reconstruction & the Experience of Loss.* Washington, DC: American Psychological Association.

Summary of Grief Theories

Grief theories	Phase 1	Pase 2	Phase 3	Phase 4
Engel 1964	Shock Disbelief	Developing awareness	Restitution Rediscovering	Outcome
Bowlby 1969–80	Numbness	Yearning Searching	Disorganised	Reorganised
Parkes 1972	Numbing	Yearning Pining	Depression	Recovery
Worden 1982	Accepting loss	Experiencing pain of loss	Adjusting to new environment	Withdraw emotion & reinvesting
Rando 1985	Avoidance	Confrontation	Accommodate	Readjusting
Stroebe and Schut 1995	Loss orientated	Grief work attending to life changes	Breaking ties Distraction from grief	Restoration orientated
Klass, Silverman & Nickman 1996	Locating the deceased	Experiencing the deceased	Reaching for connection	Remembering through transitional objects
Sanders 1999	Shock	Awareness of loss	Conservation & withdrawal	Healing & renewal
Neimeyer 2001	Disruption of narrative of life story	Change in personal view of self and others	Making sense of the experience	Moving onto a new chapter of life integrating the deceased into the narrative
Your experience	?	?	?	?

Reflections

- Which theory can you identify with the most?
- Is there an approach that fits more with your Christian belief?
- Can you recognise someone at a particular point in grief?
- Have you observed how people react differently to the same loss?

Reflecting upon your own life,

- Is your story chronological or does it follow a different structure?
- How did you decide when a chapter ended or began?
- When did your story begin?
- Is there a need for a foreword?
- Is your story evolutionary, gradual, sudden?
- If it was a novel, would it be a comedy, adventure, romance?
- What are the major trends/themes in your story?
- Where is the story anchored?
- What role does your faith play within your story?
- How does prayer affect your story?
- Is God present in every chapter?
- Who is the primary author, is there a co-author, others who deserve credit/blame?
- Who is the relevant audience for your narrative? Who would enjoy it? Who would want to edit it?
- How different would it be if you wrote it as a child, teenager or in the future?
- How different would the story be if it was written by others?
- What is the title of your self-narrative?

Part Two

Our involvement with people comes from our pastoral ability and not as a counsellor or a bereavement specialist. We may well use counselling techniques and bereavement listening skills, but this is not our primary task. We are involved with individuals because of our role within the church in some pastoral-care capacity. This clearly influences the way we approach the bereaved. In Part Two we will look at the role our faith plays when we encounter a loss situation. We will see how our faith seldom remains the same after such a major event in our lives. We will then look at a typical Christian approach in coming alongside another and offering our own unique presence. We do, of course, have a model of care that comes from Christ and so we will observe how Jesus cared and supported Mary and Martha at the time of Lazarus's death. Alas, we don't have the full skills and abilities of Jesus and therefore need guidance about when we are out of our depth and need to refer to other people with different skills to those we have ourselves. So we will clarify what we can achieve and offer guidance with an assessment tool, which will help us to know when we need to direct the bereaved to other practitioners. We will briefly look at how prayer can both support the bereaved and sustain us in this ministry. Lastly, we will look at a few specific issues that a Christian carer engages with: what happens when faith reaches rock bottom, what is our view of life after death and our involvement at funerals. Some pastoral carers will be called upon to lead a funeral, so we need to be aware of our specific role at such times.

EIGHT

The role of faith

So what difference does faith make? It will depend upon your assumptive worldview and what you expect of God. I read recently a piece in a Christian magazine, which told a story of how the day after a Christian representative had left a village in Tanzania there had been a bank robbery and many had been killed. The article ended with praising God for the Christian's safety. This kind of theology says 'I'm favoured.' I don't know what it says about those who were killed? Is our theology one that says 'it won't happen to me'? This would be a silly approach and is certainly not scriptural, but many of us function as if it's true.

What we do know is:

- God knows the meaning of grief and loss. The Bible is full of stories about death and loss. Of course it climaxes with Jesus' own death that leaves the disciples traumatised and Mary engulfed in pain. Jesus himself expressed this grief when he visited Mary and Martha after Lazarus had died. Despite Jesus being aware he was going to bring Lazarus back to life, he nevertheless expressed the pain of grief as he wept with the two sisters.

Where have you laid him?' he asked.
'Come and see, Lord' they replied
Jesus wept.
Then the Jews said, 'See how he loved him.'

John 12:34-36

- We accept that in the creativity of things, nature, life and death are entwined. Some deaths are celebrated – how was your turkey at Christmas? Try visiting a butcher on Christmas eve morning and you will see people queueing to collect their meat with a sense of pleasure in their eyes, yet they choose to ignore the fact that they are surrounded by death.
- We discriminate in our attitude to death. Death is going on all around the world but we take little notice of it till it affects ourselves. It is the emotional investment in the life of another that makes us vulnerable to the feelings of pain.
- The biblical view helps us to put death into perspective – God is involved, e.g. Psalm 90.

'All our days pass away under your wrath;
we finish our years with a moan.
The length of our days is seventy years – or eighty,
 if we have the strength: yet their span is but trouble and sorrow,
for they quickly pass, and we fly away.' Psalm 90:9-10

- God doesn't owe us a civilised 70 years. Indeed, depending upon what part of the world you come from, your life expectancy will vary considerably.
- Death comes from many causes, e.g. the judicial consequence of Ananias and Sapphira (Acts 5:1-11) or an imbalance between the psychological and the physical forces of life (1 Cor 11:27-32).
- Many deaths result from the natural law of human existence, e.g. suppressed anger, jealousy, guilt, etc.
- Some deaths advance the kingdom of God, although it may not be recognised at the time. Martyrdom is a concept that the church has recognised since its birth, e.g. the stoning of Stephen (Acts 7:54–8:1).

So what is a healthy Christian grief?

- Healthy Christian grief involves mourning
  The Beatitudes look to a healing process of mourning. 'Blessed are they that mourn' (Matthew 5:4). This involves healthy emotions. The Beatitudes generally present a guide for accepting the resources of the universe through disciplined, mature and responsive behaviour. Through a series of paradoxes, people can develop skills that can lead to the highest form of self-realisation. Jesus does acknowledge a form of blessedness in grief. He looks beyond death and the pain of grief to the healing process of mourning. Those who mourn well will emerge stronger and more comforted in life. This clearly involves personal responsibility. This means we mustn't hide our grief away. More recently, society has moved to having mini funerals without the coffin. There is a growing trend to have the funeral service quietly at the crematorium and then have a service of thanksgiving afterwards in church. Often this is to aid the logistics so that the family can meet everyone afterwards at the wake. However, it does remove the coffin from sight, the one component that says to the world,

  'Here is death, here is our death, let us mourn together.'

  Increasingly funerals can seem more about celebrating life than acknowledging death, all of which can lead to a kind of denial. Christian grief is about facing the loss and expressing the emotion that is attached to this reality. The psalmist had a good appreciation of lament and the need to cry out to God with full conviction.

- Healthy Christian grief is committed to the truth
  This means we need to recognise the fabric and structure of the universe that God has placed us in. Jesus endeavoured not to break

the natural law of his earth. He refused to change the molecular structure of cells to change stone into bread, or violate the laws of gravity. Instead he faced the journey that led to the cross and death. There were of course his miracles that did change the structure of water to wine or multiplied a few fish and loaves to feed many. Also his healings must have brought about a unique configuration to the body. However, all of these miracles, we are told, were signposts pointing to the specialness of Jesus so that we would grasp the ultimate significance of the cross and resurrection. There was a balance here between bringing in the kingdom while respecting the physical order of God's creation. There is a mystery here we have to grapple with while we respect the creator and natural order he has created. Jesus acknowledged that the sun shone on the just and the unjust and that the rain fell on the wise as well as the foolish. So we are called to live disciplined lives that are responsible within the cause and effect framework of life. Here we use God's full resources offered to us to master our lives through Christ's teachings and the power of his spirit. This is the beginning of healing when we are able to hear and accept the fact that someone has died. Jesus is 'the way, the truth and the life' (John 14:6); to find a way forward into healing requires a journey that will pass through 'the truth', whatever that might mean. There are aspects of death that we wish to avoid in the early period of loss, but sooner or later we will have to face the realities we are avoiding. The truth leads us to taking personal responsibility, to understand things as they are and not to distort our thinking or by escaping into blaming others or God himself.

- Healthy Christian grief leads to the furtherance of the Kingdom
It is as we recover and head in a new direction that we are able to care for others in grief. This means we are on a journey from

an inner focusing on our pain of loss to an outward focusing on care of others.

Praise be to the God and father of our lord Jesus Christ, the Father of compassion and the God of all comfort who comforts us in all our troubles, so that we can comfort those in trouble with the comfort we ourselves have received from God. (2 Cor 1:3-4)

- Healthy Christian Grief embraces hope
  We believe in a God of creativity who wastes nothing. Whether you believe that life after death is instant ('today you will be with me in paradise', Luke 23:43) or at the second coming, what is certain is a reunion with the Lord. It is this hope that is a comfort to believers.

Brothers, we do not want you to be ignorant about those who fall asleep, or to grieve like the rest of men, who have no hope. We believe that Jesus died and rose again and so we believe that God will bring with Jesus those who have fallen asleep in him. According to the Lord's own word, we tell you that we who are still alive, who are left till the coming of the Lord, will certainly not precede those who have fallen asleep. For the Lord himself will come down from heaven, with a loud command, with the voice of the archangel and with the trumpet call of God, and the dead in Christ will rise first. After that, we who are still alive and are left will be caught up together with them in the clouds to meet the Lord in the air. And so we will be with the Lord forever. Therefore encourage each other with these words. (1 Thessalonians 4:13-18)

- Healthy Christian grief acknowledges God as shepherd
  A biblical picture of a shepherd involves searching, healing, support, guidance, and reconciliation to troubled people. There are times when we just don't want to be found but that doesn't mean we can't acknowledge that God is still searching for us to bring us home to safety.

For thus says the Lord God: I myself will search for my sheep, and will seek them out. As shepherds seek out their flocks when they are among their scattered sheep, so I will seek out my sheep. I will rescue them from all the places to which they have been scattered on a day of clouds and thick darkness. I will bring them out from the peoples and gather them from the countries, and will bring them into their own land; and I will feed them on the mountains of Israel, by the watercourses, and in all the inhabited parts of the land. I will feed them with good pasture, and the mountain heights of Israel shall be their pasture; there they shall lie down in good grazing land, and they shall feed on rich pasture on the mountains of Israel. I myself will be the shepherd of my sheep, and I will make them lie down, says the Lord God. I will seek the lost, and I will bring back the strayed, and I will bind up the injured, and I will strengthen the weak, but the fat and the strong I will destroy. I will feed them with justice. (Ezekiel 34:11-16)

- Healthy Christian grief acknowledges God as a carer
  There is so much in scripture that reveals God's concern for the widow, the alien and the fatherless.

Do not take advantage of a widow or an orphan. If you do and they cry out to me, I will certainly hear their cry. (Exodus 22:22-23)
Do not deprive the alien or the fatherless of justice, or take the cloak of the widow as a pledge. Remember that you were slaves in Egypt and the LORD your God redeemed you from there. That is why I command you to do this. When you are harvesting in your field and you overlook a sheaf, do not go back to get it. Leave it for the alien, the fatherless and the widow, so that the LORD your God may bless you in all the work of your hands. (Deuteronomy 24:17-19)
A father to the fatherless, a defender of widows, is God in his holy dwelling. (Psalm 68:5)

- Healthy Christian grief embraces God's creativity
  God has placed us in a creative world with its seasons of spring,

summer, autumn and winter. We experience times of new birth, growth, fruitfulness and renewal, fallowness and decline. A grieving person can be aided by being immersed into God's creative order and becoming one with the environment. The creative world of art, music and nature is a healing aid. Hence the grieving spiritual self can be developed through engagement with art, music and spending time in the garden or out with nature. There is also the opportunity to perform altruistic acts, which draws us away from ourselves to begin to look outward. As this kind activity develops the self, it releases new resources to reassess ourselves. It provides space to reflect upon our past relationships, of who we are now and who we want to be. This allows us to bring a deeper meaning and purpose to our lives. We need to recognise that we can tend to see God's creativity purely through the eyes of what is useful to us and misunderstand the rest. The message that Job received after his great tragedies and the failure of his friends to console him was that much of man's grief came about through the selfishness of mankind. Humans value the use of sheep and cattle because they help to feed us but we fail often to value the crocodile or the rhinoceros, as we can't see what use they have to us. God here reminds us of our limited insight into his creation, His plans for His creation is much greater than our insight. It will only be as mankind seeks to enlarge its vision of God's creation that pain and grief will be diminished.

So healthy Christian grief:

- Acknowledges responsibility and the reality of life
- Recognises that there are other forms of love to sustain and help us
- Accepts healthy emotions

- Does not deny deep feelings but seeks to nurture them for good
- Does not retreat into cul-de-sacs of illusion but by faith is driven to the truth
- Accepts the processes of our natural world that we experience
- Doesn't make people weaker or more dependent but fosters inner courage to face the day

So those in pastoral ministry can offer comfort and challenge. We demonstrate a hope for wholeness based upon our own experience. We refuse the wish to avoid the painful reality of loss because avoidance leads to illness and despair. Here we are to prevent people from suffering for the wrong reasons. False suppositions suggest that there should be no loneliness, fear, confusion, doubt. We can't escape the pains of life but we can use the experience as we search for a deeper meaning in life.

NINE

Ministering to the bereaved in a Christian way

Come sit with me on my mourning bench.
Wolfenstorf

I was 17 years old and just finding my feet as a Christian. I started going to a local Anglican church, which at the time didn't seem to have many young people involved. I never forgot walking out after the first service with no one speaking to me except the vicar who only asked me how my brother was. It wasn't the welcome I expected. However, the curate took an interest in me and was keen to get me involved in the youth group. He invited me to visit him. I gained the courage to go and felt confident enough to begin to ask him some of the questions about Christianity that bothered me. I particularly wanted to know why we didn't see the miracles today as described in the New Testament. As a delicate new Christian with many searching questions, I didn't want to hear the reply, 'who do you think you are, you don't have the faith of the apostles!' I didn't return. My Christian journey was detoured and the church failed to gain a new member.

How can we help someone who is suffering from loss? In the midst of all these grief theories, pastoral workers need to develop their own appropriate approach. Perhaps a simple model to use would be to see three phases that we engage in with the bereaved.

Opening phase

In this open phase the pastoral worker is seeking to build up trust, rapport and an understanding of the person's history. This allows one to form an assessment of the extent of the loss and what the bereaved might be seeking from you. This then allows for clarification of appropriate expectations from each other. We have to be very careful not to promise something that we can't deliver. Often bereavement work is not a short-term fix but requires someone who is willing to journey with a person over an extended time. If we can't offer that kind of support we need to be clear right from the beginning. It is better to say that we will just be able to call a couple of times and recommend other support agencies than to promise you will keep visiting and then stop after a few weeks.

I often feel when I do a pastoral visit that I am a kind of detective absorbing information. This needs to happen in a natural and unforced way. But by simply observing the surroundings, asking open questions and developing good listening skills, it is amazing how much information a person casually shares with you. In this early stage of a relationship I am looking to gathering information relating to four specific areas.

The type of death

I'm finding out whether the death was sudden or gradual? Was it a shock or had they time to adjust? Were they able to be with the person before death and able to say goodbye? If the death was sudden and unexpected or untimely, then the bereaved may have added issues to resolve. This would also be true if it was a horrific death or perhaps mismanaged at some point.

The nature of the relationship

As previously said, the closer one perceives oneself to be like the deceased, then the greater the impact. Therefore one is looking to see what type of relationship the person had with the deceased. Were they independent of or ambivalent towards the deceased? Was it someone that they were dependent upon? This might have been for finance, emotional support, regular contact or had they simply formed a part of a person's regular daily routine. What you will not know initially is whether there had been any complexity in the relationship such as violence or abuse. It takes time for someone to trust you at this level of intimacy, for him or her to be willing to share more complex and possibly deeply painful issues. Clearly such complexities will play a role in affecting how a bereaved person recovers from their loss. If we are unaware of such issues, we may be confused at how the bereaved is behaving.

Character of the survivor
We all react to loss in a way that reflects our personality and past experience. The baggage of life we had before loss is the same baggage that we carry into loss. Therefore a grief-prone personality or a person who has is insecure and suffers from low self-esteem will undoubtedly find loss hard to handle. People who have had previous mental illnesses or show signs of excess anger or self-reproach will require particular attention. This will equally apply to people with some kind of disability, which might frustrate or confuse how they are able to express their feelings. One type of character that might easily slip under our radar might be the person who finds it hard or impossible to express their anger. We might think they are coping very well as they appear to be calm. It will only be by building up gentle trust with the person that they will gain the confidence to share with you, as well as acknowledge to themselves how they are really feeling.

Social circumstances
A key factor in how people recover from loss will depend upon what kind of social support the bereaved person has. What kind of family

support does the person have? Are there family complexities in which this death will make things worse or easier? Have they friends who will travel with them on their journey? Have they employment that will provide a sense of purpose and direction or are they unemployed with lots of time on their hands? What kind of responsibilities do they already have? Have they dependent children? Have they had other significant losses in their lives that make the situation more complex? These social issues can play a big part in how a person adapts to their loss.

Intermediate phase

This is the largest chunk of the work of a pastoral worker as they journey with the bereaved. Part of this is to begin to see what might be areas of complication or hindrance for the bereaved, which is preventing them adapting to their loss. This might include looking at what tasks the bereaved are finding difficult and helping them to find ways to overcome their difficulties. Everyone has his or her own adaptive strategy to cope. This needs to be recognised, affirmed and supported. Grief is something we 'do' rather than something that just 'happens' to us. This means we can help people make all kinds of decisions.

- Do I view the body?
- Which funeral director shall I use?
- Do we decide on cremation or burial?
- Do we use a church or not?
- What do I do with the flowers?
- What do I do with the ashes?
- What do we put on the gravestone?
- How long off shall I have from work?
- Do I need medication or will it hinder my recovery?
- Do I share my grief or keep it private?

- What about my finances?
- How do I fill in these forms?
- Do I move house or stay put?
- How do I remember yet move on?

The questions keep coming. Notice that there is not a right or wrong about what a person decides. But they may well need support to come to an answer that they are comfortable with. Along this journey we are helping people to find new meaning in life and reconstruct their own personal stories. This might mean reconstructing many times till it all makes some sense to us.

What we are also doing is gently reminding them by our presence to include God in their reflections. This involves identifying things to be thankful for, recognising his presence now and finding some hope for the future. It is by incorporating faith in our conclusions that we can come to a healthier position.

What is God saying about the past?
What is God saying about the present?
What is God saying about the future?

During this period we are providing an opportunity for people to talk about the deceased and retell their story. Sometimes they only get this opportunity when we visit and give them permission to talk about the deceased and express emotion with another rather than always by themselves. This is about being willing to use the deceased person's name and encouraging the bereaved to talk about them. Who is willing to listen to our story if we are not willing first to listen to theirs? It is very hard to reconstruct our identity alone. We need others to help us to reflect. It's like doing a jigsaw together. The person holding the pieces is the only one who can place any piece, but another person's eyes can help with suggestions of where each piece might fit and in which order. The jigsaw can never be the same, which is hard for both the bereaved and the pastoral carer to accept. As we struggle to cope with the bereaved person being different since loss, they themselves have to grapple with how their life will never be the same. There is a parallel process going on here, which is well worth recognising and acknowledging at some point with the person. Be aware that grief issues can seem far worse during the winter period. It is a time of short days and long nights. We find ourselves drawing the curtains so early in the day that it can make us feel more alone and isolated. Those who suffer from SAD syndrome will find that their grief increases the problem. A good pastoral visitor will be aware of this and will particularly keep contact with people during this period. It may be just a regular telephone call in the evenings over the first winter of the person's loss.

Is there a time to talk theology?

From my own research of interviewing bereaved parents, I have found that the early stage of grief was not the time to talk theology. At this stage the family want someone who will be there for them, to identify in their pain and to cry out with them in their despair. It is only later; perhaps three to five months on, that one can engage in a more open discussion about theology. Unfortunately, often the church has lost touch by this stage. There are, of course, stories of conversion in some bereavement situations days after the death. But the reality is that this is not the norm. If this is the case, we have to think about a better strategy to engage with the bereaved. It may be that a carer has been visiting and over time they recognise that it would be beneficial for the 'theologian' pastor to visit in order to relate to particular faith questions. This type of teamwork works well and makes the most of people's gifts and time. The key is to be still engaged with the bereaved to reach this point.

I find that faith issues arise naturally out of conversations as the bereaved share with me their story. I use a range of pointers that enable me to help a person extend their narrative. I then seek to help the bereaved weave their faith within the narrative.

- Use open questions to invite the story, e.g. what does loss mean to you? How would you describe your feelings on a typical day? How has it changed over time?
- Convey interest in the hardest part of the story, e.g. what is the most painful part of your experience? What are parts of your story that people least hear?
- Consider the impact of this loss on the survivor's worldview, e.g. has the loss changed the way you see things? About life? Yourself? Future? Prayer? God?
- Evaluate the impact of the loss on the griever's social life, e.g. how has it affected your relationship with other people? What concerns do others have about you?
- Balance the need to build the working alliance with the person with the need for sufficient information, asking more specific questions as necessary for clarity.
- Do not force questions but encourage a natural flow in the conversation, putting questions into the narrative.
- Remember, people connected with others usually experience better outcomes.

Remember to look for benefiting changes in their narrative and outlook of life. When faith arises, explore how the person views God and their faith. Bereavement counsellors have a range of open questions that they can use to help a person open up about their experience. These are helpful in giving us confidence to have a rough idea of what we can explore with a person. Although I don't have a list in front of me, I do have a series of open questions that incorporates religious questions and faith issues ready to use to help the bereaved explore their experience and how they see themselves now within their faith (or lack of it).

- What experience of loss would you like to explore?
- What do you recall about how you responded to the event of death?
- How did others respond?
- Who were you as a person at the time of death?
- What does this loss mean to you?
- What is the most painful part of the story?
- Has the loss changed the way you view life? Yourself? Your future?
- How has it affected your relationship with others?
- How has it affected your relationship with God? The church? Religious friends?
- What concerns do they have about you?
- Close your eyes and visualize a scene connected with the deceased? Who or what is your focus of attention? What is happening? Where are you? What feelings do you notice now in your body? What was the most emotionally significant part of the experience?
- Do you have trouble accepting the loss?
- To what extent has it been hard for you to trust others?
- Are there any Bible stories that relate to your story?
- How has it affected your prayers?
- Do you pray differently now?
- Do you feel angry about the loss? Towards whom? Yourself? The deceased? God? The church?
- Do you feel uneasy about moving on with your life? Which areas are difficult for you? New friends? Interests?
- Do you feel emotionally numb or feel connected with others since the death?
- To what extent do you feel life is empty or meaningless?
- Do you feel that the future holds no meaning or prospect for fulfilment?

- Do you feel on edge or jumpy?
- Have you thought of writing a letter to the deceased?
- Where is the deceased now for you?
- What beliefs do you have about life beyond?
- What philosophical beliefs contribute to your adjustment?
- How did you make sense of the death when it happened? And now?
- How has your faith changed? Do you view God differently?
- Is there anything in the Bible that speaks to your situation?
- How has the death disrupted your life story?
- How has it affected your priorities?
- What is your view of yourself before? Now?
- What metaphor, image would symbolise your grief?
- Is there a Bible story that gives you hope?
- What steps could you take to help your healing?
- How might your faith assist you now?
- What would you have said to someone in loss before this event?
- What can the church do to help you?
- What would you like me to pray for with you (or later by myself)?

These questions are just catalysts in enabling a person to see their account from a new perspective. I might only use one or two with a person that naturally arise from the conversation. There must be no sense that you are simply working through a list. People's narratives are unique and individual. The bereaved are in the process of finding out just what their narrative means, where it ends, where it begins again and what link there might be between the past and the future. If our sensitive questions can help in this, we will help the person take a step forward with their lives and hopefully with their faith.

Final phase

This phase can be difficult for both the bereaved and the pastoral worker. It is made easier if clear expectations were clarified at the beginning of the relationship. It is important always to terminate a relationship in a positive way. This requires preparation in helping the person to be aware that the relationship in its present form will end. This might not mean the worker will not see the person at church or in the community at some point, but that the regular specific meetings relating to the loss will end. Part of termination is to have time to review the progress the person has made as well as identifying issues they may still need to work on. This is also an appropriate time to point out other types of support that can be called on within the community. It is important that people know that they have other places to turn to and never feel trapped in a situation. How will we know when a person has reached a satisfactory position? After all they will never be back to how they were, coming to terms with the difference is a sign of adaptation. We can look for pointers of recovery. They will initially include going back to work, eating normally and regaining some kind of sleep pattern. Later they might include:

- Regaining an interest in life
- Finding a sense of hope and purpose to life
- Beginning to be more thankful
- Finding new roles and positions in the community
- Taking new initiatives in life
- Forming new relationships

For many, the mourning never ends but they do regain a lifestyle that provides a degree of satisfaction for themselves while playing their part within the community. When we see a person who recognises that they are beginning a new chapter in their lives, then we can be encouraged that our care has been worthwhile.

Reflections

- Think about a time when you have been in need and someone came and supported you. What was it about their visit that supported you the most?
- Think about a recent pastoral visit that you have done. Can you picture it, smell it, and hear it? Go through in your mind what you actual thought, said, did and how you reacted in the situation.
- What do you think you were actually doing in that visit and what do you think the person was expecting and wanting?

TEN

Observe the expert at work

When Jesus finally got there, he found Lazarus already four days dead. Bethany was near Jerusalem, only a couple of miles away, and many of the Jews were visiting Martha and Mary, sympathising with them over their brother. Martha heard Jesus was coming and went out to meet him. Mary remained in the house. Martha said, 'Master, if you had been here, my brother wouldn't have died. Even now, I know that whatever you ask God he will give it.'
Jesus said, 'Your brother will be raised up.'
Martha replied, 'I know that he will be raised up in the resurrection at the end of time.'
'You don't have to wait for the End. I am, right now, Resurrection and Life. The one who believes in me, even though he or she dies, will live. And everyone who lives believing in me does not ultimately die at all. Do you believe this?'
'Yes, Master. All along I have believed that you are the Messiah, the Son of God who comes into the world.'

John Ch14: v17-27, The Message

You can't get a better example of caring for the bereaved than in the way Jesus dealt with Mary and Martha at the death of their brother, Lazarus, in John Chapter 11. Let's see how it unfolds.

Building relationships

The passage begins (v2) by telling us that Jesus had already built up a relationship with this family. This is not always the case in ministry, but if we do already have a connection with people, it makes our pastoral care easier to share. Ministry is all about relationships and Jesus had clearly connected with this family. Mary had recognised his uniqueness by washing his feet with perfume and together the sisters had realised that Jesus loved his friend Lazarus. What then unfolds is the fruitfulness of what had taken place previously. Over the years I have built up a good friendship with people I had not met until death had entered their house. But it does make the first couple of meetings more tentative as trust and respect are built up between each other. If you already have a working relationship, however thin it might be, it makes the first bereavement visit so much easier. All of this emphasises the benefit of pastors getting to know their parish and building up relationships within the community. Eventually, all of those little chats at the post office or in the pub will bear fruit. Indeed it is only because of their friendship that Mary and Martha called Jesus.

You are not alone

The second thing we see (v3) is that the bereaved do not want to be alone. This should give us confidence in visiting. In many cultures the bereaved would have many people visiting in the first few days. This is far less so in Britain where the norm is to leave people in their sorrow. I have always found that people are glad of a visit (as long as you don't overstay their hospitality) and they are very capable of letting you know if it's not convenient at that moment to visit. Jesus delays here in this account. This may theologically be because He knew Lazarus was going to die and by raising him to life, it was an opportunity for the disciples to begin to grasp what Jesus himself was about to do in Jerusalem (v15). There is certainly a time to delay visiting or, more specifically, there is a time to offer brief condolences and a time to carry out a longer pastoral stay. When people are in early shock, it is not the time to be asking long questions when they are trying to arrange a funeral. It is later when people are a little calmer that they are in a better frame of mind to consider all sorts of issues.

It was a very natural reaction for Mary and Martha to send word to Jesus, after all he was a close friend. Jesus of course had no need to be told anything, buthe calls us to engage him in prayer and through his community. Not everyone believes that God is that interested in their situation to call upon Him. Often in a community, the church finds out about difficult situations at second or third hand. How are we to respond? People have the right to their privacy, yet we also have a calling to let people know that God does know and still cares. Our interest and sensitive caring response is a message to the community that God loves us and wants to engage in our suffering and struggles. This might not bring any change to the situation, but it is the spark of bringing change to the people involved. Our prayerful presence brings the message, 'though he slay me, yet will I hope in him' (Job 13:15). This might be in the form of a short visit that only gets as far as the front door, or posting a card of concern to the family. However far this initial encounter goes, it is saying loud and clear, 'you are not alone'.

A presence of love and hope

The third thing we see is the response when Jesus arrives, 'the teacher is here' (v28). It is probably the first thing we hear when we knock on someone's door, 'the vicar is here'. There is also that accusatory, embarrassed look that might communicate so much. It may be simply, 'help, what do we do or say to a vicar (or pastoral visitor) in this situation?' or it could have a deeper sense of pain and bewilderment, which Martha echoes in her words, 'Lord, if you had been here, my brother would not have died!' (v21). Yet despite these strong words, Martha still has hope in Jesus. This I'm sure is the case when we visit people. They may not be clear what that hope might be, but there is something in people's eyes that says, 'I'm hoping you can bring something to this situation'. Jesus brings the future and the present hope of resurrection (vv4 and 23). I believe by just our presence, we are echoing something of that love and hope, after all Christians are hopeful people. We develop this hope in the way we handle ourselves in this privileged position. In the way we ask open questions, actively listen and draw people out in telling us their story. We bring hope in the way we ask for permission to say a prayer (which is rarely declined) and reap an emotional response of thanks.

Acknowledging individual difference

Notice the differing reaction between Martha and Mary. We already know something of their characteristics in the account of Jesus visiting them for a meal (Luke 10: 38-42). Martha is the activist, cooking and preparing while Mary sits and contemplates at Jesus' feet. We see this echoed here with Martha coming out to meet Jesus while Mary reacts by withdrawing into herself and remaining in the house. Here is a picture of God's creativity in making all things unique and special. We have to be prepared for a variety of reactions when we visit the bereaved. But notice how, regardless of their outward reaction, they are both asking the same deep questions (v32). 'If only' are questions on all bereaved lips. Jesus' response should give us the courage to respond in the same way.

He was deeply moved in spirit and troubled (v33)

Here was a man who was not in professional mode, hiding his emotions and keeping everything under control. Jesus reveals his incarnational commitment of being the 'Son of man'. This was a natural response to seeing Mary and others weeping openly. We can't turn this on, but we can be genuinely present with people, truly congruent in empathising with the bereaved. This is not the time to take your mind off and think about your holidays but to be willing to linger, however uncomfortable it might be, and to stay with the pain that the parishioners are feeling. This is real 'incarnational' ministry. It is here where people learn how much you care that they then become willing to listen to what you have to say. This willingness to linger with the pain of the bereaved reaps great rewards when you come to speaking at a funeral or visiting at a later date (see Chapter 16).

Death is not the end

Vv11-13 convey a clear message from Jesus, that death is not the end. All of God's creativity and energy in creation does not simply disappear when a person dies. Jesus uses the term 'asleep', although he knew that Lazarus was in fact dead. He had to make this clear to the disciples who were confused. This equates well with how the bereaved are feeling. They are looking into the abyss of death, annihilation and nothingness for their relative and for themselves. It is a very dark place to be. But here Jesus brings a word that is soft and tender that has the hope of a new awakening, a new dawn. This is the hope that is at the heart of the Christian faith. Notice there is no real focus on Lazarus, about what he believed, but rather Jesus focuses upon what Mary and Martha believed. We can get very wrapped up in wondering what the deceased believed in their lives. The truth is that we don't know and are in no position to presume. This is God's business. Here, Jesus focuses upon the living, which is wise guidance for ourselves.

The comfort of others

It is easy to focus just on the role that Jesus plays within this story and miss the wider involvement of the community. Verse 19 tells us that other friends and neighbours were involved in supporting the two sisters. We need to be reminded that we cannot support a grieving person alone; the responsibility would be too great. Indeed Jesus connects with others around the family as he shares in the grief of the wider community. Here we need to recognise that the church is not the only organization that is called to care. Our ministry can be strengthened by the work of neighbours, doctors and other social groups that the bereaved are related to. It is not about competing with others to care but recognising what our unique role brings to the situation. After all, who else will open up a conversation about life after death?

Being with others

The invitation to the burial site came not just from Mary and Martha but from the gathered crowd. Jesus was being called to share in the family and community's suffering. This kind of request comes to us today in being invited to participate in the funeral or just being present in the congregation. We cannot underestimate the importance of the role a pastor plays at such corporate community gatherings. It is so easy in a busy life to pass the invitation on to others and feel we have little time for such events. Ministers can easily think, 'unless I'm doing the service or giving the talk, why go?', but we miss the point of just 'being' with people in their pain and awkwardness. This applies equally to wedding receptions. As time-consuming as wakes and receptions can be, they are an opportunity for a recognised 'Godly figure' to be present. I know in myself I have often been reticent in attending such occasions because of feeling 'ill-at-ease' with the situation. I can feel unneeded, recognising that

I might hardly know anyone at the event. There is also the difficulty that people have in not knowing what to say to you after you have led a service or given the sermon. However, learning to live with feeling 'uncomfortable' is an important part of ministry. Remember, what are the crowd wondering and asking in their subconscious?

> Is God interested in us,
> does he care,
> if so, where is he?

We may feel a weak imitation of the real Godly presence, but God uses us most when we are vulnerable and not relying on our own strength. Romans 12:13-15 encourages us to share with people who are in need, while 1 Thessalonians 4:13-18 beckons us to use our gift of encouragement with the hope God's reunion after death. Our engagement here is the beginning of 'rolling the stone' (v39) from people's eyes and hearts.

Recognising the tension of despair and hope

Martha reveals the tussle that a bereaved person has with themselves, one moment full of despair and sadness, the next holding on to hope and faith. She is disappointed with Jesus for not preventing this, yet in the same sentence she is clinging on to hope (v21). You can see a tussle is going on within her mind as she tries to make sense of what has happened. How can her belief system cope with this situation? Notice how grief and hope can co-exist together. Too often I have heard preachers tell congregations not to doubt. Unfortunately, what results is a congregation that just feels worse and guiltier for doubting. It is often our fear that someone might fall away from faith that makes us anxious to protect. Seeing people in a state of despair is frightening for all parties concerned. There is always a part of us that is self-protective; we quietly hope that if others do not despair, neither will we. Jesus did not rebuke either sister for their state of mind. What he did was to gently direct them in a hopeful direction (v23). Surely, our God is big enough to cope with our doubts, fears and anxieties without us jumping in with both feet to rescue someone who is in fact doing fine. To watch someone struggling to swim for the first time is worrying, but we won't help if we keep jumping in and rescuing them. They need to discover for themselves that they can not only float but swim in a new direction. It is as if Jesus is in the water with the swimmer, just always in front a little, beckoning the person forward.

Feel the pain

On three occasions scriptures tell us that Jesus wept. First he wept, along with others, at the effects of separation that death creates (v35). Secondly, he wept over Jerusalem (Luke 19:41) as he looked down upon a community that has lost its way and has no direction. Finally, he wept in the garden of Gethsemane (Matthew 26:39) at what lay ahead of him. There may well be a degree of anger tied up with this emotion as in each situation Jesus eperiences the effects of mankind's folly. In Genesis 6:6-7 we hear of how God was grieved in sorrow and pain at creating mankind, which had become so destructive to himself and God's creation. Being able to weep with others is an important part of empathising. Some of us, depending upon our temperament, will find this more appropriate than others. It clearly has to be natural and not forced. Identifying with people's anger is also understandable in the midst of terrible situations. There is no shortage of prayers in Scripture that involved weeping and anger mixed together. However, it is always seen in a balanced prayer that ends in comfort and assurance. We need to keep our emotions within the context of where we find ourselves. Jesus' tears were seen as identifying with the people in such a way that he then led them forward. We must make sure we don't get so wrapped up in ourselves that we forget why we are there. Any emotional expression has to be in the context of wanting to support and aid those around us.

Bringing stability

The Bethany sisters were going through a whole range of emotions. One minute anger, another despair and then they are engulfed in tears. It is into this context of turbulence that Jesus entered. Gradually, by his presence, he brought calm and assurance. Although this wasn't straightforward. Jesus' wanting to open up the tomb brought alarm to the family and crowd (v39). But Jesus brought confidence and reassurance,

> Did I not tell you that if you believed, you would see the glory of God.

Here was Jesus in control of a difficult situation. His presence enabled others to hold on to his peace and to re-find themselves. We can often say that a person is 'lost in their grief'. Mary and Martha had faith and trusted Jesus, but the situation overwhelmed their faith. They were able to express their belief that God existed and that one day there would be a resurrection, but right at that moment, doubt and fear seemed to be winning. Jesus gently reminded the sisters of the promises of God and of the hope to come. Just the presence of a Christian pastor/visitor is making a statement of God's existence and brings hope. We must never underestimate the difference that a simple, caring and loving visit can make to a bereaved person. Regardless of what the bereaved family believed, in the midst of darkness, a person of faith brings with them something of God's light.

The hope to come

The ending of this story may be a little out of our reach, but it does give us hope to convey to others. Here is the Son of God wanting to ease people's pain, wanting to bring back their loved ones. This is a picture of a God on our side. It is a blessing that Jesus chose to say his prayer out loud for our sakes.

Father, I thank you that you have heard me. (v41)

If, by our presence, we can convey the presence of God and communicate that God not only hears but understands our pain, then we will have achieved a positive outcome. What we all ponder is what happened to Lazarus? There are so many ifs and buts about his new life.

> Was he glad to come back?
> How did people treat him?
> Did his relationships change with his sisters?
> Did it take away the fear of death the second time?
> Did he still grapple with faith and doubt like the rest of us?
> Did the thought of dying again consume him in fear?
> Did he ever regret being pulled back by others?

These are all unknowns. It is unlikely Jesus would bring a man back to life to suffer because of it. Yet equally I can't see Jesus protecting Lazarus from the struggles we all encounter. It is the 'big' unknown that the bereaved have to grapple with and come to terms with eventually. As C.S Lewis puts it,

> What kind of lover am I to think so much about my affliction and so much less about her? Even the insane call, 'come back', is all for my own sake. I never even raised the question whether such a return, if it were possible, would be good for her. I want her back as an ingredient in the restoration of my past. Could I have wished her anything worse? Having got once through death, to come back and then, at some later date, have all her dying to do over again?. . . (17).

Somewhere along the line, Lazarus, Martha and Mary came to a deeper understanding of Jesus as the Christ post-resurrection. One can only reflect that faith in the resurrected Christ gave sustenance, faith and hope when death again knocked on their door (v45). This must bring hope to our entire ministry.

Reflection

- Who do you identify the most with in the story, Mary, Martha or the crowd?
- Imagine you were a member of the friends present, what would you say to Mary and Martha?
- How comfortable would you feel seeing Jesus weep at the tomb?
- How can you identify in the pain of someone whilst still being hopeful?

ELEVEN

When does a person need to be referred?

Margaret was 68 years old and was now bereaved. Her husband died after a short illness over a Christmas period. They had been married for 46 years. Margaret and her husband had been faithful members of the church, playing their full part in whatever way they could. Margaret had been healthy most of her life and seemed emotionally stable. She had children and grandchildren who were as supportive as possible although they didn't live close by. She also had a good number of friends in a village that she had lived in for over 20 years. The church pastor had conducted the funeral and began to visit Margaret once a week. As experienced as the pastor was, he found himself struggling to encourage and uplift Margaret. She seemed to be morose, lacking energy. She was having great difficulty in sleeping but didn't want to go to see the doctor. Any conversation always seemed to result in Margaret claiming that she was all right really and had no reason to complain. As the weeks passed the pastor became increasingly concerned for Margaret. He didn't think she was eating properly and along with the lack of sleep, she was beginning to look thin and drawn. It took several conversations with one of Margaret's children before Margaret gradually agreed to see the doctor and have some bereavement counselling from outside the village. Margaret found it difficult to let her guard down in a small village but gradually she got her confidence with the counsellor and began to share some of her true feelings.

First, we have to be aware of whether a person is engaging with their grief. Usually, bereaved people are able to talk about their grief in some form of activity or other. It is when they are unable to show any change in activity that grief might be becoming complicated. Grievers ought to be able to express how the process of grief is changing over time. This involves understanding how the intensity of grief oscillates. This does not necessarily mean it is getting better. As we will hear for the loss of children, people can find themselves getting worse after a period of calm. However, if we perceive a degree of movement in their grief, it does demonstrate that grieving is taking place. There are grief questionnaires[28] that measure grief factors but I would use these with caution. From a pastoral worker's perspective, we need to be seen as a support rather than an analyst. Also, such questionnaires can be unreliable if used alone to draw any conclusion. They do at least point us to relevant areas to be aware of. These include:

- Denial
- Social isolation
- Despair
- Hostility
- Guilt
- Loss of control
- Rumination
- Somatisation
- Death anxiety

It is not the presence of such components in a person's life that might bring concern, it is more the extent that one or more might begin to dominate and take over in an unhealthy, prolonged way.

From a positive perspective it is important that the pastoral worker is clear in what their intention might be in supporting a person. Are we there to help practically, to be a channel for the venting of feelings or to

---

28. Sanders, C. (1999). *Grief, the Mourning After*. New York: John Wiley.

assist cognitive thinking? We need to make sure we are using an approach that the person is comfortable with. Some will find it more beneficial if you go for a walk with them as compared to others who will value a time for open expression of feelings. We need to think about building from people's strengths. So someone who already kept a diary might find it helpful to be encouraged particularly to keep a journal through his or her grief. Others who read extensively might value the loan of a book that you can then talk about afterwards. Books can prove to be beneficial as a source of normalising and validating their experiences. They also provide additional ideas as to how to manage their own grief and offer hope that they too can survive such a loss. The pastoral worker needs to be asking not whether the book was helpful to themselves but would it be specifically helpful for the bereaved?

We do know that there are clear risk factors with bereaved people in regards to the speed of their recovery. These include:

- Attachment insecurity
- Anxious attachment leads to emotional loneliness
- Financial loss worsens adaptation
- Spirituality predicts more positive outcomes
- Low social support
- Traumatic reaction to loss
- Preoccupation with 'event story'
- Inhibited explorative system
- Anguished search for meaning
- Frozen story
- Ruminating coping – not able to transcend it
- Sudden, violent deaths
- Suicide, murder, loss of body

Grief counsellors have formulated a range of terms that we use that relate to particular behaviour types. They include:

Inhibited grief – this involves strong self-control.

Delayed grief – having an emotional reaction months or years later.

Disenfranchised grief – where grief is not acknowledged or publicly mourned.

Chronic grief – where the grief appears to be intense and prolonged.

Grief with memory – this is where someone might become tearful at Christmas or on anniversaries as they recall a loved one, but the grief doesn't seem to affect them generally.

Traumatic grief – grief is intense for a short period.

Exaggerated grief – where there seems to be an enhanced reaction to the loss.

All of these are just ways of trying to get a handle on what is going on in a grief-burdened person.

We do know that there will be more issues to handle and a poor outcome when there is/are:

Insecure attachment.

Anxious attachment, triggers emotional loneliness.

Financial loss and insecurity, worsens adaptation.

Intrusive thoughts about the deceased.

Fragmented sense of security, trust and meaning.

Excessive yearning for the deceased.

Sudden violent deaths.

This can lead to deterioration in the physical health of a person. Issues to be aware of include:

Cardiac disorders.

Immunological dysfunction.

Increased chance of cancer.

Increased use of alcohol and/or smoking.

Increased hypertension.

Suicide ideation and attempts.
Functional impairment.
Lower quality of life.

I am like a frozen computer that is busy dealing with an internal virus, unable to engage with other people or activities.

However there are more positive outcomes when there is/are:

Some presence of spirituality, which leads to a more positive mood.
Better social support and less isolation.
Financial security.
Securely attached experiences in earlier life.
Some meaning and purpose in their life.

One can see here how important the Christian faith can be in aiding a person's recovery providing it is not jut an escape in handling real issues. Although bereaved people may need additional support beyond what the pastor or a lay visitor can offer, we can provide a progressive ministry with a clear approach that will assist the individual when requiring specialized help. We need to be clear about what we are actually doing when we carry out our pastoral visits. If this is vague and confused, we are more likely to find ourselves in an awkward situation. Our tasks include ten clear aims.

	TEN TASKS FOR THE PASTOR
1	Help the survivor actualise the reality of the loss. The funeral helps with this and the language we use is important. Don't use euphemisms (and there are many). *Can you think of some?*
2	Help the survivor to identify and express feelings, venting the feeling within a safe environment.
3	Assist the survivor to learn how to live without the deceased.

4	Facilitate the withdrawal of emotional ties from the deceased and encourage the formulation of new relationships.
5	Provide time to grieve and give the survivor permission to grieve.
6	Interpret normal behaviour and affirm.
7	Allow for individual differences in the response to grieving.
8	Provide continuing support over the most critical periods at least for the first year following the death.
9	Assist the survivor in examining her or his defences and coping styles.
10	Identify any pathological behaviour and refer to an appropriate counsellor/therapist.

Caring for oneself

Pastoral workers need to assess their own grieving patterns. It is always a helpful exercise in thinking through why one has ended up in a caring profession. Often it is linked to our own grief experience of one kind or another. This means that counter-transference may be an issue to be aware of. Pastoral workers need to take seriously the task of 'self-care' if compassion fatigue or burn-out is to be avoided. There may be a need to validate one's own grief in ministry through regular rituals, supervision both in the church and from outside and quiet reflective days, etc. The pastoral worker is on a journey just like the bereaved. They need to recognise that one cannot do this job without one's own spiritual journey developing and changing. One has to develop a spiritual resilience that accommodates the existential unfairness of life. We need to be both aware and willing to allow our faith to be shaped and re-shaped through our ministry.

Remember

DO let your genuine concern and caring show.

DO be available...to listen or to help with whatever else seems needed at the time.

DO say you are sorry about what happened and about their pain.

Do tell them you will go on praying for them.

DO allow them to express as much unhappiness as they are feeling at the moment and are willing to share.

DO encourage them to be patient with themselves; not to expect too much of themselves and not to impose any 'shoulds' on themselves.

DO allow them to talk about their loss as much and as often as they want to.

DO talk about the special enduring qualities of what they've lost.

DO reassure them that they did everything that they could.

DON'T let your own sense of helplessness keep you from reaching out.

DON'T avoid them because you are uncomfortable (being avoided by friends adds pain to an already painful experience).

DON'T say how you know how they feel. (Unless you've experienced their loss yourself you probably don't know how they feel.)

DON'T say 'you ought to be feeling better by now' or anything else which implies a judgment about their feelings.

DON'T tell them what they should feel or do.

DON'T suggest that their faith must be a great help (as it might not be at that point in time).

DON'T push people to pray with you or go to church with you, you might do more harm.

DON'T change the subject when they mention their loss.

DON'T avoid mentioning their loss out of fear of reminding them of their pain (they haven't forgotten it).

DON'T try to find something positive (e.g. a moral lesson, closer family ties, etc.) about the loss.

DON'T point out at least they have their other...

DON'T say they can always have another...

DON'T suggest that they should be grateful for their...

DON'T make any comments which in any way suggest that their loss was their fault (there will be enough feelings of doubt and guilt without any help from their friends).

TWELVE

Grief factor assessment

Below is a chart to give you some framework to think about how a person might be coping. Remember, it is only a simplistic guide to help in your analysis of what might be happening in a particular bereavement situation.

	LOW RISK	MEDIUM RISK	HIGH RISK
WHO	colleague pet in-law other relative neighbour ex-partner	very close friend grandparent grandchild fiancé lover close relationship	husband, wife daughter, son sibling partner mother, father very dependant relationship
HOW	peaceful death time to prepare good support	some warning pain controlled some support	no warning painful images little support
HISTORY	good family roots good at forming relationships previous losses resolved	some family conflict finds it had to make friends unresolved losses	deprived childhood relationship breakdowns unemployment financial issues past mental and physical illness
HELP	good family and friend support support from religious groups and community good doctor relationship	little family or friend support weak community/ faith support no medical support	isolated alone negative experience or health care

Grief factor assessment

We need to remember that relationships are complex and what might seem to be a distant friendship can still have a deep impact on an individual. Someone in a supportive family, with a secure background, suffering the peaceful and predicted death of a pet might be grieving very deeply.

Grief factor case studies

Read the following case studies and reflect upon how you think the person is coping:

1. Alice

Alice is a married woman in her late 50s, who had four grown up children. The eldest son, Alex, was 30, married, with two small children. They moved in with the parents for a few months when they were moving houses. Unfortunately, Alex became ill with cancer and after 10 months died in a hospice. His mother was with him at the end when he spent a lot of time crying, greatly disturbed with fear. It is now 18 months since the death and Alice is finding life difficult. The daughter-in-law has moved away with her two children. Alice's husband is an introvert, he is very quiet but Alice believes he is in a lot of pain. The father was the main parent who brought up the children, as the mother pursued her career.

2. John

John and Susan went away with their 11-year-old son, Daniel, for the weekend to celebrate Susan's 40th birthday. They were staying with friends and having a great time when on the Sunday afternoon, Susan collapsed with pains in the chest. An ambulance was called but Susan died before getting to hospital. John and Daniel returned home to an empty house without a wife or mother. Along with the relatives, the small rural community rallied and supported the family.

John had to return to work a week after his wife's death. Over the following months he had to rely upon neighbours and friends to take and collect his son from school. Daniel was becoming increasingly moody and difficult to handle at school.

3. Wendy

Wendy had had a tough life with one thing after another. Now divorced, her pride and joy was her son, George, who was training to be a doctor. They had a good relationship and had fond memories of a special holiday in Africa. George was very conscientious in his work as a houseman but working very long hours. The hospital became concerned when George appeared to be exhausted and behaving strangely. He saw a consultant who sent him home for the weekend. That night George went to bed and committed suicide. His mother found him in the morning. Wendy threw herself into suing the hospital and starting a charity in her son's name.

4. Tom

Tom had worked abroad for 20 years when he had to return to Britain because of his mother's terminal illness. He moved in and cared for her, assuming he would go back abroad after her death. His mother made a recovery such that she lived for a further 11 years. Tom had found a new job, lived with his mother and had given up all plans of going back abroad. After his mother's death, Tom struggled to get back to work and found himself becoming more and more stressed.

THIRTEEN

The role of prayer

Lord I don't know what to say. I feel awkward at being in this situation. The thought of what has happened overwhelms me; I want to escape as soon as I can. But they are looking at me with such need in their eyes. Are they disappointed in me and my God or perhaps hoping that I can bring some healing, some peace to the situation?
Lord, you promised that when we are held to account, you would give us the words to say. Well, now is the time. Help me to listen to you at the same time as listening to them.
Only then, will I trust I have something to say.
Your will be done, Amen.

Prayer is a valid way of both expressing emotion and processing our thoughts. For some, prayer is a channel to express one's anger at the injustice of the situation. If God is not big enough to take our anger, he can hardly be God. For others, prayer is one thing you can do in the midst of a sense of helplessness. It also serves as an opportunity to reflect and review what has happened, where the deceased is located and the link you still have with them. We need to recognise that this kind of spiritual strategy can be both helpful and harmful. One person might see the death as part of God's greater plan while another may see it as a form of punishment. All loss events are a form of spiritual crisis since they involve the bereaved reviewing questions of meaning. It is here that the pastoral worker can help a person to consider whether their belief system is helping or hindering them.

If there is ever a time to pray, it is when you are bereaved, yet this can seem to be the hardest of times. The very time when you want God to feel close to you, he can seem distant and far away in your loss. We are told by James, Chapter 5:13, that if we are ever in times of trouble we should pray. But he also acknowledges the need of others to pray for you when you are sick. This highlights how difficult it is to pray when one is unwell. We mustn't be hard on ourselves when the door of prayer seems closed and double locked to us. It is why we are placed into the community of the church that allows others to pray for us. We therefore need to help to reduce the guilt that particularly bereaved Christians feel when they struggle to pray. Laziness is also a characteristic of grief; the body feels exhausted, the mind is working overtime and emotionally one feels shattered. So it is very valid to collapse and go easy on oneself, which naturally also diminishes any desire to pray. After all who prays when they are feeling lazy?

We all have our own experience of praying when life gets tough and therefore think we have something we can share with another. However, we might not comprehend how tough things are for the bereaved person. The probability is that our suffering has been nothing compared to those from the holocaust experience. We wouldn't dream of telling a victim of a concentration camp that we fully understand and can pray into the situation. We perhaps need the same tact with the bereaved.

In the midst of pain and mystery that is not to say prayer doesn't have a role to play.

First, we need to give permission for individuals to be kind to themselves and allow others to carry them in prayer. It is so easy for a Christian to visit a bereaved person and keep on encouraging them to pray. Unfortunately, we often misunderstand what is going on in the mind of the bereaved and therefore misunderstand our own role in the situation. We need to see ourselves as if we are onlookers as

'Jacob wrestles with another (angel)'. Jacob grappling with his issue did not result in what we would identify as normal prayer. All his family could do was to stand aside and uphold him in prayer. This is how it is for many bereaved people. Only as they come out of the intensity of grief will they find themselves able to relate to prayer in a way that we would normally associate with. Let's not panic because a person seems in the valley of darkness; trying to pull them out to be where we are might not be helpful or advance their development in faith. Upholding someone in prayer when they are in the midst of their struggles is both demanding and exhausting. But it is also a time of real spiritual growth for ourselves as we entrust someone to God through our prayers.

Secondly, when they do pray, we need to allow them to say prayers that perhaps we would feel uncomfortable with. Margaret Spufford, who wrote an excellent book on suffering and joy, quotes the prayers of Peter Lippert in Ladislaus Boros's book, *Pain and Providence*:

> You have created oceans of pain…and I cannot see how they were necessary to preserve your world…Lord, everything apart from you is plunged into suffering. You allow the sea to surge forward up to the steps of your throne, to the heights of your majesty; and all that goes out from you steps at once into these dark, boiling waves. You yourself, when you wanted to descend into the world, had to plunge into this ocean of suffering that surrounds you. Lord, you created pain.

> There are some who know everything, who penetrate even your great thoughts and decrees and give a nice, tidy explanation of them all. They explain and prove to me that it has to be just so and is best as it is. But I cannot endure these people who explain everything, who justify and find excuses for everything you do. I prefer to admit that I don't understand. That I cannot grasp why you created pain, why so much pain, such raging crazy and meaningless pain. I bow down before your glory indeed; but I do not now venture to raise my eyes to

you. There is too much grief and weeping in them. So I cannot look on.[29]

Unless you yourself are in the midst of this pain, we are not in a position to disagree. Here the bereaved need you to be able to say a loud 'Amen' in support of their psalm-like prayer.

The beginning of the answer may take weeks, months and, for some, years. It is unlikely you will be with the person when they begin to gain new insight in their prayers and faith. But you can through your ministry leave a wealth of resources to ponder upon from your own prayers and verses of scriptures. Identifying with the women who grieved at the tomb can be the beginning of identifying with others in their suffering. However, they did not remain in that state. The way forward was one that included confusion, alarm, heartache, rejection and final acceptance. Our prayers need to reflect something of that journey. Perhaps helping a person come to communion or to receive it in his or her own home can start the journey. The breaking of the bread can speak into people's lives in so many different ways. The road to Damascus for bereaved people can be a stony journey with no sudden dawning of light but a rather gradual awaking that seems to occur without you realising it.

Thirdly, when I do pray with an individual, there seem often to be three components. I begin with thanks usually for the deceased and their life in all its uniqueness, warts and all. That's about being honest about who the person had become. It is no good praying something that the bereaved didn't think about the deceased. Honesty has to be at the heart of any prayer. I then allow my prayer to reflect the conversation that I have just had with the person. This might well be expressing how the person feels about God at that very moment. Sometimes we have to cry out 'my God, my God, why?'

---

29. Spufford, M. (1989). *Celebration: A Story of Suffering and Joy.* London: Mowbray.

on behalf of the person. It can be reassuring to hear another echo as it shows recognition and affirmation of their feelings. I then bring to God whatever issue or problem, however small it might be, that the bereaved is experiencing. God is concerned for the small as well as the large issues. Sometimes it is very small issues that just become too big a hurdle for a person to climb over. By lifting this to God I am easing the burden within and allowing it to be shared.

It is worth having various prayer resources up one's sleeve. You may be more at ease with praying extempore while others prefer to use prayers already written down. Using the Lord's Prayer is a simple way of bringing access of prayer to others or getting them to say a psalm together. Perhaps leaving a prayer card can be helpful. It can also be constructive to leave a hymn book. Some people can find this easier to read and reflect upon than a Bible. If we are in doubt what to pray about, it is safer to ask the person what they would like you to prayer for. We can so often get a wrong understanding of what someone is conveying and end up praying totally off tangent. Being honest and open is always the best bet. People on the whole value being asked. It allows them access into your prayers, enabling them to own the prayer for themselves. As you journey with people through their grief you will find that their prayer needs to change and evolve over time. Hopefully, what we are enabling them to do is to be able to still express their love for the deceased through prayer. It is a safe way in which the continuous bond can be expressed.

Prayers that echo a passage of scripture or a verse from a hymn can be helpful anchors for people to latch on to.

Numbers 23:19
Deuteronomy 31:8
Psalm 4:8
Psalm 36:5-6
Psalm 41:3

Psalm 91:1-2
Psalm 48:14
Psalm 55:22
Psalm 73:23-24
Proverbs 3:24
Isaiah 26:3
Isaiah 43:1-2
Isaiah 63:9
John 13:7
John 14:2-3
Acts 20:24
2 Corinthians 1:3-5
2 Corinthians 4:16-17
2 Corinthians 12:9
Hebrews 5:8-9
Hebrews 6:18-19
1 Peter 4:12-13
1 Peter 5:7
Revelation 7:15-17
Revelation 21:4

The Prayer of the Chalice

Father, to thee I raise my whole being
A vessel emptied of self. Accept Lord
This my emptiness, and so fill me
With thy self, thy light, thy
love, thy life, that these thy
Precious gifts may radiate
Through me and over-flow
The chalice of my heart
Into the hearts of all
With whom I come in
Contact this week
Revealing
Unto them
The
Beauty of thy
Joy
And
The
Serenity
Of thy peace
Which nothing can destroy. Amen

FOURTEEN

When faith hits the rocks

Sarah and John were regular attendants at the local church along with their two small children, Clarisse and Peter. They made friends and participated in the church with helping to run the crèche and then a toddler group. Life changed suddenly when Clarisse at the age of five was diagnosed was cancer. For the next 18 months, mum spent most of her time with her daughter, in and out of hospital. All of this put great pressure upon their marriage and young three-year-old Peter began to play up, wanting more and more attention. The church supported the family as best they could especially when Clarisse finally died one weekend at home. The funeral was sensitively carried out by the minister, but from that day forward John never entered the church. Sarah continued to hold in with friends being supportive but she didn't find it easy. Any discussion in the local homegroup just resulted in Sarah bursting out in anger and disbelief in God. 'Where was he when we needed him', she would demand. A couple of friends from the church maintained long-term contact with the family but eventually the church seemed to forget about this family, but the family never stopped thinking about God and the church.

How can one continue to be a Christian after a major loss? This is a question many have to grapple with.

> Does my faith remain the same?
> Why is it I seek God out in my loss only then to pull away?
> How can the death of anyone bring glory to God?

I accept the death but why did God allow all of the pain before death?

Why is church not the same anymore?

For some Christians, they become defensive of their faith, not allowing doubt to linger one moment. There are some questions they will simply not attempt to answer. This keeps them safe within the parameters of the faith that they have. Others become more aggressive as they lash out with a tirade of questions. These are often questions that no one can answer and often lead the bereaved into a dead end cul-de-sac of grief. Others hold onto their faith and remain in the church but keep their questions, doubts and concerns to themselves. I wonder just how many are in church in this position? The concern is that they can continue in the church for years, while the leaders fail to scratch where they are itching. We preach over their heads or on subjects that just don't relate to them. It becomes hard to sit in church each week if you're angry with God and no one seems to share your anger. Hence it becomes easier to just drift away from church, often unnoticed.

Faith can find some deaths easier to cope with than others. If it is someone who has reached what might be considered a good age, suffered little pain near the end and had an opportunity to put their house in order, then it is hard to rant and rail against God. But if the death is untimely, traumatic, happens to the young, follows considerable pain, or was preventable, then look out God, here comes a storm!

People ultimately have six choices in loss:

1. They find that their faith is deepened. I can think of several people who, when illness struck, or a relative or friend had died, found themselves seeking to develop their faith. When death occurred, they found that their faith sustained them in their loss, and over time they become more committed as Christians.

2. They find that their faith is challenged but renewed. It could be said that this is what happened to Job or C.S. Lewis. For both, they found a deeper sense of mystery in their faith. Others like Kushner revised their notion of God's character while holding on to faith.[30] Here they may change their perspective of what we mean by God's omnipotence. This might result in someone still praying to God but not seeing him as a kind of genie who does what you ask.

We have come to believe that in God's gift of a free will, by which we become humans instead of robots, good and evil co-exist. With this disease, death and famine become part of our world scene. We have experienced some of the ashes of the fallen world these past two years. In all we have seen there is nothing happening, as a result of the fallen world, that God in His sovereignty cannot help us cope with, or no situation in which He will leave us alone.[31]

3. They have no change in their beliefs. This might be when a son dies from a drug overdose. This only re-affirms the belief that bad actions lead to devastating consequences. The bereaved faith is only confirmed and is secured. Membership in a church remains the same.
4. They redefine their spirituality. Here a person might find that they have made a spiritual shift. This may be a minor one, such as moving from one denomination to another where they feel more comfortable. It might be going from a busy noisy church to somewhere they can find contemplation and space to just be themselves. This is especially true if previously the person had been very active in the church. For others it could be finding

---

30. Kushner, H. (1981). When Bad Things Happen to Good People. London: Pan Press.
31. Giesbrecht, P. (1988). *Where Is God When a Child Suffers?* Hannibal: Hannibal Books.

> faith in a totally new way. Perhaps they might become a Quaker, Buddhist or seek to express their faith in a very individualistic and private way rather than associating with a group of people.

I have come to believe that the work of an artist helps me to understand God. The artist chooses a certain size of canvas and oils or water-colours for a particular project. However, because of what he has chosen, he has imposed a discipline upon his creativity. He now has the problem of working within this self-induced framework. Any solution to the problems he faces must be worked out in this setting. The artist's problems arise not because he has done anything wrong but simply because he had to choose a form to work within. The challenge for the artist is to overcome his problems in such a way that creates a new and richer form of work. A good artist doesn't give up on his painting but leaves no problem unresolved. I believe that my God never abandons us but is seeking somehow to redeem all evil.

5. Find their faith inadequate and fail to find a suitable replacement. As one bereaved parent put it,

I have come to terms with the death of my child but not the loss of all that I had believed.'

> Here, the church can be a difficult place to be unless someone is willing to grapple with the issues being raised. The bereaved person becomes a kind of agnostic Christian living with more doubt than faith.
> 6. Find their faith false and actively stand against religion. Here a person might become a humanist or just campaign against the affects of the church and religion at large. In this context, God is no more, we are all 'home alone'. There is no hope of reunion here; death is simply the end for their relative and themselves.

Never shall I forget that night, the first night in camp, which has turned my life into one long night, seven times cursed and seven times sealed. Never shall I forget that smoke. Never shall I forget the little faces of the children, whose bodies I saw turned into wreaths of smoke beneath a silent blue sky. Never shall I forget those flames which consumed my faith forever.[32]

There is a degree of similarity here in the concepts of developmental faith. John Westerhoff saw faith developing rather like a tree.[33] As the tree grows, it adds rings to expand and mature while holding onto the previous rings in the core of the tree. So a person's faith expands and develops while retaining elements of a previous view and belief system. Westerhoff identified four styles of faith: experienced faith, affiliative faith, searching faith and owned faith. Fowler[34] identified these changes in a slightly different way using six stages: Intuitive-Projective Faith, Mythic-Literal Faith, Synthetic-Conventional Faith, Individuative-Reflective Faith, Conjunctive Faith, Universalising Faith.

Charles McCollough's has simpler titles, which are easier to grasp:

The Innocent
The Literalist
The Loyalist
The Critic
The Seer
The Saint[35]

---

32. Wiesel, E. (1972). *Night*. New York: Hill & Wang.
33. Westerhoff, J. (1976) *Will Our Children Have Faith?* New York: The Seabury Press.
34. Fowler, J. (1987). *Faith Development and Pastoral Care*. Philadelphia: Fortress Press.
35. McCullough, C. (1983). *Heads of Heaven; Feet of Clay*. New York: Pilgrim Press.

We need to be careful here that we don't fall into the same trap theologically as the bereavement specialists did with their stage concepts. People are just not that simple. But this approach of looking at faith from different perspectives can be extremely helpful to the bereaved and those caring for them. It may provide a way of getting a handle on what's going on in the bereaved with their faith. Rather than condemning or rejecting a person as they grapple with faith issues, we can empathise with where they are sitting at this point in their faith journey. It is recognised that many people have a change of career or embark on an education course of instruction after a major crisis in their lives. This is as equally true for the bereaved in the world of faith and religion. The result might be a 'weaker' or 'stronger' faith or just a 'different' faith. Kenneth Stokes[36] suggests that the key is not that a person has experienced a crisis that affects their faith but rather the way the individual deals with it. He or she learns from it and grows spiritually because of their experience. Stokes recognises that after a crisis we tend to talk about our faith in descriptive words such as either 'weaker', 'stronger', 'not as much', 'more than'. Any of these descriptions could mean that the person is growing and maturing in faith as much as losing their faith. Whenever we are thinking through our faith it will involve perhaps rejecting some of our older models that we used to cling to. This can create a feeling of guilt especially if it leaves us uncomfortable with those we associate with. If it creates a dichotomy with our family, friends or church, then it becomes a difficult place to sit. Stokes suggests that this might be the time of the 'still small voice of calm' amidst the earthquake, wind and fire.

> My idea of God is not a divine idea. It has to be shattered time after time (C. S. Lewis)

---

36. Stokes, K. (1994). *Faith Is a Verb: Dynamics of Adult Faith Development.* Connecticut: Twenty-Third Publications.

There was once a man who had been brought up without learning how to swim. One day a friend invited him to try a simply course called 'Alpha swimming course' that would allow him to learn the most basic of swimming, the breast stroke. The club proved to be friendly and safe and the man quickly became accepted and a part of the club. He felt secure with his new friends and the regular routine of swimming and social friendship. But one day at work a colleague shared with him that he was also into swimming. This surprised the man and they began to share experiences. This new acquaintance invited him to his club where they practised the crawl stroke. This proved invigorating and he was keen to tell his friends back at his old club. However, not everyone was so keen on the 'crawl' and some seemed hesitant to talk about it. As time went on the man found himself getting rather frustrated with the breast stroke which seemed to result in giving him aches and pains. However, he didn't tell his friends. Gradually he met others outside the club who enlightened him about other swimming strokes such as the butterfly. One day he took a big step and attempted to swim in the sea. Others had told him that this was very dangerous and shouldn't be attempted. But the man seemed to be asking questions that others in the club were not interested in. The man learned that to be content in the swimming club, it was best not to mention that he sometimes swam in the sea or did the butterfly. He was fully committed to the breast stroke club and enjoyed the friendship and activities, but he also knew he didn't always think in the same way as others.

What twists and turns the bereaved finally take might well depend upon the pastoral carer as to whether they are willing and able to journey with the person on their 'faith' venture. Are we willing to stick in when the bereaved adopts a 'temporary atheist' position or seem to become a great theologian and proclaims God is dead? If we are willing to act as a bridge with the bereaved, we will allow them to be able to remain in a church after a period of absence.

In these situations, we need to offer neither platitudes nor certitudes nor arguments. But we can still minister with sensitivity, bringing something about engagement, allowing questions without answers and sowing seeds of hope and purpose.

When Jesus died the disciples were devastated. There is an old English word, 'reaved', which means torn apart or robbed, plundered. They were not ready for Easter Sunday and the resurrection hope.

In the past, clergy used to be called at the point of death. Today, however, people look elsewhere.

Ezekiel (Ch 34) outlines what the duty of a shepherd should be: strengthening the weak, healing the sick, binding up the wounded, bringing back the lost, being kind and caring, gathering together.

We must never forget that the bereaved can teach us much. Just because we have had an experience of loss it doesn't mean we understand another person's loss. We need to be careful we don't fall into the trap of some of Job's friends who after seven days of sitting silently began speaking in a way that hindered Job's recovery. Whereas Jesus' ministry to Mary and Martha was so genuine that onlookers made comment of it (John Ch 11). When a person's faith is shaken, it is often linked to the concept of suffering. This is a subject for another occasion but it is worth recognising that one element attached to this issue is often the role of forgiveness, be it of the deceased, one's self or of God.

Can I forgive?

Wrestling with forgiveness is a big issue when it comes to loss situations. We can find ourselves struggling to forgive God, the deceased, others and ourselves.

If the loss is due to the malicious, foolish behaviour of others, then most bereaved victims want to see justice prevail. For some, this is not enough and they require revenge. This can become a great preoccupation that can poison their recovery. Unforgiveness can become all-consuming.

Unfortunately, life is just not fair and even when we get justice, it doesn't necessarily remove the desire for revenge. At the heart of this is a person's unforgiving heart, which can smoulder for years, corrupting a person's life. One can identify this if we look out for the following symptoms:

- The bereaved can feel as if no one understands what he or she is feeling.
- When someone is in this condition they are quick to claim their rights.
- They can be very sensitive to wrongs done to them even if it seems something small and insignificant.
- They can become obsessed with injustices done to them in the past.
- They may seem to gain pleasure in being a victim.
- They may enjoy the power that they gain by being in misery.

Unfortunately, unforgiveness does not stop the pain of loss but only spreads the misery to others. It is a form of pollution that affects the whole of the community.

The road to recovery only begins when the person realises that there is nothing they can do to reverse the wrong even if justice and revenge took place. Nothing will bring the person back. By not forgiving, one is simply prolonging the pain of loss. This for some is exactly what they want, to endure pain for the rest of their lives. The reality is that forgiveness is also costly. To give up the right to get even is not easy, it is surrendering power to a higher source. We have a high example of this in Jesus as he surrendered his power at the cross. Those who have been able to let go and forgive talk about a liberating experience. Letting God be God releases us to get on with living and just being human.

What will forgiveness look like for the bereaved?

- First, forgiveness is never instant. It is more of a process than an event. There will be the need to go on forgiving at many different levels.
- Although forgiveness may not have a clear ending, it does require a willingness to begin at some point.
- Forgiveness is not the answer to all the questions. It won't put the past right, or bring back what one has lost. There will still be issues to work through on a daily basis.
- Forgiveness can cancel the consequences between the victim and the wrong-doer.
- Forgiveness attempts to wish the wrong-doer well, with an opportunity to make the most of their lives.
- Forgiveness does not mean we forget.
- Forgiveness allows us to enlarge our experience of life, which may not diminish the loss but does bring more colour to our existence.
- Unforgiveness is often tied up with anger.

The Christian is always on a journey in their relationship with God. There may be times when we deeply believe that God will not allow us to be tempted beyond what we are capable of resisting. Perhaps we often underestimate our resources or those that He supplies. We are all surrounded by the divine activity of God's endless creation every day. But we also live amongst signs of a failed creation. When we are staring into that failure and someone says to us that 'our faith must be such a comfort to us', it might be far from the truth. One Christian put it this way:

> My problem is not to comprehend, but to avoid over-identification, or mis-identification. I do not regard the evil, which torment me as punishment from God or signs of his anger. I do believe that these evils can be turned to His purpose.

Reflections

- How has your faith evolved over the years?
- Can you think of a time when you had a crisis of faith?
- How did it affect you?
- How has your experience equipped you for pastoral situations?
- How can your church keep links with people who have 'lost their faith'?
- What resources do you have that you could lend someone grappling with theological issues of suffering?

FIFTEEN

Life after death?

Heaven is a wonderful place, filled with glory and grace,
I want to see my saviour's face cause heaven is a wonderful place.

When a person sees their loved one die, they are hit with a string of questions:

- Where is the person?
- Why didn't God heal him or her?
- I thought God was all-powerful?
- How will God square up to the person's lack of religious belief?
- Will I see the deceased again?
- Can I communicate with them?

We know that locating the deceased is an important step for the bereaved. So the more we can engage in these spiritual questions, the more we can help the bereaved adjust. For an atheist, death is simply returning to where they were before they were born, back to nothingness. But for many Christians, life after death is very clear and solid. However, between these two positions, there is a whole spectrum of beliefs.

Most people adopt a particular stance when it comes to the subject of death.

- Death is being with God in heaven.
- Death is an invisible force that takes you when it is your time to go.

- Death is the grim reaper.
- Death is a time of judgement during which your life is evaluated and you are consigned to either heaven or hell.
- Death is non-living. It is the ultimate existential experience.
- Death is being elements in the form of the protons and electrons orbiting around forever.
- Death is elevation to another life, a continued existence in a realm without consequences of human frailty – hostility, materialistic values, etc.
- Death is rebirth. It is beginning again in a new and different life.
- Death is the state between two other states, as sleep is the state between two waking states.

There seem to be questions that revolve around what, where and when.

What is heaven?

A Hindu would say that the next life is either becoming a higher being or perhaps sliding down the life scale to be a pig or a slug. A Buddhist talks of a spiritual nothingness, but a Christian speaks of a place that is very much physical and concrete. Over the Christian history, the concept of heaven has evolved.[37] There seem to be three types of approach rather like the three sides of a triangle:

- This approach is based on the physicalness of Jesus after the resurrection. Geographically, this is more of a western approach. Although Jesus was clearly different on Easter Sunday, he was nevertheless physical enough for the disciples to see, hear and touch him. This gives rise to heaven having a physical appearance. A place of detailed afterlife with work, family, progression and development. A never-ending journey that is onward, upward and

---

37. McDannell, C. and Lang, B. (2001). *Heaven, a History.* New Haven: Yale University Press.

always higher. It is a place where you can enjoy the best of what life can offer. A place of eternal activity and eternal social concern. It is the kind of place that you can hug God. In Revelation, it is a jewelled city, where there is no more weeping or crying or mourning. Augustine saw it as the City of God. Blake saw it as a place where we reunite with our loved one. Swedeberg in the enlightenment era saw it as an ever-expanding universe. The Mormons see it as a place of family progress with fields, forests and lakes, full of remarkable buildings.
- Modern day fiction writer Philip Pullman uses symbols such as light, altimeter, knife and torch to reach the other side.
- What we see here is a portrayal of heaven that often reflects the best of human civilisation. It is based on the fact that the creator God, who made plants, animals, colours and taste, would surely express his creativity equally in heaven. So if you take the best of God's handiwork on earth, then as with any artist, we would recognise God's handiwork in heaven. Perhaps the key thing about this view is not so much what heaven is like but, as one old Priest put it,

    …it is not important to have a precise idea of the future life,
    what counts is that the future life itself is certain.

- Others see heaven just as real but as a more theocentric heaven, with a heavenly light, incorporating angels, praise, vision, which is far more of an abstract approach. This, geographically, is more of an eastern view, which incorporates the flavour of a dynamic continuity. It is just as real as the first concept but less physical and more mysterious. Some might see it like a water droplet merging into the ocean, thus being one with God. Others, like Paul Tillich, saw heaven as a symbol and not a location. This approach focuses more on the spiritual aspect of heaven along with its holiness. It reflects the mystical knowledge of God.

> Heaven is not like a bird in a cage, but more like water in a sponge.

- Finally, others see it more as 'a new heaven on earth' that we are all building towards. Here it is a quality that can be experienced today in the life of the Spirit. This is a driving force to work to make life better today, more heavenly for our children's children.

> Heaven isn't a private possession, any more than music, any more than food.

Over 10 years I have been asking ordinands what they think heaven is like. Regardless of their churchmanship, they inevitably spread themselves out somewhere between these three stances or may want to hold onto more than one approach. Tom Wright talks about heaven as a place where we are with Christ, where we are rested and renewed.[38] Wright focuses more on what comes after heaven, when heaven and earth is united in a new way. This combines the hope for the future while also doing all we can to bring about God's kingdom in the present. Here, those who know God now will be key in caring and managing the new heaven and earth in the future. Others believe that Christians will be caught up in the rapture in which all are taken to heaven in one grand swoop by God. Earth will be left for a final battle before it is finally destroyed. If our future leaders of the church believe a variety of perspectives, all equally argued from scripture and church history, then we have to be open to engage with the laity who will equally express a range of views. Perhaps the key thing here is being able to help a bereaved person express what they believe heaven and the after-life is all about, rather than projecting our own views.

---

38. Wright, T. (2007). *Surprised by Hope*. London: SPCK.

Where is heaven?

Again the location of heaven reflects the previous views. Some see it above (whatever that means), while others see it more on earth, near by. Voltaire said, 'Heaven is where I am', whereas John Bunyan saw it as a heavenly city on a tower beyond Jordan, Dante saw it as an ocean above purgatory, and Columbus set sail to find heaven on earth. Jesus talked about the kingdom of God being at hand with you now if you have eyes to see. The Gospel of Thomas says:

> Heaven is laid out upon the earth, not a place to go to but a spiritual awareness now.

Or as Elizabeth Browning puts it, 'earth is crammed with heaven and every common bush is afire with God'. Perhaps we can't go wrong if we believe that heaven is where God is.

> Heaven is going to be with God in the place where He has been all along.

Since heaven is where God is and he is both in space and outside of it, one might suggest heaven is as close as possible to each one of us. Scientists seem to come close to this with their belief that multiple dimensions may well exist.

When is heaven?

Some perceive heaven being the moment you die. This is based on Jesus' words to one of the men on the cross, 'today you will be with me in paradise'. Others believe it will be at the second coming when all will rise and be judged accordingly. Paradise has been explained as a beautiful garden where we find rest. The thief on the cross was offered this on Good Friday before the Easter Sunday resurrection. Does this mean paradise was just an interim resting place or was Jesus talking about what he was about to achieve through the resurrection for all before and after this time? It was to describe this state after death and before heaven that the historical church invented the concept of purgatory, being a state in which we are incomplete. This equally applies to life now on earth as we grapple with seeking holiness, while at the same time experiencing sin and selfishness. Perhaps it doesn't matter whether heaven is in 1000 years or one second after death, provided God is in control. After all, he is both in time and out of time. For Jesus, the eternal was constantly near. God's endowment of consciousness is always immortal. God is clearly committed to mankind. He has invested something of himself into his creation. We might like to think the upper level of our consciousness is the spiritual state. Death is therefore seen as a transition from the physical to the spiritual. Immortality is not so much an extension of time and restored relationships but an enlargement of spirituality that encompasses space and time.

What about hell?

Hell seems to be out of favour in our present society and is rarely mentioned in the church. It was not that important in the early days of the church either. It had more significance in the middle ages, when the two extremes became important. The Eastern Church has never really had this separate concept. Perhaps latterly, we have had too much of hell in the two great wars to make us grapple with it today. It might be said that hell focuses less on the duration and more on the finality of death. Fire, which is so often associated with hell, is seen as something that consumes and brings the end of something, whereas heaven is seen more as a new beginning. C. S. Lewis didn't see the two as opposites but rather that hell is the outer rim, where being fades away into non-entity. A typical view of hell today would be simply non-being, an atheist's heaven where we choose not to be with God. Yet even in this context, there is still life in one form or another. Ashes to ashes and dust to dust may seem lifeless, but they consist of elements made up of electrons and protons moving in a wonderful rhythmical dance.

All of these concepts reflect how we are just grappling at something that is beyond our comprehension at this present time. It is something that the bereaved certainly grapple with. They want to work out where the deceased is and whether they will see them again.

The pastor can find himself or herself caught in a difficult position. If one is dogmatic and simply expresses one's own convictions about heaven, we may find it does not satisfy the bereaved. On the other hand, if we convey the fact that it is all mystery and we have no answers, then the bereaved quickly turn to others who do offer certainty. The spiritualist movement has fed off the bereaved for many years. However, the reality is that neither the church nor other religious movements can actually offer what the bereaved are seeking, that is their loved one back here on earth. We have to learn to sit at times in uncomfortable positions, just like the bereaved.

Although I may have a very strong belief in the reality of heaven, it is not my faith that will help the bereaved but the development of their own. My role is to help a person take one step towards God rather than move nearer my belief system, which might be a backward move for the person. What they require is someone who is willing to reserve their own opinions and be willing to help the bereaved formulate their own. Preaching about these concepts offers a very different role as compared to working pastorally with an individual. Often, projecting our own views will leave the bereaved cold. If we are able to help the individual grapple with scripture and express what they think without fear of judgement, and give them room to juggle and change their mind, we will allow for seeds of faith to develop. I find the power of prayer, after such discussions, has a deep affirming effect upon the bereaved. In the end, all we can do is to direct people to focus and trust the God of all knowledge and wisdom who knows all the answers to these challenging questions. After all, we cannot pass judgement on where anyone is after death.

Only God truly knows peoples heart's. But if one is in communication with God through prayer, then one is in touch with all that the afterlife might hold, including our loved ones. Certainly over the years when I have interviewed atheists and agnostics, they have expressed a deep envy for those who have the comfort of a belief in heaven and the afterlife.

What about my relative?

At the heart of the Christian message is the belief in the resurrection. If Jesus was not raised from the dead then our faith is shallow indeed and has little to offer others in grief and loss. How can we begin to help people to imagine the future in a hopeful way? 1 Corinthians 15 outlines a description of one way of understanding what happens to us after death. It begins by being clear that what happened to Jesus would also happen to all of his believers. Secondly, Paul reminds us that our thinking on this earth is rather limited and confined. If we are to begin to grasp what is in store for us beyond, we will have to stretch our imagination (v36). A God who has made the galaxies has little problem with bringing together that which He has created. After all, God created His universe out of 'nothing'. So what problem is it to Him to bring back to health that which He has loved? That is not saying all will be the same. Paul uses the illustration of a seed that looks dead to help us begin to use our creative imagination (vv.38-42). The seed, when it comes to life, is changed; it is on a journey from death to life (vv.51-52). This change involves four things:

- Perishable to Imperishable
  From the moment we are born our bodies are decaying. Yes, it is constantly renewing itself but gradually this degradation gets the better of us. Scientists are busy looking into genetics to prolong cells, but here Paul tells us God's new creation will consist of some kind of eternal freshness.

- Dishonour to Glory
  We all have our own views of our lives of when we are at our peak or at our most attractive. But we also know that there are times when we are far from attractive to others or ourselves. When the body itself breaks down through infection, it can become hard to look at or endure. We can struggle to look in the mirror. After death, relatives will often say that they want to remember their loved one as they were rather than how they look now in death. Paul is trying to get us to capture a time when we will always be at our most attractive to God and therefore to ourselves. Here is a picture of humans with no shame or embarrassment.

- Weakness to Power
  One of the hardest things to watch is a loved one deteriorating physically and becoming weak. A terminally ill person is on a journey from strength and energy to a position of weakness, frailty and finally to a lifeless form. Here, Paul tells us new life will be breathed within us that will give us a vitality and energy of our youth. As Isaiah puts it:

They will soar on wings like eagles. They will run and not grow weary, they will walk and not faint (Isaiah 40:31)

- Natural to Spiritual
  The difference between the natural and the spiritual is that one is constantly affected by the magnetic pull that steers us off course into self harm; while the other is always attuned to the Holy Spirit and remains true to itself as it aims for what is true and whole.

Paul concludes this passage with a cry of triumph that God has removed the sting of sin and death (vv.55-57). He then encourages us to stand firm in this fact and allow it to motivate us to a useful future life. This balance between Christian hope for our loved ones and a motivation to use our time now effectively is a healthy position for any bereaved person to arrive at. The more we can assist the bereaved to own this for themselves, the less our long-term work will be needed.

> I have witnessed heaven in experiencing the tragic beauty of grace through grief.
>
> Benjamin Morse

Reflection

- If you were the great creator, what kind of heaven would you create?
- Where do you think your deceased loved ones are right now?
- What do you think is the distance between our world and the heavenly realm?
- What in your life now has elements of heavenliness?
- What do you think you could do to bring in God's heavenly kingdom within your small geographical world?

Key verses to relect upon

John 3:16
John 12:24
John 14:1-6
Matthew 28:20B
1 Corinthians 2:9
1 Corinthians 15:20-28
1 Corinthians 15:35-46
1 Corinthians 15:51-58
Psalm 23
Revelation 21

SIXTEEN

Funerals

It was a cold wet day in November as I drove to the large crematorium on the edge of the city. I was about to conduct a funeral of a type I had not done before. As I arrived, the funeral directors were waiting for me, not that I was late, in fact there was 15 minutes to go. 'You're early,' I remarked. One of the men just nodded at the car, 'we want to get this over with as quick as we can'. I knew what he meant. This wasn't my first baby funeral as I had led several baby and child funerals, being a part-time chaplain to a maternity and children's hospital. However, this felt very different. It was the first time I had done a service in which no one wanted to be present. Sometimes when the baby is very premature, families choose not to attach to what were their hopes. So the hospital takes responsibility and it is left to the funeral director and a chaplain on duty. I robed, prayed and gave the nod to the director attendant. One of the men carried the tiny white coffin up the isle and placed it on the small table. Now what? I asked the attendants if they wanted to stay but they declined and went out for a smoke. Just me, the white coffin, an unknown name – what until days ago had the potential of life, and hopefully God. I decided to do a full service, to the annoyance of a couple of the attendants. It wasn't an experience I would forget in a hurry.

William Gladstone believed that the way a community dealt with their dead reflected upon the nature and beliefs of that community. Certainly the role of a funeral provides an opportunity for a family and community to spiritually, psychologically and socially begin to adjust to their loss. It is at a funeral that we seek to acknowledge the reality that someone has died. It is also here we hopefully realise that we are not alone.

There has been a big cultural change in the funeral industry over recent years. Cremations have increased rather than burial, we now have natural burial sites, people have more choice about who does the service, there is more a focus on thanksgiving rather than mourning and the laity participate far more with eulogies in the service. We now have full-time priests who have become professional funeral service takers employed by funeral directors. Along with this, people's expectations in a consumer society have changed. The bereaved want much more of a say in terms of what happens at a funeral and often a clergyperson can become nothing more than a master of ceremonies. There is also a tendency to dress less formally at a funeral, somehow deadening the pain and significance of the loss.

Churches and their leaders have also changed, with more of a focus on growth and happiness rather than the needy and the poor, and there is little space in services for lament. The church at large seems to be unclear as to whether it really wants to be involved in the funeral business at all. Many Anglican clergy who in the past would have officiated at all the funerals within their parish are now being more selective, with some only doing funerals for church members. This inevitably will lead to more secular funerals and the development of funeral firms employing their own service officiates. Whether this is a good thing I will let you decide. For clergy, they have the tension of whether they are willing to officiate at funerals where they have no church or personal contact. For some this is simply not an issue, as they will see it as their calling to serve all. Others will be more church-orientated and perhaps resent being used almost as a conductor of semi-secular services. How flexible a minister is willing to be with the chief mourners as to how much Christian content a funeral should contain is a real issue.

Some church leaders are preachers, others administrators, some are leaders, teachers and others are pastors. Some attempt to fulfil all of these roles. The question is, 'who will be the grief carers in the church?' 'Who will do the funerals and the aftercare?' Not necessarily the leader of the church. Whoever it is, it is important that they are identified within a church to carry out this ministry and are trained to the highest level. We need to see the importance of the funeral ritual that we provide as 'doorways to healing through which grievers walk'.[39] We are increasingly in Britain in danger of losing our rituals, allowing the community to collude in minimising, avoiding and denying death issues.

For those who do officiate at funerals, we need to recognise that we have differing groups of people at funerals, each with their own requirements.

- The chief mourners
- The friends of the deceased
- The friends of the bereaved
- The wider community
- The officials

We need to recognise that the needs of these differing groups require a different focus. The chief mourners are probably still in shock and numbness. From my own research I have found that with their higher degree of attachment and unexpectedness of the loss, the bereaved family recalls little of the service. They do appreciate the numbers of people who attend. What the minister says tends to go over their heads and thoughts. They appreciate what we do but will

---

39. Wolfelt, A. (1994). *Understanding Grief: Help Yourself Heal*. London: Routledge.

find it hard to forgive us if we make a mistake. Here, we have people who need recognition of their intense pain and grief. The minister needs to stand alongside them in their pain and be their voice as they cry out, 'my God, my God why?'. I personally find myself doing one thing for the chief mourners at the church, another for the wider gathered community and something different again when I'm just with the key members of the family at the committal. At the church I am identifying with them in the pain, but at the crematorium, I use this as an opportunity not only to say goodbye to the deceased but also briefly prepare the main mourners for what lies ahead of them on their journey. Here, I am sowing seeds of offering further support in the months ahead.

However, the wider gathering is in a very different place. They are one step removed from the bereaved family. They may be grieving for the person in the coffin or they may more likely be thinking about other losses that this service reminds them of. They may also be thinking about their own mortality. Here, the minister is communicating in a different way. This is the place where bigger issues of life, death and what might lie ahead can be addressed. This is the group of people who have the capacity in a service to reflect about 'who am I?', 'who are you?', and 'where am I heading?'.

The friends of the deceased may take this in or they may be very focused on the life of the deceased and be wanting something significant said about the person. To achieve this I use a simple technique from Post Traumatic Stress Debriefing (see Chapter 27), which allows me to be accurate when speaking to the congregation. I particularly write down the very words that the bereaved use when describing the deceased. By feeding this back in the service, I know they will accept and agree with what is said, thus providing comfort and acceptance.

With regards to the friends of the bereaved, they may or may not have known the deceased. Their focus will be about caring for their grieving friends. Here, they require resources for how to assist someone in grief. We also need to be aware of the need for balance between those who want a reserved, 'common prayer' format, where every funeral is identical, and those who want it more personal and expressive.

What we are unaware of is the one individual who feels left out in their grief. Perhaps they were very close to the deceased but no one recognises them. The funeral is their opportunity for being drawn in to something bigger, to have their moment of expressing their thoughts and prayers, be it through hymns, words or prayers and to finally say 'goodbye'.

So the role of the minister at a funeral is varied and, if done well, achieves communication across the congregation. One is also communicating to other officials at the funeral as well as to oneself. Here, the engagement therefore needs to be real and congruent to oneself, otherwise one is just going through the motions, which can easily be detected. I have found myself in this position at times, which has left me feeling very frustrated and unfulfilled — who knows how the congregation felt?

The funeral acts as ritual, as Walters puts it, 'to transport the deceased to the land of the dead, and the bereaved back to the land of the living'.[40] There is also a kind of conveyer-belt process going on here. We start out as chief mourners in a daze, only to find ourselves in the months to come attending other funerals, only this time sitting further back from the coffin. Each time we attend a funeral we will be processing different aspects of the event and what death means to us.

So to summarise, what are we doing at funerals?

- We are acknowledging the reality of death.
- We are providing a vehicle to express emotion.
- We are recalling and recollecting our memories of the deceased and their significance in our lives.
- We are providing an opportunity to reflect upon other previous losses in life.

---

40. Walters, T. (1999). *Funerals: And How to Improve Them*. London: Hodder & Stoughton.

- We are helping people to acknowledge that we are in a process of change.
- We are opening up possible ways of bringing change in our lives.
- We are recognizing that we are not alone but part of a community.
- We are opening ourselves to the unknown, to wonder, awe and mystery.
- We are saying, 'I am not an island but I need others to successfully journey in life'.
- We are teaching a sound Christian approach to God's creation, forgiveness and hope.
- We are celebrating God's involvement in our lives and the work of Christ.
- We are providing an evangelistic opportunity by being pastorally sensitive.
- We are producing a 'good enough' service that will sow seeds of positive attitudes towards rituals, faith and the church.

Memorial services in church

There has been an increase in memorial services some time after the body has been taken to the crematorium or cemetery. The main reason for this has been logistics. When I ministered in the countryside, it could take an hour and a half to get to the crematorium and back in time for the wake. By then, most of the congregation had moved on. So it is understandable that people might want to do the Committal first, just for the closest family members and friends and then have a Thanksgiving service afterwards, perhaps days or weeks later. There seems nothing wrong with this provided it is not a community collusion in not handling the reality of death. With no coffin, we are softening the impact that death has upon us. I have had it said that 'it is too upsetting to see the coffin in church'. Yet one of the purposes of a funeral is to have an opportunity to express emotion in a safe way.

Without that opportunity of release, we can be simply lingering in denial and storing up emotions for the future.

The role of thanksgiving and memorial services can be therapeutically beneficial. In Britain we only have two yearly occasions to remember the dead. The first is Remembrance Day in honour of those who have died during wars or armed conflict. This is very much a national occasion. The second is more of a church event on All Souls' Day. This doesn't leave opportunity to remember the dead at other times of the year. Hence memorial and thanksgiving occasions can be very helpful in the grieving journey. Both of these events occur at a similar time in the year, namely in the autumn (November 1 or 2 and November 11), which leaves a large part of the year with no special occasion of recall. In Poland, All Souls' Day is a huge national event and an extremely moving occasion. It is likened to going to a football match with crowds of people blocking the roads as they carry flowers and candles walking to the cemeteries. We may not have such an occasion here in Britain, but we can mark time out for special thanksgiving events over the calendar year. More will be said about such occasions when we look at developing a 'church policy' on loss issues (Chapter 40).

Roadside memorials

Today it is impossible not to notice roadside flowers marking the death of an individual. It is complex why this has developed in recent years. It may be partly linked to the mass of flowers that arrived at Buckingham Palace at the death of Lady Diana. It may reflect that people feel less in touch with the church as a sacred place of remembrance. It may also be due to how the world communicates today, where one event is quickly shared with the world through the media and the World Wide Web and is then instantly copied over and over again. What is special for the bereaved is that this spot is where the deceased was last seen alive. This is now a place of significance. If the church seeks to engage with the bereaved who identify and mark such places, we need to also recognise them as temporary sacred places. How do we then help these families transfer their grief and remembrance to the church? We have to engage where they are at when we first meet them. This might mean being willing to go with the family to the location of death and carry out a short, prayerful, solemn service of remembrance. By making a link with the bereaved, the deceased and the location, we are in a better place to then help the family move forward and make a connection with the church for the months and years to come. Finding meaning for the bereaved will involve understanding what took place at the point of death. We need to be willing therefore to engage at that point. The heart of ministry is always being willing to go where people are at, before we are able to move them forward in their faith towards God.

By offering the church and our ministry as a gift to the bereaved and the local community, we are both avoiding any criticism that might be levelled at the church for being uncaring and offering up a good example of loving our neighbour.

Reflection

- What role do funerals play within the life of your church?
- Is this a responsibility carried only by the minister or do other lay workers offer support?
- Does the church see funerals as one-off events or the beginning of a pastoral journey with the community?
- How do the following two verses reflect your church's funeral ministry?

We want to avoid any criticism of the way we administer this liberal gift. For we are taking pains to do what is right, not only in the eyes of the Lord but also in the eyes of men. (2 Corinthians 8:20)

Because of the service by which you have proved yourselves, men will praise God for the obedience that accompanies your confession of the gospel of Christ, and for your generosity in sharing with them and with everyone else. (2 Corinthians 9:13)

Part Three

Death comes at every stage of life but we fall into the trap of thinking it will only occur when we are at least three score and ten years old. However, our society has changed considerably over the last hundred years, not least in regards to how people die and the effects it has upon the bereaved.

This next part of the book will look at some of the more traumatic losses we will encounter in our church and pastoral patch. We will look at the impact of a loss of a premature baby right through to an older teenager and young adult. We will then look at loss through the eyes of a child and the consequences that this can have on someone so early in their development. We will finally recognise that it is not always the obvious that has the big shock impact. Sometimes it is the loss of a friend which seems to undermine our very being.

SEVENTEEN

The loss of a child in a modern society

In the 1900s, Sicilians would place the deceased in tombs with the bodies upright and they would visit them regularly. It was a very different approach to Britain. The way we have dealt with death has changed over time.

When my grandmother was ill in the late 1950s, I was just a toddler. I recall seeing her in the lounge in a single bed, both breasts removed through surgery and the ravages of cancer. I can recall the nurse coming with the morphine injections, the curate coming and kneeling in prayer with holes in his shoes. The morning after she had died, I saw her in her open coffin laid out in the dining room. The downstairs curtains were all drawn closed. A few days later, everyone went to the funeral except the food, the women who laid Gran out and myself. The funeral directors would all have a dram of whisky before sealing the coffin. People gathered outside, mostly wearing black or black armbands.

Twenty years later and just married, my mum died of a similar type of cancer, in another single bed in the lounge of the same house. This time we had the funeral director to lay her out but still kept her in the house. However, the three daughters-in-law refused to sleep in the house, so dad and his three sons stayed. This time, the funeral directors didn't have a dram of whisky and people didn't wear as many dark colours. But people still bowed their heads and the cars just about stopped to let the procession by.

Today it's very different. It has all become far more clinical. Most people die away from the home, not everyone visits the deceased, cars overtake the hearse, and you have about 20 minutes at the crematorium to say your goodbyes. No one wears black afterwards, no armband, life just moves on, or so it seems, except for the flowers in their cellophane strapped to lampposts where the car accident took place.

But there is another big difference. Fifty to a hundred years ago, people lived with their families, cousins, aunts and uncles all around them, they had a greater support structure to lean on and to share in their grief.

The role that different members of a family played has also changed. In the past, families might have had several children to counter the fact that there was a high death rate for the young. Then, the children played a much smaller role in life, being expected to 'be seen but not heard'. Today children are big business; if we do have children it will be generally when we are older and we tend to have only one or two. But once born, they play a greater part in their parent's lives. There is the assumption that the children will not only live to adulthood but will also see their parents into old age. There are also now so many activities for children. Simply transporting them to various events can be time-consuming. Children are now also targets for the marketing world, whether it is magazines, clothes, radio or TV. All of this puts pressure on parents to get things right. Unfortunately, for most, they don't have parents close to them to advise and support. With the development of patchwork families, relationships in the wider family can be rather complex. All of this means we put greater expectation on the family unit, particularly on the parent-child bond. There is the danger that a parent can, often without realising, expect their child to be a partner, friend and only then a child.

All of this has an impact when we begin to talk about how people react to loss in a family, especially to the death of children. In a symbolic way, the death of a child represents the death of the self.

This can result in the parent losing something of himself or herself, with little desire or motivation to live in the present or the future. The high profile the media give to violent deaths may seduce us into thinking childhood deaths are rare. Sadly, that is far from the truth. The death of a child is seen in the community as inappropriate, unnatural and unacceptable in the modern age. It makes everyone reflect upon the fragility of life.

How are we to cope with such losses? Parents don't know what to do; friends feel awkward and neighbours often want nothing to do with the situation. On top of this, the caring professions of doctors, nurses and clergy, can feel that they have failed in preventing such premature deaths. Unless the Christian community is prepared to engage with such losses, we will not only be ostracising the bereaved but will be giving a negative message to their many friends and acquaintants.

John and Sue

It was approaching Christmas and life was hectic in the Smith family. John and Sue's marriage was not the happiest at the time. John was at work till late while Sue, after a busy day herself at work, was coping with her son and daughter. Anne, who was seven, said she had a headache. She never really seemed to be poorly, unlike her brother, so mum simply gave her an anti-headache tablet. Over the next few hours Anne's pain became worse, with a rash and blistering in her mouth. By the next morning, Anne's skin was beginning to peel away from her body. She had developed a rare toxic skin disease. The first week was critical, but Anne seemed to be holding her own. However, her parents had been told to expect the worst. After ten days, Anne seemed to be recovering when she had a fit and died suddenly from a heart attack. She had been released from her agony, but the family pain was only just beginning.

How can a family cope with such a loss? Whatever problems families have before a child dies, it is clear that they will carry such difficulties with them into the future. How do parents relate to each other when they seem to be grieving in different ways? Is it possible to prevent the guilt and fear from affecting their other children? In what way can the church help? How would you support this family if they were in your church community?

Fred and Alice
It was the first time Fred and Alice had left their son alone in the house for a weekend, the first real break they had had in 19 years of marriage. The couple were glad to get away from the constant family squabbles. Their eldest son, Ian, was busy working and wouldn't be home much over the weekend so the younger son went to stay with a friend's family. Ian had a motorbike, which had been a worry for his parents. How many times had the son heard the parents say, 'be careful!'

When the parents returned home from a magnificent weekend, they were relieved to see the bike in one piece in the driveway. But seconds later, they discovered their son in the bathroom, dead from a drug overdose.

When parents see all their hard work in parenting over many years disappear in seconds, can they ever recover? What do you do when you have a house full of belongings relating to your dead child? How do you react when your relatives cannot relate to your loss? If you were invited to visit Fred and Alice hours after they returned home, how would you cope and what from the church could you offer?

Alan and Martha
Alan and Martha were full of hope. Life had been tough, building up their business while at the same time being lay leaders in a church. Despite a recession, they had survived and now their estranged son had come home and had joined them in the business. The son, David, was married with a young baby. A keen cyclist, each day he

would cycle to work with his father not far behind in his car. One day the father had noticed an ambulance speed past him. Thinking nothing of it, he continued to work only to find his son had not yet arrived. Unfortunately for David and his family, he had been hit and killed instantly from behind by a car that hadn't seen him.

What would be the outcome of the family now? Would the business survive? How would Alan and Martha's faith survive such an event? How would they cope when the daughter-in-law moves away taking the grandchild and all of David's possessions with her? What impact would these events have upon the local church fellowship?

Here, we can see that bereaved parents are multiple victims. They lose not only their child but also their hopes, dreams and self-esteem. Parents fulfil the role of protector, provider, problem-solver and advisor. Now they can feel an overwhelming sense of failure, attacking their sense of power and ability. On top of this the remaining siblings can experience a double loss. They not only lose a brother or sister, but also now lose their parents in grief.

> Death is awful, demonic. If you think your task as a comforter is to tell me that really, all things considered, it's not so bad, you don't sit with me in my grief but place yourself off in the distance away from me. Over there, you are of no help. What I need to hear from you is that you recognise how painful it is. I need to hear from you that you are with me in my desperation.[41]

The next few chapters will attempt to summarise my own research looking into the long-term effects of the death of a child. We will then think about how the church can respond. I wanted to know what was the difference between losing a baby, a five-year-old, ten-

---

41. Wolterstorff, N. (1987). *Lament for a Son*. Grand Rapids: Eerdmanns.

year-old, a teenager and a young adult. And what was the impact two, five, ten and fifteen years later? I have been interviewing parents for more than 20 years. At one point I interviewed 100 parents throughout the country as well as using two questionnaires, and then interviewed 200 families in Lebanon, three countries in Africa, and Japan.

EIGHTEEN

Miscarriage, stillbirth, abortion and infant death

We had our little baby girl.
We never brought her home.
We have no little hands to hold,
No pretty hair to comb.

Now our dreams are all we have
Of how you would have grown,
The places we'd have taken you,
The love we would have known.

If tears could turn to raindrops
And thoughts become a storm
There wouldn't have been a sunny day,
Since the day that you were born.

We love and miss you very much,
Is all we have to say.
You're in our thoughts,
You're in our hearts.

A mother whose baby lived for 30 minutes

George and Rachel were looking forward to the birth of their second child. Rose was only three when her mum became pregnant again, but she picked up her parents' excitement. All went well for the first 18 weeks, until Rachel noticed that she could not feel any kicking in the womb. At first the GP felt that there was nothing wrong and Rachel was making a fuss. Eventually, however, the hospital gave Rachel another scan and very quickly she found herself having an emergency caesarean. By the time Rachel came round from the anesthetic, her baby had died. She was still in a daze when she was allowed to hold her baby girl. The hospital took photographs, but it was all too much for Rachel to take in. Over the next couple of days she felt safe in hospital, in a small room on her own. Unfortunately, one nurse came into the room and asked, 'Where's your baby?' Rachel just couldn't stop crying. The baby girl was buried in her grandfather's grave after a service in the hospital chapel. Only the immediate family was present. Those around Rachel tried to support her by saying what they thought was right.

'Someone said to me, "are you better now?" as if it was a cold. Another said, "at least you didn't get to know it". I felt like hiding in the house. You have months of excitement and preparation for the birth and suddenly it was all gone. I'd just assumed that the doctor would be able to make the baby better.'

Rachel lost a stone in weight over the first year and began to worry about losing Rose. George and Rachel did find that other people began to talk to them about their own experiences of losing babies. It was four years later before Rachel had another child, although the pregnancy was a worrying time for both parents. Rachel joined a self-help group called Stillbirth and Neonatal Death Society (SANDS). Here, she was able to share experiences with other mums who had similar experiences.

'I still think about her every day. She would have been at school by now. I try and imagine what she would be like. I guess I idolise her in a way.'

In 2008 in England and Wales there were 3617 stillbirths, 2261 neonatal deaths (up to 27 days of life) and 3284 infant mortalities within a year after birth (Office for National Statistics). In most cases, the church has some connection, however loose with the parents or grandparents. Sooner or later someone will talk to you about his or her experience.

Miscarriage

A miscarriage or spontaneous abortion is the unintended ending of a pregnancy before the time the foetus could survive outside the womb. This usually occurs some time before the 24th week of pregnancy. Although miscarriages are common, the grief associated with it is often misunderstood. Since the baby has not been seen or recognised by other relatives and friends, there is the assumption that the pain of loss is not great. How often mums are told, 'you've been spared from an imperfect baby, don't worry, you can always have another'. However, often the baby can appear to have no deformities and at this stage it is not another baby they want but the one that died.

If there has been a deformity, parents can be encouraged not to see the deceased baby. However, the mind is able to create and imagine grotesque pictures, which can cause more problems than seeing the baby. I have never forgotten meeting a mother who had been carrying twins. Unfortunately, one of the twins had died in the womb several weeks before his twin was born by caesarean section. The mother wanted to see the dead baby even though his condition was not the best. When she was finally allowed to see him she immediately commented about how he looked just like his twin. She proudly took her healthy baby home along with photographs of his twin.

A common reaction to miscarriage is nagging fear and the continual question 'how did this happen?'. Since the baby was so much part of the mother's physical body, it is natural for her to blame herself. Was it a result of lack of sleep, smoking, drinking, sexual intercourse, curry, working too far into pregnancy or even her age. The list of possible factors a mother can contemplate is endless.

She will naturally also wonder whether the hospital, GP or health visitor made a mistake all of who might have thought she was just a fussing mum-to-be.

For many, having a child is a sign of being a normal human being. Therefore, when it seems to go wrong, mothers can have strong negative feelings about themselves. They have no control over their loss, so they can feel helpless with low self-esteem. On top of this, they have been nurturing a source of expectation and excitement, which was ready to explode into joy at birth, only to find it evaporating into sadness. Maternity hospitals can be an extremely difficult place to be for a mother without a baby. Even in a quiet room of their own, bereaved mothers can hear newborn babies crying. Staff are unsure how to handle the situation and may feel more comfortable if the mother goes home, since they too can feel as if they have failed. The pressure is not only on mums; dads also can feel that they have failed. Although less involved in the pregnancy, they can feel guilty that they didn't support their partner enough. 'Why didn't I go with her to the scan?' 'Why didn't I insist she went to the doctors sooner?' It can also challenge the male ego not to have produced a healthy baby, tarnishing pride and status.

There are other aspects of miscarriages that have their own particular issues. When IVF is not successful, it can result in a hollow phantom loss, which is unfocused. Here, there are often cost implications, all of which can put a marriage under extreme pressures.

We need to remember, too, that many miscarriages don't take place in hospitals but in the home. They can happen very early in pregnancy when a woman is unsure she is even pregnant. Miscarrying at home can mean that the loss is even more secret, isolating the loss. The home also becomes a place of tragedy and can particularly become an issue for the woman.

Stillbirth

A stillbirth is when the baby dies before birth but has usually reached at least 28 weeks of gestation. For parents, it becomes the time when the beginning of life is the same as the end of life; when the cry of a 'longed for' baby becomes the sob of bereavement for the parents. Instead of the anticipated baptism and celebration, there is a sombre funeral.

For months parents have been preparing the home for the arrival of a new family member. A growing attachment has begun between the patents and the baby as they feel and see the movements of the baby in the womb. Every moment of the labour process is recalled as they rushed to the hospital when the contractions began, only to find that their baby has died at some point before birth.

For some mothers they are informed that their baby has died before they give birth. The size of the baby means that the mother has to give birth through normal contractions. Here, the womb becomes a place of death, something the mother has to carry with them throughout their lives. For others, their baby survives for only seconds or minutes.

> I just couldn't believe what was happening. All was going well and then suddenly there was a panic. Moments later I was holding my ill son, but fifteen minutes later he was dead. I couldn't believe the nurse was taking photographs.

When the mother has had a caesarean section under anesthetic, the situation is further complicated with a drowsy mother recovering from a major operation and wanting her baby.

The possible reasons for such a death again play heavily on the minds of the parents. The short journey a baby makes through the narrow birth canal from the warm womb into the cold outside can be the most hazardous of all journeys. Unfortunately, there can be many reasons why the journey can be unsuccessful.

Within hours, a new parent suddenly has to inform relatives and friends what has happened, contacting a funeral director and registering perhaps a birth and a death.

The thought of the autopsy can be extremely stressful to the parents who want their almost perfect baby untouched. There is the tension between wanting to know why the death took place and yet not harming the baby. However, the pathologist is most skilful at hiding any autopsy incisions and the knowledge it provides can compensate in the long run. If genetic reasons are given for the death, parents have to face the statistics of whether such a death is likely to recur if they try again. For some parents, they have to endure multiple losses over the years before they achieve a healthy living baby. Each time there is failure, there is the enormous pressure of whether to try again.

There comes a point when the mother has to leave the hospital for home. The feeling of walking out without your baby is a hollow one, but walking into an empty house is worse. Then, the couple has to decide what to do with the cot, pram and nappies.

> As soon as I got home, I went and washed the pram and cot thoroughly and then put them in the loft.

The father is often lost for what to do at such a time. Some mothers prefer to have baby things around them, holding on to their hope, while other want nothing to remind them. There is suddenly time on their hands with no nappies to change or feeding bottles to prepare. Talking to relatives is difficult, for often the wider family have not seen the baby. On top of this, the woman has to cope with not just emotional pain but also physical pain. She may have stitches in her uterus and pain in her breasts from the production of milk.

If there are already children in the family, then there is the question of what they should be told.

Children have many questions at such times:

- Where is my brother now?
- Can I see him?
- Why can't I play with him?
- Is it my fault?

More will be said about supporting children in loss situations in Chapter 23.

Many parents end up bearing their losses silently, never referring to the painful event/s again. When I was a hospital maternity chaplain, I would meet expectant mothers who would suddenly begin to share their experiences of previous losses. Expecting the birth of another baby brings back all their memories, fears and hopes.

> You go through so much and it's all for nothing, it makes me feel so annoyed. Pregnancy is all we have of our memories.

> When I became pregnant again, I felt disloyal to my dead child.

Abortion

It is very easy to think that people do not grieve when they actively choose to abort a pregnancy. However, such decisions are never clear-cut. Even when someone chooses to abort early in the pregnancy and the parent doesn't believe that the embryo is a distinct person, one cannot assume there will be no emotional sadness about what has taken place. The more complex situations are where the couple or one of the partners doesn't believe that abortion is right, yet feels that they cannot cope with the pregnancy and all that might follow. I recall journeying with a couple in my parish that had three children when the wife became pregnant again. She felt she just could not cope with another child. The couple believed that abortion was wrong but the consequences of another child for various reasons seemed unbearable.

After long discussions, my wife supported the wife through the abortion process. It was a secret that was not shared with their church friends or the wider family. Carrying such secrets is exhausting. For the wife, she had to see other members of the church give birth about the same time as she would have done and to then observe from a distance the development of the children. The support required in this pastoral situation lasted several years. From a counselling perspective, one is trained to empathise with the client. You may not agree with what the person believes or chooses to do, but the premise is that unless you put yourself in their position, you are not in a framework to help. This can be a big issue for Christians with a clear belief system that opposes abortion. We need to be clear when we engage with people whether we are acting as a true counsellor or are being asked for advice from a Christian position. There is a big difference between the two approaches. If I am a counsellor, then I believe an individual has the freedom and autonomy to make their own decisions regardless of whether they agree with my own. If, however, I am offering Christian guidance, I am trying to explain a Christian perspective that might steer the person to make a particular decision. If we are clear in our own mind what we are doing right from the beginning we will not find ourselves in a conflict situation later on. It is possible to do both although one has to be very careful not to leave the individual just feeling judged by you.

Prenatal loss

Prenatal loss comes usually after parents have already had several, perhaps many, near death moments. The journey of a premature baby is precarious. Before the baby is strong enough to be able to breathe by itself and to have put on enough weight to go home, it may have several difficult moments to frighten the parents. Here we have parents who are hopeful, yet have also been warned clearly by the doctors and the nurses of the difficulties that lie ahead.

MISCARRIAGE, STILLBIRTH, ABORTION AND INFANT DEATH

As a maternity hospital chaplain, I was often called in to be with the parents of a neo-natal baby at the point of death. Sometimes I may have met the parents previously and may have already baptised the baby but usually I have never met the couple. The noise of the equipment can be frightening to the uninitiated and so is the sight. Complicated equipment surrounds tiny babies and creates an intimidating picture. Tubes, IV bottles, wires, drainage jars, oscilloscopes, heart stimulators, blood pressure monitors and respirators are everywhere. When you focus in on one premature baby, you see a tiny baby weighing just over one kilo. There will be plasma and glucose tubes into both arms, oxygen fed into both nostrils, a respirator tube down the baby's throat, a blood pressure cuff on the wrist, which is constant feeding information to a digital machine that seems to have a life of its own. There are electro-cardiogram patches on the baby's chest and there is a little gauze protecting the baby from the bright lights. The room is full of buzzing, hissing, wheezing and thumping noises of the support machinery. If you stand close to the baby, you can hear the air being pushed in and out of the lungs by the respirator.

My role at such times was to take the parents into a waiting room, while the nurse decoupled the baby from all of the machinery. I quietly listen to the patents' story, whilst the nurse put doll's clothes onto the baby and placed him or her into a wicker basket. With parents informed of what to now expect, the baby was brought into the room. The parents and I, along with the baby, now waited for death to arrive. One might think there is very little one can do in such a situation. Gradually I learned that there are several things one can do to help and ease the journey that the parents are on:

- I would encourage the parents to pick up the baby, perhaps for the first proper time.
- I would encourage the father particularly to engage with the

child. Men seem to find such situations particularly hard to endure.
- I would encourage the parents to tell me their story from the time of conception.
- I would reassure them that the hospital had done their best.
- I would help them to wonder at the uniqueness and the beauty of their child.
- I would baptise the baby if the parents requested it.
- I would help them take photographs of the baby with each other without all the equipment in the way.
- I would ask the parents if they wanted me to pray for them. Usually they would say yes. I would say a prayer of thanks for the specialness of the child, for the baby's parents and their love of the child, thanks for the care of the nurses and doctors, that this time would draw the parents close together now and in the future, and I would commend the baby to God and his new creation where He makes all things whole and complete.
- I would, as appropriate, cry with the parents.
- I would sit in silence and just 'be' with them.
- And I would begin again, talking to them and getting them to share their story in a new way.

This process may repeat itself several times before the tiny baby finally dies. How long we would continue in the room would depend upon the parents, but eventually with the help of the staff, the parents would eventually say goodbye to their child and go home alone. Hopefully they would be able to take with them photographs, hair clips, hand and foot prints, artifacts that will help them to remember in the future. It is not unusual for parents to have formed such a good bond with the ward unit and a particular nurse that they keep on returning just for a chat and a cup of coffee.

Cot deaths

It is worth mention cot death at this stage, as it has some similarities to a loss at birth whilst still being a unique type of loss.

Peter and Lynne were on holiday for the first time since the birth of their second child. A typical family of four, they had gone to Cornwall to visit their parents. Their first child was a healthy three-year-old girl. The second child was a boy, only weeks old. He was a healthy baby, the pride and joy of his father. Baby Thomas was still at the stage of having four-hourly feeds, but in the early hours of one morning, when mum realised she had not been wakened by crying, she went to investigate. All seemed fine, so Lynne left Thomas to sleep for an extra half hour. But half an hour later was too late. Baby Thomas had died of cot death syndrome. The ambulance driver tried to resuscitate the baby to no avail; the policeman enquired to see if death had occurred through natural means and the parents were left with an empty carrycot and grieving grandparents. The events of that day are engraved upon their memories.

Such a death raises imponderable questions for the parents:

- Could the death have been prevented?
- Why did the police come?
- Was it the parents' fault?
- Why is there no clear known cause?
- Can we believe what we hear about cot deaths?
- Should we have more children?

The sudden death of an apparently healthy baby is so unbelievable, so shocking, that parents are dumbfounded. Sudden Infant Death Syndrome (SIDS) is baffling, as it seems to strike with no warning. The baby that is fulfilling all the normal expectations of a parent is suddenly found dead when mum goes to feed it. It may happen during the night, in the daytime, in the parents' home or in a friend's home. I have even known it to happen in a ten-minute car journey.

Unlike miscarriage or stillbirth situations, the baby has been with the parents for some time. During this time the mother and father, as well as the wider family, have formed strong bonds of attachment with the child. They have not only performed the basic parental duties of feeding, cleaning and protecting; but have watched the baby develop its own character, forming a unique personality.

On discovering the baby, there is a natural tendency not to believe he or she has died.

> I'd never tried to resuscitate anyone, let alone my own baby. I just kept going until the ambulance arrived. I could hear my wife shouting to stop, but I couldn't. I was frightened of hurting my baby's chest but I thought what's a few broken ribs if he's alive.

> It was awful. One moment my baby was dead and the next a policeman was trying to find out if I'd murdered him. They took the cot and mattress away; we didn't even have time to say goodbye.

It is traumatic enough to know your beautiful baby will need a post mortem, but when there is no cause for the death it sets in motion a never-ending search for the reason why. It is understandable that parents can blame themselves:

- Was the baby too hot in the cardigan knitted by grandmother?
- Was the baby too cold?
- Had we started to feed him too early?
- Did I pass on my flu bug to him?
- Was it our smoking or the cat's hairs?
- Did he not feel loved enough?

Parents rerun the events of the moments before discovering the baby dead over and over, searching for a reason.

> I feel angry at the medics who said it was okay to lay my baby on its tummy.

The fact that the coroner is involved only increases the feelings that someone must be to blame. The sense of guilt does not just stop with the parents. The ambulance attendants, nurses and doctors can all feel inadequate. Grandparents can blame themselves, perhaps thinking it was genetic, while siblings can feel guilty for resenting the intrusion that the new baby made in their lives.

Later, there is the difficult decision of whether the parents should have another child. If they do, then they have a sword of Damocles hanging over them. They have to decide whether to use pulse monitors each time they lay the child down to sleep or wake the baby frequently to observe any sudden changes. For some parents this is a comfort, whereas for others it only heightens their fears.

At whatever age a baby dies, parents never forget the specialness of the child. However, as the years go by, they inevitably carry their memories more alone.

> So few people knew my baby, but with older children, others can share your memories.

Many feel a sense of injustice as they hear in the news of battered babies or parents who neglect their children or leave them with nannies.

> I feel as if I have lost my luck. I'm more morbid and bitter; things happen to me now not to other people.

Whether the death of a baby comes through miscarriage, stillbirth or cot death, the effect upon the parents is one that leaves them with deep scars.

Pastoral implications for the loss of a baby

The probability is that in every church community there will be someone being affected by one of the many types of death that can occur for pre- and post-birth babies. The impact is not only on the parents but also on the grandparents and less close relatives and friends. There are several issues we need to think about pastorally:

- When do you name a neo-natal baby? This will require sensitive listening skills to the parent/s to see how they perceive their relationship to their foetus/baby. I have known people who have wanted to name an early miscarriage, while others have lost a premature baby later in the pregnancy and have not wanted to identify the baby with a name. It all depends upon the parents' beliefs and assumptions that they have formulated. If a parent has not identified the foetus as a person then we are not helping if we try and encourage a deeper attachment. Equally, if a parent has named the lost foetus and we think this is over the top, then we will appear to be insensitive. We need to remember that people's belief systems, whatever they might be, can aid recovery. So we need to carefully draw out from the parent how they view the situation so that we can help them adjust to the situation.
- Do you offer a thanksgiving service? Thanksgiving services provide a channel for parents and the nearest relatives and friends to have an opportunity to acknowledge what has occurred. Often this can take place in the hospital chapel but can be just as appropriate in a church afterwards. I have often carried out such services with just a mother and father present. It can be an occasion to express emotion, to open up one's loss to the family and community, to bring God into the situation and to seek comfort and hope. The key is that it is a catalyst to help a couple move forward with their grief. It may involve nothing more than a few prayers, a reading and the placing of

a flower on the Lord's Table. But here we are recognising, in a special place, that something significant has happened to a couple and can draw on God's presence to comfort and give hope. Sometimes these services are less about thanksgiving and more about acknowledging the truth of the complexity of a situation. This might be so with a person who has had an abortion but still wants to bring to God all of their complex emotions. Forgiveness is something that we all need, whether we feel we need it or not. Since guilt is often present when a baby of whatever age dies, a service is an opportunity to seek absolution from God and, importantly, from ourselves.

- Baptism is an issue that often arises in these situations. We will all have our own moral and faith code of practice here. For myself, I have always offered baptism for individuals when they have requested it. At a time of crisis, it is not the time for deep theological discussion but for a compassionate heart. Baptism is about death and life, which is exactly the situation we often find ourselves in. Whether the premature baby is alive, at the point of death or has just died, I personally feel I am not equipped to judge. What I am equipped to do is to lift to God that which he has created, for his healing, whether it be on this earth or in the kingdom to come. What is evident is that the way we handle this situation can determine how parents recover and find faith and hope.

- What can you say at a funeral of a premature baby? It is something I am often asked by ministers and lay leaders. The one aspect of a funeral that is missing is the historical eulogy of the deceased. So what can we say?

- First we need to recognise and acknowledge how painful the situation is for all who are present. The big shock that people have at a baby funeral is the size of the coffin. One just naturally expects a usual-sized coffin rather than the tiny white box. This alone creates tension at the occasion. So being honest at the beginning of the service can at least put people at ease. Secondly, we still need to recognise that what was created was a unique individual with his or her own history, if only in the womb. Actually the person began to exist right back when a couple talked about or dreamed about conception. One can give thanks for the hope, conversations, planning, and the feeling in the womb with the kicks and turns, all of which brought pleasure to the couple. Indeed it hurts so much because of these hopes and desires. So we need to recognise this and tie the pain together with the love. In this way we don't fight the pain but recognise why it exists.

- Thirdly, we can also give thanks for those at the hospital who tried their best along with family and friends who want to support now and in the future.
- Finally, we need to recognise our faith in a God of hope who in his creation wastes nothing. Indeed it is out of nothing that he creates and recreates. So we need to commend the premature baby to God in the hope of God's new creation. Does this mean we are saying that perhaps the tiny foetus will be made complete? Only God knows, but there is usually a deep desire in the parents to hope so. We can only put our hope in a God of creativity and hope. It is in his character that we put our trust.
- What if the family doesn't want to attend? I have carried out a number of services where there has only been the tiny white coffin and myself. Even hardened funeral directors can find such occasions difficult. It is at such occasions I would like to think the heavenly host surrounds me as I continue to complete a full service that this small creation deserves.
- If the family recognises that they have lost a member of their family, it is helpful as a pastor to remember the date of the occasion. It is not onerous to record the date and remember to

- visit or make a caring comment on or near the anniversary when you see them.
- We need as professional carers to recognise the tension the death of a baby or miscarriarge creates between a couple. One might assume such a loss draws couples together but it can more often drive them apart. Helping couples to acknowledge that tension at such times is common and normal can help enormously. It says that they are not alone and someone cares.
- Relating to couples in loss may not be our own particular ministry, but it doesn't mean we cannot be a channel for healing. There are so many self-help support groups today to direct couples and individuals. We are also a resource of information and may, with the right permission, be able to link people up with others who have had similar experiences.
- The church has an opportunity here to take such losses seriously, to offer ongoing care and to be a place of remembrance for as long as the family requires it.

Reflections

- Imagine you are the neighbour of a couple returning home after a miscarriage. How would you feel about visiting?
- A mother has a baby that is diagnosed with a severe genetic disorder such that that the baby can't communicate, see and will die before he is four years old. The mother is a professional child-minder in your church. What issues is she facing?
- Having lost a baby two years ago, you now have a healthy baby girl. When asked how many children do you have, how do you answer?
- Your eight-year-old son has asked to see his baby brother who has died at birth. The baby has a deformity. What are the reasons for and against your son seeing his brother?

- You are asked to lead the funeral of a premature baby, which the parents choose not to attend. What are the implications?
- What can you give thanks for at a baby's funeral?

NINETEEN

The death of children

> Oh call my brother back to me,
> I cannot play alone.
> The summer comes with flower and bee,
> Where is my brother gone?
>
> *Felicia Dorothea Hemans*

Life had not been easy for Margaret since her husband left her with two children, Carol, who was thirteen and Simon seven. Although there were fewer arguments for the children to hear, after only six months Margaret had an even bigger problem to face. Her daughter had been complaining of backache for some time so they decided to see the doctor. At first the pain was diagnosed as being caused by a virus, but finally it was discovered that Carol had a brain tumor. After a five-hour operation, the doctors were unsuccessful in removing the tumor. Carol was expected to live for only a few months. However, her mother would not give up hope and went on a search to find a cure for her daughter.

'I felt so resentful towards the doctors who didn't know of any drugs to give her.'

During those difficult months, her husband applied to the court for custody of his son. Margaret didn't know which way to turn. She was still hopeful when Carol came home with her oxygen cylinder. A Marie Curie nurse came each day to help.

'I never told my daughter as I wanted her to think she was getting better.'

The night Carol died her mother sensed a presence in the room, which gave her strength.

> 'I'm not a religious woman, but I just knew Carol was going to die that night. I suddenly felt at peace. Carol had matured so much during those weeks. It was as if she had an old head on her shoulders.'

At first Margaret had a sharp pain within, but gradually over the months after Carol died the pain became a deep ache. She still felt this ache eight years later. Margaret describes the first year of her loss as one in which she hid in the house, apart from going to the cemetery each day. The second year she read every religious book she could get her hands on. Five years later she was still on anti-depressants, still hoping that each year she would feel better.

By the time a child starts school, the mother has usually formed an incredibly strong bond with the boy or girl, often stronger than the bond between husband and wife. Family life very quickly begins to revolve around attending to the child or children, making meals, washing, ironing, transporting them to various activities. Most parents' aim is to provide the very best for their child. Therefore, when parents discover they have a terminally ill child on their hands, it's as if life itself has stopped.

> 'Suddenly nothing in the world seemed important except the care of the child.'
> 'How we got home from hospital I just don't know, we were in total shock.'
> 'It is not only the emotional pain you feel but actual physical pain, which is excruciating.'
> 'It was like watching a piece of paper with all your hopes and plans on it go up in smoke.'

When a child dies suddenly there is not time to prepare for the loss. However, when illness is diagnosed, the family has the task of changing direction as they focus inward towards the child. In a sense, the terminally ill child becomes special as it receives not only the extra attention of parents but also relatives and the medical profession. As Knapp puts it, 'this modification of parental and family activities must occur, because in the normal world activities are geared to the future'.[42]

Suddenly only the day at hand is important. At first, parents of a child diagnosed as terminally ill react in a similar way to parents who have suddenly lost a child. Shock and disbelief, accompanied by moments of anger and hostility, are common.

> 'You're just not prepared for a Doctor to tell you your child is terminally ill.'

It can take days for the diagnosis to sink in. Indeed, some parents simply will not accept the diagnosis. The thought of their child dying is too much to bear. Whether or not parents acknowledge the facts, they tend to begin a search along with the medical profession looking for a cure. The parents grope for anything that will help them understand what is happening to their child and themselves. This is probably a good thing as this positive attitude is passed onto the child indirectly and gives the family a sense of confidence to continue.

One of the difficulties parents have to adjust to is knowing that their child is terminally ill while perhaps showing no visible symptoms. On top of this, the medication can give a false hope that the child will fully recover. For the children who do enter remission, although joy and relief is experienced, the sword of Damocles still hangs over the family. A remission is the parents' dream, but even when it does occur there is the ongoing fear that the illness will return.

A dying child is not only sensitive to what message the parents convey but also picks up the 'covert vibes' that are given off by the

---

42. Knapp, R. (1986). *Beyond Endurance: When a Child Dies*. New York: Schocken Books.

family, hospital staff and other patients. Parents have the difficult dilemma of whether to inform a young child that he or she is dying. This might be an area where the local church might be able to help. A children's worker able to use creative tools can be able to engage with a child in a way that is different to the parent. The growing knowledge that the child acquires tends to contribute to a rapid maturity. Many parents begin to allow the sick child to control large sections of their lives. They begin to listen to the child as if he or she were an adult. Large portions of family time are spent focusing upon the sick child, and this can lead to neglect of the other children. This can cause resentments in the siblings, later leading to anger and guilt when they lose their brother or sister. Parents can ease the situation by explaining to their other children why they are behaving in a way that seems unfair. They need to create a regular opportunity for the children to discuss their own feelings. Once again this can be an area where the church can help.

It is common for parents to seek some kind of miraculous recovery. This may lead to a long search for alternative treatment to what the hospital offers. Changing the diet, seeking herbal cures and religious intervention may all play a part as the weeks progress. Although these may not prevent the death, they do give purpose, direction and hope. A pastor has a delicate role here in providing ongoing support to the family. Our role is to listen to what the family want. Our prayers are to be directed to their requests rather than our desires. Over the course of time these desires change such that we need to be sensitive to attune to them. It is only in this way that we will still be effectively ministering to the family long after the death. Along the path of this journey we have to be prepared to engage in hope and expectation, fear and guilt, disillusionment and reconciliation.

When the death of a young child occurs we need to recognise some of the particular issues families have to face.

- Mothers have often given up their career to look after a young child and then to provide twenty-four-hour care.
- During the illness, parents often find that other friends with children of similar age tend to distance themselves from the family. This is a result of helplessness as well as fear that such an event could happen to their child. No one wants to be reminded of one of the worst fears of your life. This certainly doesn't help the family, as it only increases their social isolation.
- After death, mothers particularly can feel isolated. They have lost the contact at the school gate with other mums. They now have time on their hands and do not feel able to re-embark on their careers.
- Fathers are often still continuing at work with all the added stress that this entails. After death they have to continue in this routine with diminished enthusiasm, coming home often to a wife who has not left the house all day. It is not surprising that tension in the marriage increases at such times.
- When families lose a young child, the parents are often young enough themselves to be able to have other children. However, as with the loss of babies, it is essential that the dead child does not become some kind of 'perfect child' in the mind of the parents that all other children can never live up to. I have personally counselled a number of teenagers with eating disorders who feel never good enough for their parents who had previously lost a baby or young child.

In light of these developments the church can have a key role in helping such families both survive and recover in the years ahead. The chart below gives an idea of the emotional rollercoaster the parents are experiencing.

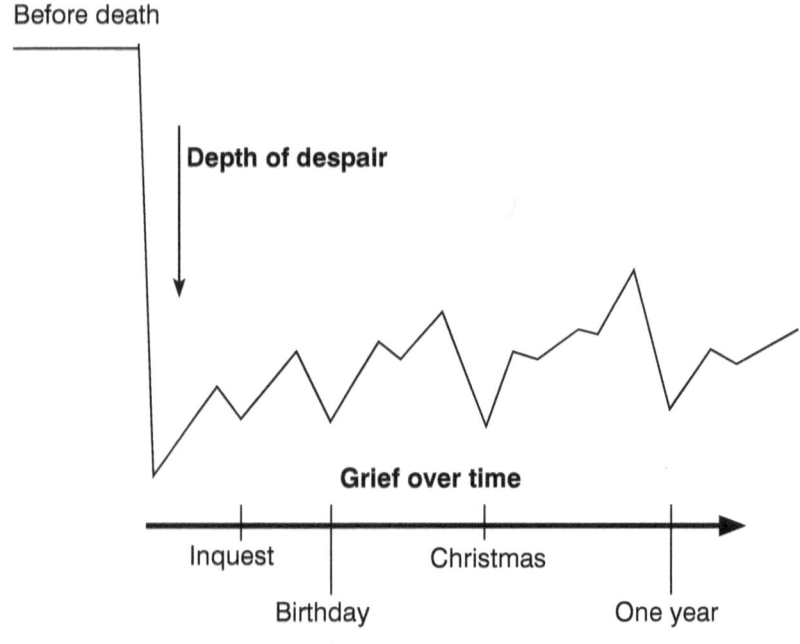

Grief trajectory after a sudden death of a child

Here you can see the difference of the grief experience depending upon whether the death was sudden or after a period of illness. Note how the depth of despair oscillates constantly. Key times can affect the bereaved parents enormously. The main difference if the child dies after an illness is that the parents have a period with the child before death. Here the biggest shock is the discovery that your child is seriously ill and might die. There can hope and remission before the slow realisation that your child is dying. This at least provides a period of adjustment to and reflection on what is occurring as compared to the sudden death of a child. Slowly parents begin to contemplate what is going to happen and consciously or subconsciously prepare themselves for the death.

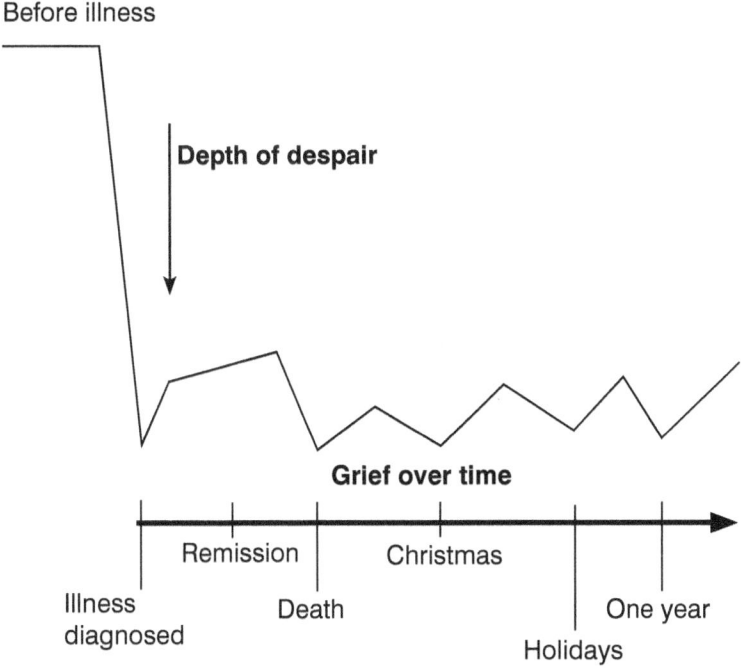

Grief trajectory of death of a child after an illness

If the church can provide a consistent supporter over this turbulent time then they can be there for the family at the key difficult times and may help in preventing some of these problems from developing. This supporter is not usually the minister or leader but a layperson who can make a long-term commitment to the family. We fail to have the right to speak in such situations if we have not previously journeyed with the family. However, if we have offered support to the siblings in particular, then we will be able to offer effective support when appropriate to the whole family.

Reflections

- What do you think are the key factors in telling a small child that they may not recover from the illness?
- Your child has been ill for three weeks. You get an appointment at hospital but it is in four weeks' time. How do you feel?
- Your child's best friend has been diagnosed with cancer. How do you feel about letting your child play at his friend's house?
- When a child is terminally ill, should a parent change the way they discipline the child?
- A mother has stopped work to care for her dying child. The husband is under pressure from his work and works long hours. What expectations might a couple have of each other and how can the church help?

TWENTY

The death of teenagers

> Why should we want to see them again?
> Because we love them.
> Where did we get the capacity to love?
> Surely it was the gift of God.
> How could God foster within our
> Hearts the capacity to love, letting it grow stronger
> And more perfect with the years,
> If at the end He meant to destroy it by death?
> That would be futile, cruel and unthinkable.
> He gave me the gift of loving,
> He will give me again my beloved.
>
> *Leslie Church*

Sally was the boss of the family. She had just celebrated her seventeenth birthday with an enormous party. The home had been full of excited teenagers bursting with energy. Sally was the sort of girl that always had friends around her. She was doing well at school with her A levels; that's not to say everything was plain sailing in her life. Her strong-willed character created a few frictions in her home with her parents John and Mary. Sally had got herself hooked on diets. As soon as she finished one diet, she would start another. Not far from anorexia, if it hadn't been for the support of her parents and Sally's determination, she might well not have recovered. But now her confidence was restored and she was back to the usual tussles with her younger brother and disagreements with mum and dad.

The main argument one weekend was her boyfriend. Dad was not keen on him, which only pushed sally closer to Ian. Mum would encourage Sally to spend time with her in the kitchen baking cakes as an opportunity to get underneath the fiery character and find out what Sally really felt.

One night after Sally had been to school and finished her part-time job, her boyfriend rang, wanting to take her out with a friend. Dad immediately said no, but mum, realising that Sally was under pressure, said yes. As they left in the boyfriend's car, the atmosphere was tense between dad and mum. Several hours passed and Sally hadn't returned home. The parents reluctantly went to bed, half sleeping, when mum suddenly awoke. She hesitantly went to Sally's bedroom and for the first time opened her diary to find Sally's friends' telephone numbers. No one seemed to know where Sally had got to. Minutes later the police arrived. The three teenagers had given a lift to a friend and were on their way home when their car collided head-on with a taxi, which was on the wrong side of the road. Three people, including Sally, had been killed. The boyfriend and the taxi driver had survived. Sally's father had to go to hospital to identify Sally's body.

The next few days were traumatic with many relatives, schoolteachers and friends visiting their home. At times, Sally's mum was supporting and calming down Sally's friends rather than the reverse. It was all so trying. It was difficult to patch together Sally's last few hours of life. Sally's parents wanted to know whether it was Ian's fault, but Ian was in intensive care, so they had to wait.

It was a small town but the church was overflowing for the funeral. Everyone seemed to want to share in the parents' grief. However, as time went on, they found themselves feeling isolated. Several friends of the parents kept away altogether after the funeral. It was as if Sally had never existed. Friends would ask after the son, but not mention Sally's name, while others would come out with painful experiences of their own.

'They would tell me about the accident they had, or encourage me to let go of my daughter as if I could forget her. One friend suggested that her divorce had been much worse.'

Sally's grandparents and relatives also found it difficult. John's father had been ill before Sally's death but he seemed to give up after the funeral and died months later. Another relative that lived a distance away didn't go to the funeral. This created ongoing tension in the family.

There were positive things that arose. A grandmother began to talk for the first time about how she had lost a child when she was younger that Sally's parents knew nothing about. Some of Sally's friends would visit and share stories of Sally at school. This was a comfort to the parents. The house now was full of pictures of their daughter. They had acquired a cat, as it was something Sally had always wanted. However, for Sally's brother this was all too much. He eventually left home and went to a university as far away as possible.

After five years, the couple was still together with their son living away from home. The couple had gone through ups and downs in their marriage and work was now less important to both of them. They had a simple attitude to life, living day by day. The contact with Sally's friends had dwindled, which saddened them. They still felt a strong sense of anger at the taxi driver who had fallen asleep at the wheel, at the boyfriend, at God, at Sally and at themselves for past mistakes.

'The most upsetting thing is when people deny her reality; they think we're contagious so they keep away. We've lost not only growing up with her, her exams, marriage, children, but most of all we've lost a friend, our best friend, who influenced us for good.'

Sally's story is typical of the events that follow the tragic loss of a teenager. To appreciate the impact of such a loss, we need to understand the intense and complex relationship that has been forged between parent and child. By the time a teenager has reached 14 years old, their parents have invested thousands of hours in caring for them. However, adolescence brings with it a degree of conflict as the child grapples for independence. They are neither children who need constant supervision nor adults who are ready to take on the full responsibility of life. They are in a kind of in-between time straddling play and responsibility as they experience physical and emotional changes. Hence parenting teenagers can be a time of both pleasure and tension. Parents have to give up their position as a role model as the teenager look elsewhere for inspiration, guidance and support. Teenagers are grappling with a number of big questions that they won't share with their parents:

- Will they pass their exams?
- Will they ever get a job?
- What career should they pursue?
- How will they cope with leaving home?
- Will their parents divorce?
- Are they capable of having sex?
- Should they masturbate, try drugs and travel abroad?

Such thoughts and questions inevitably begin to separate the teenager from the parent as they look for answers away from home. Arguments are fairly common as disagreements arise about beliefs, behaviour and attitude. In the past, adolescence seemed to last till the family celebrated the child's 21st birthday. By then the son or daughter would have a steady career path, be fully aware of their sexuality, probably be in a stable relationship and would have left home. Today, however, it is rather different. It has been suggested that adolescence now lasts into the late twenties. Young people take this time to finally settle down into a permanent work position and a more stable relationship. In the midst of this complex parent-adolescent relationship, the death of a teenager can leave a parent totally vulnerable and grief-stricken. Death rarely arrives at the door when we are ready for it. It is understandable to find parents in a state of shock and dismay.

If illness precedes death, then there can be time for parents to clear the air with their child. There is an opportunity to apologise for regrets and a chance to listen afresh to the desires and wishes of their child. There is also the chance to begin to come to terms with the forthcoming death and begin the grief process. Parents may find it extremely painful to sit alongside a son or daughter in a coma or going through chemotherapy, but years later they find it a comfort to know that they had been with their child at the end, fulfilling a parent's role of care.

When a teenager dies, there is usually a high level of sympathy and support by the community. Parents begin a journey of discovery as they find out new facts, events and talents about their child.

'I didn't realize how clever he was until afterwards.'

The bedroom can be a source of information and comfort for the parents. Here, the sense of sight and smell draws a parent to feel close to the child. Some parents sleep in the room or simply keep it untouched for many years. Funerals of teenagers are usually standing-room only occasions as the church is filled with young people. A recurring fact is that many parents have told me that after the funeral their friends struggle to keep in touch. Either they find the recurring thought of losing their child too upsetting or they get tired of the ongoing support needed by the bereaved parents.

'My son was taken to school for years by his friend's parents.
Yet from the moment of his death they have not spoken to us.'

Parents appreciate hearing from the child's friends, as they are able to add information about their child's life. However, as time goes on, it can be painful to observe from a distance these young people getting on with their lives, getting their A levels, going to college and getting married. The care of the siblings now becomes complex. Do parents loosen their control over the other children so that they don't argue or do they tighten their control in fear of another loss? Another factor at this stage is that parents are now at a different stage of life. They are now too old to invest in more children yet it can feel as if you have wasted many years investing in a child that has now died. This leads to an increase in rumination.

> 'I think about him daily, in fact more so now he's dead than when he was alive. You don't need to think about them if they are alive.'
> 'I can't rebuild my life now, I'm too old to have children.'
> 'I think nicer thoughts about her now she's dead than when she was alive.'

The loss of a 'problematic' teenager leads to prolonged pain. It affects the parents' motivation at work, as suddenly all incentive to succeed seems so shallow. It also affects the social life of the parents. At social occasions with contemporaries, the conversation often revolves around their children. This leaves the bereaved parents more inclined to stay at home. They will find themselves often sitting near a door for an easy exit when they feel uncomfortable.

> 'Any social event we went to. We made sure from the beginning we had an escape route if we needed it. In the first three years I don't think we saw any event right through to the end.'

In the end parents are left with the ongoing ache of 'shadow grief'. This is where a parent's life never fully recovers to what it was previously.

THE DEATH OF TEENAGERS

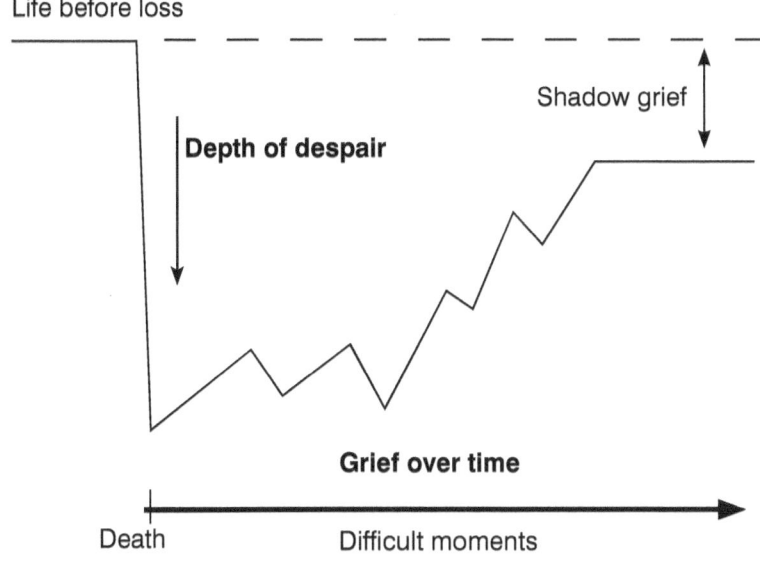

Shadow grief

One can see the need for a long-term strategy if a church is to engage in supporting these parents. Otherwise we end up behaving just like the bereaved parents' friends who become support weary.

Reflections

- When a teenager has died in the family home, what are the issues involved in deciding to move from the house?
- Can anything beneficial result from the fact that a teenager ends up in a coma for two weeks before dying after a car accident?
- What feelings might arise when a mother decides to read her deceased teenager's diary?
- What would you say to a mother who tells you she is very angry at her deceased son who was killed in a motorbike accident?

TWENTY-ONE

The death of young adults

> Were a star quenched on high,
> For ages would its light
> Still travelling downwards from the sky,
> Shine on our mortal night.
> So, when a good man dies,
> For years beyond our ken,
> The light he leaves behind him
> Shines upon the paths of men.
>
> *Anonymous*

Fred and Violet were a typical couple with two children. Alice was 16 and still at school and Alan was 20 and studying at university. Alan was deaf in one ear but he seemed to cope with it admirably. He was a tall, handsome, blonde-haired young man with a marvellous future ahead of him. It was the end of the term and he was returning home by train. Unfortunately, he was standing too near the edge of the line when a train travelling through the station caught his side. His parents arrived at the hospital only minutes after Alan had died. His face was unmarked by the accident as Fred and Alice held his still warm hand. Alan's parents were not new to bereavement. They had both lost brothers in the war and their parents were dead. The events of the next few days were a blur to Violet except she could remember how beautiful and at peace her son looked.

> 'For the first few years if I saw a blond person I would look intensively to see if it could be Alan. It all seemed false somehow, rather like living in a bubble. I was not suicidal but extremely angry with God. But because Alan had faith, somehow my faith grew.'

Some friends were helpful but most didn't seem to have a clue how to help. One even asked Violet to watch a movie about a train! Violet eventually ended up in hospital with a minor mental health problem. Alan's sister Alice felt neglected for months afterwards. She had been especially close to Alan. She remembers playing his music over and over again in her bedroom. She had always wanted to study medicine but suddenly changed her mind. However, after a couple of years she changed her mind again and finally became a doctor. She fell in love with a tall blond man and settled down into family life. However, after giving birth to her first child she became ill with cancer. She struggled for nine years before she finally died. Once again Fred and Violet were thrown into grief. This time the son-in-law organised the funeral. He decided to keep away from his distraught in-laws and kept his child also away. Now Fred and Violet had not only lost two children, but also possessions belonging to Alice and contact with their only grandchild. They had been left with a peaceful picture of Alan but since their daughter had had such a battle with cancer all they could recall was a painful scene.

Now in older age Fred and Alice have time on their hands, and it is difficult not to dwell on the past. They rarely see their grandchild. The deaths have created a sort of distance between the couple, a constant strain of communication between them.

> 'I was in a shock for a long time after Alan's died, whereas for Alice I knew it was coming, although it affected me just as deeply. I feel guilty I never spoke to Alice about dying. The only thing I have left now is Alan's ring.'

We might think that the death of an older child might leave fewer scars than the death of a young child or teenager. However, having talked to a good number of older bereaved parents, such a loss is still catastrophic. The age of an older parent may bring wisdom but it also brings with it more regrets and less to look forward to in the future. One particular difference here is that often the parents are not the next of kin. If the child was married then the daughter- or son-in-law is the legal next of kin and therefore organises the funeral and holds on to all the possessions. This may be correct but it leaves parents with the potential danger that they have nothing physical to hold on to despite years of investment into their child. This can lead to resentment between the parents and the in-law.

All parents expect to die before their children. They may have already prepared their will leaving their children as executors. When the tables are turned and the children die first, the parents can feel cheated. They may even end up inheriting possessions and money from their children. The result is often a high level of guilt, guilt for inheritance but more so for just being alive instead of their child.

Perhaps one of the greatest difficulties older parents have with loss is that they have more time on their hands to reflect. Younger parents have less choice but to keep going to care for other children and to keep paying the mortgage to keep a roof over their heads.

> 'At the very time I found space and peace in my life,
> suddenly that space and peace were totally shattered.'

There is a deep wish in most parents of whatever age to be with the child. Many contemplate suicide with a few succeeding.

> 'I can see no point of living, I just want to be with him,
> wherever he is.'

Some parents end up having to look after grandchildren. This requires a role reversal in habits, routines and goals that they had lost when younger. However, it can provide a means of motivation to continue with life. This does inevitably bring with it added stress, responsibility and financial commitments. In one case, grandparents had acted as support parents to their grandchildren when their son's wife died. Years later the son remarried allowing his parents to now enjoy their retirement. Unfortunately, nine months into his marriage the son's second wife suddenly died. The grandparents had to cope once again with bereavement and to summon up physical and emotional energy to now support their son and his teenage children.

> 'I feel diminished as I look at other families playing in the park. It reduces my identity of who I am.'

Older mothers are perhaps having to cope with going through menopause while parents generally are also having to face up to handling their ageing and perhaps dying parents. The loss of a child intensifies the situation. At a time when they should be getting life under control, parents suddenly find themselves very much not in control.

Reflections

- What hopes and expectations do parents have when their children graduate?
- What emotions might arise when parents are financial beneficiaries from their 28-year-old son's will?
- What issues arise with the death of a 20-year-old son who was an atheist for Christian parents?
- A son who was in his late twenties dies leaving a wife and a small baby. What are the issues for his parents when the mother moves away taking the baby and all their son's possessions?

TWENTY-TWO

Common issues the church needs to be aware of with the loss of children

> Life may be understood looking backward,
> But life must be lived looking forward.
>
> *Anon*

In looking at how parents cope with the loss of children there seem to be several common factors.

The need not to forget

Whenever you visit a home where there has been a death of a child, there are usually photographs visible. Artifacts of the deceased and sometimes their bedrooms are preserved as a memorial. The longer the child has lived at home, the longer it seems to take the family to remove the child's belongings. A person's bedroom portrays something special about them. The older the child, the more they have made the room their own. The décor and personal belongings give a feeling that the person is around. When it comes to the death of that person, relatives want to be as close to them as possible, and this is best achieved by being in the bedroom. Several families have told me how they would just sit in their child's bedroom taking in the smells and atmosphere that remained. Although many parents may not redecorate their child's room, none would see it as a shrine but simply a place of identification, a place of pain, but also a place they could walk out from and get on with their lives. Those who have not lost a child may find all of this strange, but if you get a group of bereaved parents together, you begin to see that it is perfectly normal and natural. There is also a deep need to talk about the child. Unfortunately, most people try not to use the deceased's child's name as they feel it will make the parent upset. It probably will, but they would prefer people not to deny the existence of their child. I have spent many hours travelling the country talking to bereaved parents. The one thing I have discovered is that if they think you are interested, they will talk to you for hours about their child. All that is required is a willingness to actively listen. It seems that parents can deal with the emptiness of the future produced by the death of a child only by filling those voids with images of the child they once had, through thoughts, memories, and open discussion. Only in this way does such a loss become reality.

Dreams

Dreams and premonitions are recurring themes when talking to parents who have experienced loss. Such vivid experiences may occur before death, at the moment of death or afterwards in grief. The majority of mothers, as opposed to fathers, are often able to recall their experience.

One mother dreamed of her baby choking in the middle of the night. She rushed to the child to cuddle him. The mother often said to the child, 'you mustn't die'. Then one day the child died of cot death syndrome at the babysitter's house. Another mother was busy teaching when she suddenly felt faint and had to sit down. Later that day she was told that her teenage son had died in a car crash at the very moment she felt unwell. Clearly, such experiences may be post-created subconsciously as a mechanism for accepting that the death was inevitable. However, those who experienced such incidents were convinced that they were real events. From a pastoral perspective, we have to take what a person says as the truth and work with their perspective in a way that enables them to move forward.

The majority of parents I've talked to could remember dreaming of their child after the death. They could recall the dreams with fond memories and saw them in a positive light. Many parents would wake feeling more awake and peaceful.

> 'When I dreamed of my daughter, I felt better. I'd see her in a field with her favourite dress on. I'd say "you're all better", and she would reply, "I love you": and then walk away.'

Some recalled always dreaming the same dreams in the same location.

> 'It was as if it had a healing effect on me. It was not a familiar place, but each time I dreamed it I felt better.'

Dreams are not always positive.[43] In a few cases parents would wake up crying because of a dream. But in the majority of cases parents were glad about the dreams and wished they had continued.

The wish to die

For many parents, particularly mothers, there is an almost overwhelming drive to be with the deceased child. This is irrespective of whether they have other living children. One might have thought that losing a child would make you more focused upon your other children. This is not always the case. I have spoken to mothers who have told me that they believe that other relatives can look after their children but, from their perspective, no one is looking after the dead child. This can become a fixated approach that occupies a great deal of time for the bereaved mother. If there are no other living children and perhaps the mother is divorced and is feeling isolated, then they can be at very high risk of suicide. The pain of separation can just become too much to bear. Many parents interviewed said that they still had remnants of their desire to end it all several years after the loss.

---

43. Mallon, B. (2000). *Dreams, Counselling and Healing*. Dublin: Newleaf.

> 'I just wanted to die in the first year. Breast cancer, anything – just to be with my son.'

There are two phases at work here. First, there is the acute phase – feelings of desolation and wanting to escape from life. The bereaved parent can teeter on the brink of self-destruction for anything from two weeks to three months. The chronic phase is much longer, but is characterised by less intense feelings. In my own research, I have found this chronic phase lasting much longer than many realise.

> 'I would lie in the bath and wonder whether I had the nerve to drown myself and end it all.'

Where a mother, three or five years later, is thinking about ending her life and has friends and relatives preferring not to talk to her about the past, one can see how she will be experiencing considerable stress. This chronic phase, I suggest, lasts up to five years or more before it gradually subsides, but it never fully disappears. The parents' reaction here is one of a 'take it or leave it' attitude. They tend to have less fear of death in any form and even though they may no longer contemplate taking their lives, they would still not resist it.

> 'You can go for weeks and suddenly the events go round and round in your mind and before you know it you're getting depressed.'

Suicide can remain high on the agenda if the parent has other negative factors also affecting them. For example, one mother reached breaking point because of the way her husband was treating her.

> 'He made me feel worthless, because he ignored my feelings, my child's birthday's, anniversaries and her photographs.'

When parents are plunged into a pit of intense despair and depression, it is certainly clear that they lose their zest for living. With a society that often ignores their cries for help, most end up wearing an outdoor mask which says 'everything is okay'. This leads to a mundane 'plodding on' existence exhibiting a decrease in motivation and determination.

'It's like a great big hole blowing through you all of the time.'

A change of values

> At some point there is a moment at which you realise your child is not coming back and your original self is never going to be complete or the same. You will spend the rest of your life living with a major loss and it is going to be okay. You can do that. It's not going to be so aching and so terrible that you can't function, that you can't re-create your own self.
>
> *The mother of a teenage accident victim*

Tragedy jolts people into a deeper perspective of life, they gain new insights, skills and a change of lifestyle. They are given no choice but to rethink their goals, to reorganise their priorities and to move in a new direction. This takes time, courage, patience and support. Many parents become more altruistic in their approach to life. This is where they practise an unselfish concern for the welfare of others. This action not only benefits those they support but they themselves reap a positive outcome. This altruistic behaviour may take many forms whether it be joining a support group, raising funds for charities, writing self-help books, or campaigning against injustices in the world.

All of this is a worthwhile attempt to bring good out of a disaster. In no way does it compensate for the loss but it does give a focus for living. One can see where the church can help by supporting the parent in their social charitable action.

Other changes for bereaved parents often include a less materialistic approach to life. If you have worked for years in a mundane job so that you can pay the mortgage and care for your family only then to see this family torn in two by the death of a child, it certainly changes your perspective on work. In some respects bereaved parents become more tolerant in life, yet they also suffer fools less gladly. Time is now something not to be wasted on things you might not like or believe in.

Shadow grief

Shadow grief is what can result from the loss of a child. It is an emotional residue that hangs over the parent for the rest of their life. This shadow appears after a traumatic journey. If we are to engage in supporting bereaved parents, we need to be aware of this journey they find themselves on that results in this grief residue.

Events Before Death

The events immediately before the death of a child can influence how families cope months and years after. When a child has an extensive period of illness, parents begin to fear the worst. Some parents describe hearing the news that your child is terminally ill as worse than the actual death. The family can feel as if they have all been put into a liquidiser with everything in turmoil. Although caring for the terminally ill child can be a gruelling ordeal, there are positive aspects, which assist relatives in their bereavement. From parent interviews, I found that where the parent had time to adjust to the impending death, they were able to talk about the period before death with some positiveness. Generally, where there is anticipatory grief, parents show less self-blame, less extreme emotion at the time of death, less anger and fewer depressive symptoms. There is also a greater tendency to formulate some way of handling the event that makes it more real, with less likelihood of reacting with disbelief and shock. However, if illness is prolonged, then it can cause an increased likelihood of marital tension and depressive symptoms. What is 'prolonged' is difficult to say and will vary in each case, but we are thinking in the order of over 12 months.

The Moment of Death

Although the first reaction at the point of death is a temporary state of shock, parents do recall these moments vividly. No matter how much preparation one has, there is something in us that clings to the concept of immortality, especially for our children. It is almost inconceivable for us to acknowledge that we have to face death.

> 'I can remember every minute of the first two hours after hearing of his death.'
>
> *A mother five years later*

If we are willing to understand how the parent felt at the time of death, it will help us in understanding their reaction afterwards.

> 'It was the first time I felt release since my child, 12 months ago, had become ill. However, later I felt guilty because I felt like this.'

> 'For six weeks I sat with my son, holding his hand while he was on the life support machine, I talked and talked to him, so that when it came to switching off the machine, I felt ready.'

The Days that Follow

It the early days after a child has died, it can feel as if the world has stopped spinning. It is understandable that a parent might feel as if they will never encounter a semblance of enjoyment again.

'Silent, swift, irreplaceable, the scythe has swept by, and we are left…the mail comes, the phone rings, Wednesday gives way to Thursday and this week to next week. You have to keep getting up in the morning and combing your hair (for whom?), eating breakfast and making the bed (who cares?).

'It can seem 100 years ago and at times like five minutes. I lost interest in everything except day-to-day necessities.'

It is in the midst of this that family and friends gather, a funeral is to be arranged and the death registered. We need to remember, if we get involved with funeral preparations, what state of mind the parent might be in. Rather than celebrating eternal life or giving thanks for the past, a parent is simply waiting to hear the child's voice enter the room. We, along with the funeral director, may well be seen as an intrusion

'I kept expecting him to walk into the room or receive a telephone call saying he was okay.'

A mother who had lost her baby in a car accident couldn't sleep without holding onto the baby's baby-gro pajamas. The smell of the cloth was a comfort to her. Weeks later she washed the pajamas only to find that the smell had gone, something she regretted ever since.

The First Few Months
The early months are a fog of rare pain, guilt, anger and fear.

'I cried every night for six months.'

'I constantly cry, I'm afraid of stopping in fear of forgetting him. When I do stop crying, I feel guilty for showing signs of getting better. If I love him how can I possibly get better.'

In the early months parents have to adjust to post-mortems and perhaps inquests. At a time when friends hope the parents are adjusting, the situation may appear to be getting worse. Physical pain remains along with the mental strain of constantly thinking about the child. There is also the added strain of having to go back to work and pay the bills. As the weeks go by, it can appear that the world just continues as normal while the parent feels trapped in their experience. Contact with family and friends tends to wane inevitably as there is a limit to how much support people can offer. Alas, it can be a time of disappointment in friends that a parent felt could have been more supportive.

The first few months involve getting used to a very different routine and lifestyle. It might mean the parent is not visiting the school any more, not being needed as a taxi driver or having the house full of the child's friends. The one place the parent dreaded going, to the hospital, may now be the very place they miss.

> 'We went to hospital every Tuesday for four years with our daughter. It left an enormous gap; in the illness we at least had a routine. We chose Tuesday for the funeral.'

The first year is full of past memories of what the parent did with the child in the previous year. It is not uncommon for parents to go through their minds and recall exactly what they were doing with the child this time last year. Birthdays, anniversaries, Christmas and holidays are often the worst times.

> 'I hate birthday parties and holidays. They are the very time when the person who would love it most is missing.'

Marriage Relationships and Siblings

When you get married, the Scriptures say that two become one, but when there is death in the family, the two grieve individually and in their own unique way. This inevitably often results in conflict in the marriage. In the back of the person's mind is the belief that one's partner is there to lean upon but what do you do if that person is already bent double in pain? If there were cracks in the marriage before the death, then this baggage is carried forward into the grief situation.

> 'Our marriage had cracks but our daughter cemented over them until she died. Our other child was hyperactive, so his father felt he had been left the "booby" prize.'

> 'When my son was in hospital, I wanted to stay with him but my husband, not liking hospitals, always wanted to leave early. This created conflict and later I felt bitter and angry towards him.'

> 'My husband was not so close to my son so he reacted differently. It made us feel further apart. I felt bitter that he didn't care. My husband just didn't want to talk, whereas I couldn't stop referring to our child. This was a major factor in our divorce.'

Others persevere in their marriage but recognise that it is just not the same.

> 'My husband would not talk about our dead baby. I felt hate for him because of it.
> Our marriage has never been the same.'

Lack of communication is one of the major factors in the breakdown of marriages where a child has died. If you can help a couple to take turns each day in talking (or not talking), it can give each permission to express themselves without swamping the other. This can be difficult if one partner just refuses to talk, but it can be at least a starting point and bring recognition that each have different needs that have to be recognised. As said earlier, we mustn't just assume because one partner is not showing signs of tears that they are not hurting intensely.

The majority of couples I have talked to have expressed how the loss of a child had not especially made their marriage stronger because of what they had been through. To survive together can be seen as an achievement in itself. Where marriages seemed to have very few tensions was where there was good communication, a willingness to listen to each other's feelings, recognition of the different way that they handled their grief, willing support when one partner felt low, an agreement about where they were heading and manifestation of signs of affection each day.

Siblings have a double loss as they lose not only a brother or sister but also their parents in grief. It is easy to feel left out with nobody interested in how the sibling is feeling. Parents can hide their grief, which also makes it confusing for a child to know what is normal behaviour when a brother or sister dies. More will be said about this in Chapter 24.

> 'My daughter seemed to take the loss in her stride.
> It was months later when I realized how sad she had become.'

Siblings will experience the same pain, anger, guilt and fear as the parents. They will have fears about a parent dying, or whether they will now die, fear about their parents' marriage failing and fears of being alone.

One of the commonest experiences described by children is feeling totally isolated in their grief when all the attention seems to focus upon their parents. One teenager said to his parents,

> 'Why is it people come and talk to you about your loss but not to me?'

When children feel ostracised, it only leads to more complexities later. One teenager in his desperate need left a message in his sock drawer where he knew his mum would find it. It simply said that he missed his brother and how wretched he was feeling. In the first year it can seem that the conversation is always about the dead child rather than those alive. Increased numbers of photographs around the house only intensifies the confused emotions the surviving children feel.

Parents are caught betwixt and between whether to be more disciplined or lenient with the surviving siblings.

> 'I was afraid to argue with my son, so I gave in to all his requests. You hesitate to disagree, provoke or argue, and you become more liberal because of fear of losing another.'

Other parents choose to be more cautious and protective.

> 'Because of my daughter's car accident, I didn't want my son to learn to drive. I even hoped he would fail his test.'

It is in situations like this that children need to be a part of a wider group of friends and support. Here the church can provide a good resource of care and a listening ear to hear their story. Sometimes it is the church's responsibility to gently draw the attention of the parents to the needs of the siblings before further harm is caused.

The Following Years

The first anniversary doesn't suddenly make the pain go away, despite everyone saying that things will be better when the first year has passed. This may be wishful thinking by the friends and family. No one likes to see people continue to be in pain and there is a degree of fatigue of caring for bereaved parents. In reality the parent is now further away from the deceased than ever. Now they have no memories of caring for their child in the previous year. Now all they can recall of last year is being 'lost in their grief'. On top of this they will have had the sad experience of people avoiding them in the street. This might seem far-fetched. I certainly struggled to believe it at first but so many parents have recalled this experience. It is understandable if you think about it. What do you say to a bereaved parent? How do you cope if they start crying? Do you want to be reminded that your child could also die? Hence it is easier to slightly avoid the issue. All of this goes with the package that people stop using the deceased child's name. Again people think they are easing the pain of the parent. If we don't mention him or her then they will think less about the child. Unfortunately, since the child is always close to the parent's thoughts, the absence of people using the name only increases the pain.

> 'You begin to learn that you will have good and bad days, you can't predict which they will be, but at least you learn that, like the weather, there will be continual change.'

> 'I believe that just as the clouds come and go, so I have good days and bad days. There is no logic to these days. I now at least know that if it's a bad day it will pass. This is the only way I can have any hope.'

> 'We talked a lot to each other and just expected everything to get better. After three years I realised it wouldn't. I had to just get on with life as it is.'

> 'I feel that I have lost my luck. Things happen to me now not other people.'

After five years, over 54 per cent of parents told me that they were still experiencing grief and loss. After ten years the figure dropped to 20 per cent, which is still very high. After both five and ten years, 60 per cent of parents expressed to me that there were issues still unresolved from their child's death. Listen to how parents spoke after ten years of grief.

'If final acceptance is getting over it, then I never will.
But if acceptance is missing him, then I am there now.'
'I still have off days, especially when I see mums with children the same age as my child.'
'When someone comes up to you and asks, "how's your daughter?" it's like a dagger turning in me.'
'I still avoid pregnant women.'

By now, parents have realised that although they may be coming to terms with their loss, they will never get over it. They continue to hold on to the picture they had of their child at death. Contemporaries have grown and changed, but parents find it difficult to imagine their child anything other than how he or she was the day they died. This is 'shadow grief', where life has grown and changed but the thoughts of the child are always just under the surface. This is normality, it is normal to surely want another five minutes with your child, it is normal to hold on to fond memories, it is normal to want to acknowledge your child's past existence.

'I still feel resentful for the loss of my four-year-old. I don't go over it but still live with it.
You can't put it behind because it's all too precious.'

There is no balancing the books here but we have to remember that these bereaved parents also contribute significantly to the community. What with their altruistic attitude, starting charities, caring themselves for individuals and writing self-help support books, they give much to those around them. One person explained their grief as something that had not decreased, but recognised that their life experience had been enlarged. The diagrams below try to capture this experience.

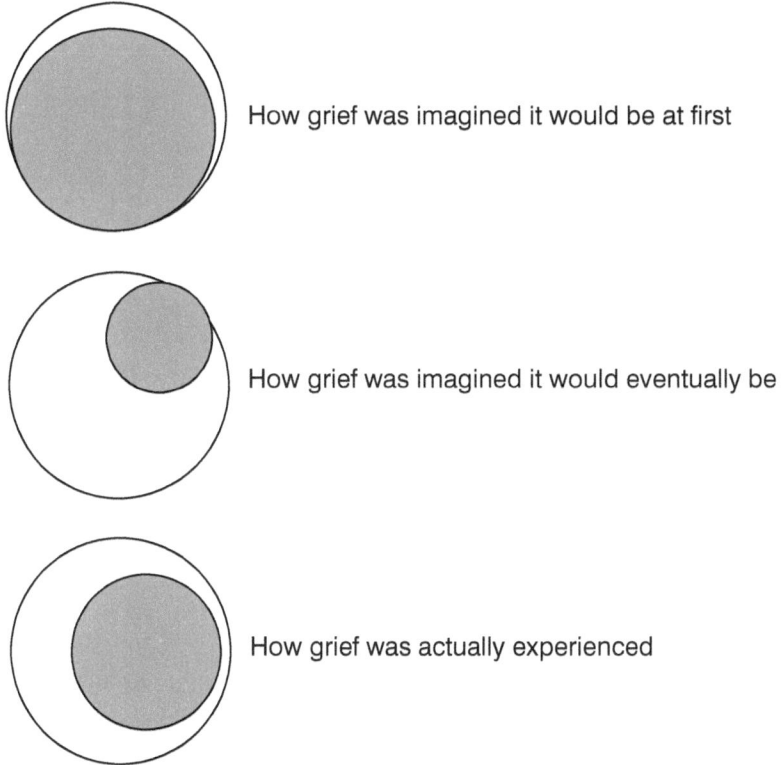

How grief was imagined it would be at first

How grief was imagined it would eventually be

How grief was actually experienced

A Religious Perspective

> The wind bloweth where it listeth,
> And thou hearest the sound thereof
> But canst not tell whence it cometh, and whether it goeth;
> So is everyone that is born of the Spirit.
>
> *John 3:8*

A child's death seems a strange, unnatural disaster. It perplexes us and makes us aware that, in the end, we have no power to control our own lives or our children's. Inevitably, parents attempt to search for some reason for the loss and many questions are raised in their minds as they dwell on the child's death, trying to find some comfort, peace and hope.

- Is the death fate or just bad luck?
- Where is my loved child now?
- Does he or she still exist in some form that I can relate to now and in the future?
- What happened to the personality of my child?
- If there is life after death, will I recognise my child?
- Will she or he continue to grow and change in heaven?

I have often heard it said in churches that people turn to God when they experience the death of a child. In America, 70 per cent of parents are believed to turn to religion for comfort and hope when they lose a child. In my own research I found different results. 84 per cent said that their religious belief in God had remained the same or increased and only 16 per cent said their faith had decreased. This tells us that most people's assumptive worldview remains relatively the same at a time of a disaster. We tend to cling to what we know with some small variations.

> 'It was all for something, although I don't know what. I get annoyed if someone says, "it was all for nothing".'

There will be those whose faith is strengthened while others will feel that God has placed the mark of Cain upon their foreheads.

> 'People say how can you believe in God now? But I say how can you not.'

> 'When I needed God the most, I felt as if He put up the shutters.'

Although parents became angry with God, this did not surface as much as one might expect. Believers were frustrated at the thought that God seemed to be saying that the child was okay, when the parents felt such an enormous personal loss.

'How can my child be all right? If he was, he would be next to me – not with God.'

What was a common factor was that people's faith had changed in its nature.

'Our faith has been pulled to shreds. It is now back together, but certainly not as it was before.'

'Our attitude has changed. God didn't make it happen, yet He didn't prevent it. I now see a picture of life with free will and a God without power.'

Some of those who said they were atheists or agnostics revealed how envious they were of those who had faith. The thought of acknowledging that your child is dead and rotting in the ground with no hope of a reunion is hard for anyone to accept.

One recurring theme among parents was their determined belief in the afterlife, even if their understanding of God had become rather shaky. 81 per cent of just over a 100 families said that they believed in the afterlife compared to 74 per cent who said they believed in God. This reflects the very deep longing within parents to have a reunion with their child in some form or other.

Bereaved parents continue to pray to God but in a less 'genie' type of way. Prayer is seen as a way of keeping contact with the dead child and maintaining hope of a reunion. It is very common for parents to want to talk to their child and prayer is one way to do just that. Here, continuing with the bond and link with the child serves to be a comfort for the bereaved. Here God has become less omnipotent but more of a safe keeper of the dead.

One might think this would direct such parents to the church; however, bereaved parents seem to have a difficult relationship with gathered religious communities. This complex relationship all begins with the funeral. On the whole, the main thing the parents remember from the funeral are the flowers and the numbers that attend. This is understandable, as we tend to have the funeral in Britain within five to ten days of the death when the parents are still very much in shock. What they don't forget is if the clergyman or funeral director makes a mistake. This becomes impregnated in their minds. Parents then find that going to church reminds them of their child's funeral and therefore can be just a too upsetting place to be. Hymns are also emotional things to sing if your nerves are on edge. On top of this churches today tend to focus on a successful, cheerful image, all of which passes these parents by. The greater the praise event, the greater the despair the parent can feel. You then have well-meaning Christians who long to see the parent getting better which gradually wears the parent down enough to just keep away from church. You might be thinking 'Is there nothing then we can do for these people?' In the next chapter I will suggest a strategy of care, but for now let us just acknowledge the reasons why church can be a difficult place not only for bereaved parents but also for people who are suffering in whatever way.

All of this can drive parents to seek answers elsewhere. A good number of parents told me how they ventured temporarily to see spiritualists or mediums to seek some comfort that their child is safe. Ultimately, no one can give the parents what they are seeking, that is to have their child back, and so such contacts seemed not to last.

Historically society placed its trust in the church for healing as well as mental and emotional support. There was hope either in healing or in life after death. Indeed, people were encouraged to be prepared to die a good death. Elaine Tierney notes that in the 13th century popular preaching instructed parishioners to remember death.

Gollfried wrote, 'Preachers advised people to go to sleep every night as if it was their last and as if their beds were their tombs'. Thomas à Kempis wrote of death, 'He who is dead in the world, is not in the world, but in God, unto whom he lives, comfortable, and your life is hid in Christ in God.' Preparation for death was important. To die without having confessed one's sins would submit one to eternal damnation. So the emphasis was on death, and from this developed the concept of dying well, what the guide would describe as the 'art of dying'.

Today people are just not prepared to see suffering as anything but negative and certainly not to consider death unless one is absolutely forced to. Instead, at times of crisis, society has replaced its trust in religion with science and specifically medicine. Instead of praying longer we now seek more and more chemical treatment. When this fails and the child dies, instead of focusing on the concept of heaven, we are encouraged to give to appropriate charities so that one day we will solve this problem of death. Alas, for now at least, both religion and science fail to provide what the parents want. It is not surprising, therefore, that parents can have difficulties both with churches and medical centres. Yet both provide a glimmer of worthwhile hope, hence parents maintain some faith and some charitable action for the hospitals.

A strategy of support

How can you as an individual or as a church support bereaved parents? Perhaps the first thing we need to recognise is that if we want to get involved in this kind of ministry we need to understand that it is not a 100 metre sprint but more of a marathon both for the parent and the carer. Let me just outline a few pointers to consider.

- We need to recognise the importance of being involved in support right from the beginning. However, this is the most vulnerable point. The parents and family are in shock, therefore this is not the time for long conversations. Too often people visit the bereaved and stay far too long, start sharing

their experience and even get so upset that the bereaved has to care for the carer. The parents very much resent this and this may discourage the church from any future care of the family.
- Don't promise something that you cannot deliver. It is easy to fall into the trap of offering all sorts of activities only to find that you can't maintain this over a period of time. If you offer support, be specific and clarify for how long you can offer it for. In this way both sides do not disappoint each other.
- Don't say, 'just ring me if you want anything'. Remember that the parent is in shock; they are therefore unlikely to have the energy or wit to think about you. You needs to be proactive in what you offer provided they accept the offer, be it providing meals, doing washing, ironing, etc.
- When it comes to the funeral, remember that you are doing one thing for the parents and family, while doing something else for the wider community at the service. Anything you can do to make the service go smoothly without problems will be appreciated. Help the parents to think through a range of options:
  - Remind them that there is no rush to make decisions.
  - Involve others in organising the service, e.g. siblings, school, friends, etc.
  - There is no rush to choose a stone for the burial or deal with the ashes if the body is to be cremated.
  - They can choose what the child is to be dressed in and what artifacts to go in the coffin.
  - Parents can visit the child as often as they want before the service.
  - Parents can ask the funeral director to get them a lock of hair to keep.
  - The service can involve modern music, photographs and contributions from various people.

COMMON ISSUES THE CHURCH NEEDS TO BE AWARE OF

- Parents can arrange for the service to be videoed or recorded.
- A copy of the talk and eulogies can be provided.
- If the parent chooses to read/pray/give a talk, then the leader of the service is willing to step in at any point to complete the task.
- If large numbers will be attending, attendance cards can be filled in or a remembrance book with photographs can be signed and written in as a keepsake.
- Parents may be offered drugs or alcohol 'to help them through'. If they can manage without these it will be better, because using them can impede their ability to make important decisions, and delay the grieving process.
- The parents' family or friends can carry the coffin. The coffin can be placed in the church the night before or just before the service.
- The parents can keep the flowers or press some as a keepsake.
- The parents are welcome to throw flowers, feathers, seeds, etc. into the grave.
- The parents can help in filling in the grave.
- Parents are welcome to release a helium balloon at the end of the service.
- All of these decisions can reduce the helplessness that parents may feel.

- At a funeral one is trying to give thanks for a unique life, acknowledge the depth of pain for all and yet also offer a glimmer of hope. This balance is not easy to achieve. I offer one image at the end of this chapter to help you think about how to give thanks for a life cut short that seems to have been appreciated by parents. Acknowledging the depth of pain is easier; one simply has to be honest about how you and everyone present feels. No one wants to be present at such a funeral. Therefore, by acknowledging this and declaring that there is no easy answer, one is identifying with the whole congregation and putting everyone at ease. At a Christian funeral we need to fulfil our duty of expressing the Christian faith and hope, as you perceive it. However, we need to do this with gentleness. The parents are unlikely to hear it. Their time comes later, as will be explained. So a long theological talk can possibly antagonise. A shorter message of hope and purpose for the wider congregation that attempts to reach into their thoughts and questions will more likely sow seeds of faith.

- Parents do want to talk about theology at some point. Often this is about three to six months after the death. Unfortunately, churches have often lost contact by this time. We inevitably move on to other funerals and perhaps easier pastoral care situations. However, if we are still engaged with the family at this point and are willing to give the time, you will be able to share a fuller Christian understanding, along with hope and purpose with the parents. But you have to have stick around enough with the pain and the mess and confusion to have the right to speak into the situation. Those who try and talk theology in the first few days tend not to get invited back.
- We have resources and knowledge about support agencies, which we can link families up with in the future. Compassionate Friends can be a great help here. This is a group of bereaved parents who agree to meet approximately once a month to simply share their grief journey together. This provides, especially for single parents or in cases where one partner won't talk, a chance to normalise their experience. I recall one parent telling me how she had torn off all the wallpaper in her house. She thought she was going mad until she shared this at a self-help group. She heard others

talk about their moments of frustration and anger. One lady told how she destroyed every plant pot in the house. If we can link individuals up together it can prove to be a turning point in their lives.

- We can help to provide a strategy for the difficult times ahead. For example, many mothers dread Christmas. The thought of buying presents while not acknowledging their dead child is just too much. I have often suggested that the parents buy a present for the deceased as a way of recognising their presence in their lives. This can then release the mother to focus on the rest of the family without feeling guilty. The present might simply be a plant or a donation to a charity.

- If we remember to visit just before crunch times in the year (holidays, birthdays, anniversaries, etc.), the family will appreciate it. We can then provide an opportunity to talk about the day/s that they are dreading. Often the lead up to the day is worse than the day itself. Again, if we can help the parent to plan the day beforehand, then we are providing them with a strategy to cope. A good secretary can organise your diary to accommodate this approach.

- Remember when you visit to use the name of the deceased child. Don't be afraid to talk about them and, more importantly, be willing to listen to the parent talk about them. You may be the only person who actually allows the parent to talk freely about the child without judgment or restriction. It may mean you will have to be comfortable with a parent crying but the fact that they do is a sign that they trust you.

- Be conscious of the siblings in the family. Link them up with a child bereavement agency that might support them. I often do small exercises with a parent and child together which allows the family to talk freely together when I'm with them and afterwards. More about working with children is explained in the next chapter.

- To enable a bereaved parent cope with church, it is easy to provide seats at the back of church that allow the parent to arrive late and leave during the last hymn. For a period of time they will appreciate this protection.
- Provide a book of remembrance in the church. This will bring the parent back to the church time and time again.
- Remember to keep a note of the bereaved families so that when a new leader of the church arrives, they are able to follow up your good practice (remembering the computer laws about confidentiality, etc.).
- Try and appoint two people to share the responsibility of care over a period of time. In this way they can support each other and share the load over a longer period.
- Have a church care policy as outlined in the final chapter.
- Beware that parents are more vulnerable in large towns and cities than in small-knit communities where they are recognised and more supported.
- Remember the Do's and Don'ts:

Do NOT say:

Why are you crying?
It was worse for...
I understand.
Good will come out of this.
It was the hospital's fault.
He/she is better off dead.
He/she has gone to a better place.
My divorce was more painful.
Look on the bright side.
It could be worse.
Call me if you want anything.
Try and be wise.
I know because I lost my dog.
At least he reached 16.
He was just a trouble to you.
It will get better.
Time will heal.
It will be better after the anniversary.

Things to DO:

Listen.

Ask how the child died.

Use the dead child's name.

Allow yourself to be upset.

Allow parents to react in their own way.

Offer to do specific jobs.

Allow moments of silence.

Recognise that you do not have answers.

Seek to empathise rather than sympathise.

Remember:
It is not a situation that needs answers,
it is a reality that needs a presence.

Reflections

- How different is it to be a parent losing a child through a terminal illness as compared to a sudden death?
- It is now eight years since your friend's child died. How do you feel about mentioning the child's name to the parent?
- Why do you think people cross the road to avoid bereaved parents?
- What would be your reply when a parent asks, 'where is my deceased child now?'
- What are the signs that a bereaved parent requires additional medical help?

An illustration of a life cut short

The life of a baby or a child can be compared to a portrait of someone special. There are some portraits we see in museums, which are large and perhaps dark in colour through wear and tear. We have other portraits and pictures that fit on our wall in our homes that are perhaps more special. We also have very small paintings, perhaps in a cameo form, that we can keep in a locket around our neck that capture someone very special to us. All of these portraits are complete, yet their size varies enormously. The life of a child or baby is more like the cameo portrait, it may not consist of many years but, nevertheless, the life can still be complete and somehow even more special.

TWENTY-THREE

Supporting children in grief

Will was a slightly overweight nine-year-old boy, the only son of Alex and Fiona who spoilt him rotten. He, like his dad, had a great love of cars and motorbikes. Will didn't seem to have a lot of friends in school and because of this often came home upset on the school bus. It was his mother's fortieth birthday and the family decided to go and visit friends for the weekend. Unfortunately his mother had a stroke over the weekend and died within minutes. Days later Will and his dad returned home. The funeral was filled to the brim with local people all offering support to Alex and his son. Alex would need it, as he had to return to work promptly if he wanted to keep his job. Each school morning, Will would have to go to the next door neighbour's house after dad went to work and he waited for the school bus. In the evening, he would go to different homes for his tea until his dad returned home after 7 o'clock. The school was supportive, but Will found it difficult to concentrate and even harder to make friends. He began to get into trouble with bullying smaller children in the school. He was also being a distraction in the local church's Sunday school. The dad, the church, the school and the community were unsure what to do with Will; but what was clear, he needed some help.

Although many adults would like to protect children from the impact of grief and loss, alas this is not possible.

- Two children under 18 are bereaved of a parent ever hour
- There are 20,000 newly bereaved children each year

- Risk of parental death by the time you reach 16 years of age is 6 per cent
- One out of five children will experience divorce by the time they are 16 years old (in England and Wales, National Child Bereavement Network)

On top of this we have a large number of refugee children who have experienced a range of losses. Over 90 per cent of teenagers who get involved in youth offending services have had a significant loss of some kind. One has to wonder whether their behaviour is partly a means of working out their own anger and frustration, unaware of what is happening to them.

We know that if children are to grow up emotionally and socially healthy, they need a good dose of appreciation, approval, attention, encouragement, respect and security. Unfortunately, when it comes to supporting children when death occurs in the family, we tend to ignore their needs. Our culture has developed its own way of treating children when they have to cope with loss.

We tell the children not to feel bad, but alas they do. We encourage them to be strong, which inevitably encourages them to hide their pain. As adults, we tend to hide our grief and moments of tears away from children, which gives a confused message to children. They either think that the adults just didn't care about the deceased, which creates anger; or they think it must be their fault that they are still upset.

This means that children do a lot of their grieving alone in their bedrooms. When it comes to funerals, the trend is to think that it is better to keep a child busy and send them to school. We seem to think that if one is busy, you won't think about the loss. This only means that children are robbed of saying goodbye to a relative at a funeral. They are not given the chance to develop healthy coping mechanisms, which will equip them well when they experience further losses in adulthood. So what goes on at a funeral remains a mystery, full of apprehension. Unfortunately, I would find that the apprehension already in the adults had been passed onto the children by the time I visited the home to talk about the funeral. When asking whether the children would be attending the funeral, I would often hear that the child doesn't want to go. But how does the child come to such a conclusion? They clearly pick up the vibes from the family. So they go to school and we then wonder way they can't concentrate.

Bereaved children tend to do less well at school, are more likely to drink and turn to drugs and are also more likely to be bullied. As a result of the adults' uncomfortable feelings that they cannot ease the child's pain, they then buy them some kind of substitute replacement. Unfortunately, a dog or cat is no replacement for a mum or dad. The reality is that just as for adults, time heals no wounds; it is what we do with the time that makes the difference.

Children are on a journey of learning and development. They are moving from perceiving that life revolves around them to being able to see things from another point of view. What is clear is what we would want to see children achieve in their lives. We want a child to be able to deal with painful emotional issues. They need the skill to be able to handle their thoughts, emotions and behaviours. A child has to become aware of their limits and strengths; we want them to have the ability to change so that a positive consequence will result. The conclusion of this development is that children begin to function comfortably within their world and are able to reach significant milestones in their lives.

Children of all ages need the opportunity to grieve like adults. They need to be able to say goodbye, to share how they feel, to vent their emotions and to adjust to the loss.

There has been a big debate about what is the age at which children begin to grieve. It revolves around how children see themselves and their caregivers and to what extent they are able to comprehend the finality of death.

Infants

Infants up to two years of age begin to show the first signs of grief and mourning. They will pick up all the feelings of their chief caregiver and this will initiate an alarm reaction as they call out for the caregiver so they can feel safe and secure. If the loss is of the chief caregiver, then the young child will protest with feelings of despair. With very young losses it is easy for the child in later life to fantasise about their 'perfect parent'.

Children up to about five years of age are primarily concerned with the here and now; the concept of the future hardly exists. They have what is called 'concrete thinking'. They struggle with the idea that death is final. This means that they will keep expecting the deceased to return. A typical reaction might involve a child asking questions about the deceased, and then getting straight back to playing with their toys. But this doesn't mean that the child understands. They may ask the same question over and over again. There is also the tendency to personalise all events, which can result in a child thinking it was their entire fault.

> A mother who had experienced a cot death with her second child told me of the older four-year-old who said that if he had been at home with his Fisher Price medical kit, then his baby brother would not have died.

Young children often take throwaway comments that adults make seriously. So when we say things like, 'death is like sleeping', or 'not waking up again', or 'gone on a journey', or 'Jesus took him', a child can take it literally. This creates great confusion and frustration when they are told to go to sleep, or be taken on a car journey or told to pray to Jesus.

It is important that they are told:

- The truth in simple language.
- That they might be upset and have their own feelings.

- That other people are upset too.
- That they can talk about the loss for as long as they want.
- That it is okay to ask questions.
- That it wasn't their fault.
- That they will be safe and cared for.

Older children

Children of about six to ten years of age are developing fast. They tend to think of death as a person, a shadowy figure that can be thwarted or outsmarted if they only knew how. At this age it is difficult to understand that someone can be happy and worried at the same time.

It is also hard for them to understand that when someone is dead, they are not coming back to life. For a child, a world without a parent may be beyond their thinking. He or she has to grasp that they are a separate entity from their parent and without them they will still exist. This is a time when the imagination is very busy, with facts and fantasy often getting confused. They may think 'magically', that if they only perform a special task, then the person will return. Magic thinking is not reserved only for children, most adults think magically when they fill in a lottery slip each week, and may find themselves making wishes after the death of a loved one just like a child.

A child is at an inquisitive age, and can bombard you with endless questions, which are difficult and painful for an adult to answer.

- What happens to the body?
- What's it like to be in a coffin?
- Can they breathe?
- Where is the deceased?
- Can I see him/her?
- What's heaven like?

- Can I go to heaven?
- Why did they die?
- And many more ...

We can only be as honest as we can and say that we don't know if that is the case.

As the child grapples with the feeling of guilt, they can also be confused between feelings and actions. So a child could easily feel the death is their fault because they cried, or got daddy cross. Children may educationally take a step backwards with daydreaming, bed-wetting, sucking thumbs, biting nails, sleep disorder, symbolic stealing or generally forgetting things. This regression is not negative but a healthy way of handling the feeling of being overwhelmed. Relatives should not chastise but give space for the child to return to their normal age behaviour. Children require permission to express their feelings, but in an environment where there are clear ground rules and limits. All of this leads children to express their grief by being over-dependent on the chief care-giving parent. The child might also develop a range of somatic illnesses that might need the doctor's reassurance. Headaches, stomach upsets and general aches and pains are common. Children will often manifest the same symptoms as the terminally ill relative. We don't help if we fail to take the child seriously and bring reassurance.

As a child reaches 10 to 12 years of age, they become more aware of the future rather than showing only concrete or magic thinking. This awareness can reawaken feelings of childishness and helplessness. A child may show outward coping behaviour but be denying their feelings within. At this time children may also be handling a growing sexual awareness, which may complicate relationships. Children are also now becoming more aware of the possibility of their own deaths, which can be very frightening.

Again, children need consistent care:

Give the child the basic facts of what has happened.
Reassure them that they are not alone in this and will be supported in the future.
Include the child in the funeral service (take toys and have someone the child is comfortable with to look after them).
Encourage the child to hold on to their memories. Give them a chance to talk about them.
Validate their emotions and allow them to express their feelings.
Explain that life will go on and they will always remember their loved one.

Adolescents

Adolescence is a period of loss and gain. The child is passing from childhood and closeness to the family to developing closer peer relationships and more sexual awareness. Death therefore can come at a very challenging time in their life.

The concept of finality develops with age. As a child reaches 12 years old, they are still taking things at face value but are also developing skills in deduction. As they move into adulthood they are beginning to think like adults though not maturely. The ability to reason in the abstract is developing as are concepts of idealisms. Judgement becomes more internalised with independent decisions reached by weighing up pros and cons. Wanting to be independent is also a sign that the young person is taking control of their lives. This often leads to clashes with family and authorities. Mood swings are common. Here, there is an understanding of death and an ability to ponder on such concepts as an afterlife.

However, when a close parent dies, a teenager can take on board aspects of the deceased. They can take on the role of mother or father thus protecting them from the pain and emptiness that they feel.

Older teenage girls may even become pregnant as a way of 'filling the gap', while boys may become aggressive and hard to handle.

If these wounds of loss go unrecognised, they can remain under the surface for years with the teenager's behaviour not being connected with his or her loss. This is then carried into adulthood having a negative affect upon the person's life.

It is not uncommon for teenagers to have school problems for two to three years after a significant loss. This results in learning difficulties, poor attendance at school, lower school grades and a general sign of disorganisation. What is required is an understanding school, setting lower targets and providing regular breaks. Unfortunately, I have come across headteachers who give no allowance even when a parent has died. This is where a church leader can be helpful in supporting a family in communication with the school. Teenagers need to know what caused the death and particularly whether the illness might affect them in the future. A helpful local doctor can put young people at ease or initiate tests to clarify the situation.

It has been found that girls, regardless of age, exhibited more anxiety and somatic problems than boys.[44] Girls can idolise the deceased parent more and show an increased sensitivity to change in the family setting after the death. Boys, however, are more likely to say themselves that they get into more trouble at school, which suggests that they express their grief by acting out their behaviour. Girls generally are more able to express their feelings and receive sympathy as compared to boys, who are more likely to be told to be strong and cope. But we mustn't overestimate the difference between boys and girls. A large study found that there was only small difference in characteristics between the young sexes. Even when a small difference develops in the area of mathematics, verbal

---

44. Worden, J. (1996). *Children and Grief: When a Parent Dies.* New York: Guildford Press.

reasoning, the difference at puberty is still small. We must remember that many girls love rough play and can be very competitive while some boys just don't relate to rough games and are very sensitive and caring. While at the age of five, boys and girls show an equal interest in babies and the care of infants. So we need to hold on the saying,

> Gender influences patterns of grief, but gender (at whatever age) does not determine patterns of grief.

All children, of whatever age, will be affected by any change in the family. Change of routine, moving house or school will add to the loss experience. Sometimes children are expected to fill the role of the deceased, adding to their pressure and expectations. I recall an 11-year-old girl who had lost her mum. Just starting her secondary school, she had to pick up her younger sister from a neighbour, then travel home and prepare tea till dad arrived home at 7pm. A tall order when you've lost your mother. There is also a double loss if a parent dies, as the child loses the normal behaviour of the parent remaining as he or she gets consumed with their own grief. It is no wonder then that children become worried about losing the other parent.

In some situations the death of a parent may bring a positive outcome for the child if it removes abuse, violence, etc. However, that does not mean that the child will not grieve; they may feel guilty at being pleased that the problem has been removed. In the end, integration can often involve the child seeking meaning in their loss. They, like adults, are on a journey, trying to make sense of life, why we are here and where we are heading. What is required is a development of a sense of pride that they have coped, risen to the challenge and survived. Only then will a more hopeful and resilient child result.

Over recent years there has been a growing number of child grief charitable agencies working with children. What they have found is that children will grieve in stages over many years. They will reprocess their experience at each stage of their lives. As they gain new thinking and insights they will try to reach a more satisfying explanation of their loss. Therefore, if a child has had loss as a young child, one still needs to be aware of the issues they may be carrying with them into adolescence and adulthood.

The church can play a key role in helping these young people become resilient caring adults with hope and purpose in their lives. The church can help the child know that you care and are concerned about what has happened to them. That you want to do your best for them to help, that you are willing to listen, without judgement, how the child thinks, feels and what needs they may have.

A church children and youth ministry can be a place to fulfil four essential needs:

- **A listening ear.** This needs to be consistent, without judgement, recognising that we do not understand their position without empathy. Here we need to be consistent with our children's worker who is assigned to care for the child. Consistency is important at a time of change in a child's life. This involves regular contact, interest if the child is missing from a regular group, and a healthy dialogue with the family. We also need to make sure that future youth workers are aware of the events in the life of this child.
- **Information.** Often young people are not given the information that they require. This gives room for the imagination to run wild and room for misunderstanding and lack of trust. The information might consist of reasons why the person died, medical information, religious beliefs, understanding about grief, what will happen in the future. A church group can be a good place for children to work through such issues. We need to be careful we do not give platitudes to comfort the child. It

is essential that we give space for the child to work out their own belief system. What we can do is create a safe place to ask questions that are often not asked elsewhere. Questions about:

Where is the deceased?
Is there life after death?
What is heaven like?
Can my relative see me?
Will I ever see them again?

These are questions that children think about, but they are often not tackled in secular support agencies. The church has to be willing to engage with such questions without giving blanket answers. In child bereavement groups I have run, I have been fascinated by how children think about these questions. They do not come to my conclusions and I have to be at ease with this. Who am I to say I know any better? What I can do is to help the children think through the many possible answers to these deep questions. I have to be relaxed to know that whatever conclusion they come to, it will probably change as they develop educationally. Indeed, these children are on the same journey as the rest of us as we grapple with such questions throughout our lives. That doesn't mean the child cannot develop a faith that can sustain them through this journey. However, if we are dogmatic and simply have fixed answers, which the child does not feel comfortable with, then we will see less of them in our children's ministries.

- **Companionship**. A child needs someone who will travel with them into the future with knowledge about their loss. This means the church ministry needs a clear procedure of support for children. Someone needs to remember the child at birthdays, Christmas and anniversaries. We need to be willing to use the

deceased's name and allow the child to talk if they want to. We need a teaching programme that yearly deals with issues of loss. Other children will all participate, as they will have lost pets and perhaps grandparents as well experience living losses when parents separate and divorce. The church's link with the local school can also provide ongoing support: regular school assemblies, offering to do a teaching session or opening up the church for a teaching session and running after-school clubs. The church may even have someone with play therapy or Godly play experience who might offer to run a small after-school group just looking at loss issues.
- **Space**. Children need room to be themselves. This includes letting them talk or be silent, to cry or to shout, to let off steam or to hide in a safe place. They don't want to be patronised. Again, the church is a safe place for children to both feel safe but also to express themselves freely. A key aspect of recovery is the ability to play normally and safely, and surely the church should create such a place. It is also a place where alert sensitive workers can identify ongoing negative signs that might require additional professional help.

Signs when additional support is required

Support may be needed by children when they:

Remain angry or depressed.
Suppress their feelings.
Are unable to move on.
Feel that they are disloyal if they give up the pain and are happy.
Lack the ability to be involved with others.
Lack observable development at school.
Persist in unhealthy preoccupation, e.g. physical pains and aches.
Are fearful of additional separations.

Are difficult to control.

Are helplessly discontent and appear to give up easily.

Discount themselves and underachieve.

Behave in a destructive way towards themselves or others.

Fail to maintain a good relationship with the caregiver.

Indulge in activities that indicate that they are trying to relieve distress and anxiety, e.g. picking at themselves, licking, sucking, biting, twiddling, soiling, or reverting to the behaviour typical of a younger age.

Show distress or refusal to talk about the loss, or not allow others to talk about the loss, e.g. agitation, leaving the room, changing the subject or distressing others.

Set fire to things.

Show disregard for personal safety.

Indicate that the caregiver does not have the ability to allow the child to express feelings.

Prefer isolation.

There may be signs that we can look out for well before these symptoms develop. Children will be more at risk if:

Death is unexpected, sudden or violent.

There is no funeral involvement.

The child idealised the deceased parent.

The child can't speak about the deceased or is not allowed to.

There is family stress.

The child's parent is depressed.

There is poor peer support.

Techniques that children/youth workers can use

In all of my play therapy work with children, I follow a simple pattern. It begins with building a relationship with the child/children.

This focuses upon exercises that build the child's self esteem. I then develop the idea of stories and story-telling which lead the children towards sharing their story in a creative way. This allows the children to have an opportunity to talk/draw/express their own memories, which until now may have been trapped within them. This naturally leads on to exercises that focus upon understanding and expressing feeling. I then focus the children on thinking about how to move on in life with their life experiences in such a way that it doesn't hinder them. Finally, I make sure there is a planned enjoyable ending of the sessions. Remember, children often have not had a good experience of a positive ending of a relationship. We need to model good behaviour to them.

Self-esteem exercises

- SELF-ESTEEM: Food, drink and more snacks! Children like treats and snacks; it puts them at ease.
- SELF-ESTEEM: Rules of the game. It helps to break the stereotype of school by affirming that it is okay to be messy, you can colour outside of lines, experiment etc.
- SELF-ESTEEM: Make your own birth certificate in a colourful way, adding additional information than a normal birth certificate.
- SELF-ESTEEM: Any game that builds up self-esteem.
- SELF-ESTEEM: Write your name as a bar code.

Storytelling and memory exercises

- STORYTELLING: Losing something special – glove puppet, tell a story of how the puppet lost something special, pass the puppet around to share feelings of loss. Second time around, ask how they feel about the loss. Lead to drawing the story or writing the story. End with puppet saying how they feel now.

- STORYTELLING: My coat of arms. Symbols of things you do well, a goal you accomplished recently, that remind you of the person who died, the worst thing about grief, etc.
- STORYTELLING: Draw a self-portrait – introducing the concept of change. How might you look in the future?
- STORYTELLING: Introduce the concept of change, e.g. egg, caterpillar and butterfly.
- STORYTELLING: Use a story like the Lion King/Bambi story on video/booklet. Start with a happy time in the story. How did Simba feel? Pass the puppet around. Draw your happy feelings. Follow this with the death of Simba's dad, etc. What made them special, what did they miss about the person? Make this into a booklet form.
- STORYTELLING: Changes that create loss – e.g. crib, bottle, dummy, teeth, haircuts, going to school, etc.
- STORYTELLING: Energy within – running with the pen. Think of some of the movements you have done today – walking, running, turning, jumping, kicking a ball, etc. Can we put this movement down on paper?
- STORYTELLING: Make a newspaper of your story. Include good news and sad news, facts and feelings, pictures and photographs.
- STORYTELLING: Changes timeline – you could do it in the form of a tree. Roots where you were born, trunk, growth, and branches with things hanging down and pointing up, positive and negative changes.
- STORYTELLING: Make a calendar of special events. What can we do to help difficult days?
- STORYTELLING: Make a memory jar with coloured chalk and salt. Each colour represents special memories.
- MEMORIES: A memory tree. Roots represent earliest memories, trunk represents early years, with branches representing more

recent parts of your life. What is your earliest memory? How do you remember hearing about the illness or death? Where is this in the tree? Draw a branch of 'if only'. Something you wish another did or didn't do, said or didn't say. Make a branch of good memories.

- MEMORIES: Talk about the funeral. Draw or write about it. Imagine what it was like if you were not present. Can we find out more facts about what happened? How would you redesign the funeral?

Feeling exercises

- FEELINGS: Make a First Aid kit. What do you need for a physical injury? What do you need when you are emotionally injured? A friend to talk to, a book to read, a diary, computer game, photos to look at, music to listen to, paint, bubble bath, write stories, poems, feelings, grow a plant exercise, pray, have a cuddle?
- FEELINGS: Light a candle. Blow it out again. Where did it go? The light? The flame? The smoke? The warmth? The specialness of the flame? People have something special too – the warmth, love and care (sometimes called the soul). When someone dies this too leaves the body. Draw…discuss.
- FEELINGS: Shake a soda can up. What's happening inside? Relate this to our emotions of hurt, anger, guilt, fear and stress leading to physical problems. How can we let the gas out slowly so that no one gets in a mess? Relate this to our emotions.
- FEELINGS: Make a grief jacket. Roll up different coloured papers representing feelings and place these in different pockets. Explain how we carry feelings within us.
- FEELINGS: Make a spinning wheel of feelings.
- FEELINGS: Make a patchwork quilt made up of different feelings put on sticky patches. These can change over the sessions.

- FEELINGS: Putting anger on paper doesn't hurt anyone. How do we show anger? Hitting, running, kicking, punching, screaming, etc. Express anger with a red crayon on paper. Fill as much space as you want to. Then crunch the paper up to throw as far as possible.
- FEELINGS: Make a paper aeroplane and draw/write on the plane everything that makes you angry. Now enjoy throwing it as hard as you can.
- FEELINGS: I'm not alone. Using animal finger puppets to think about the different members of your family. Who represents which family? What about the deceased? Place them into a special box. Who is with whom? If you take one animal out of the box, who is still close to you? What do you worry about...?
- FEELINGS: Trampoline drawing. Who is supporting you?
- FEELINGS. Drawing our fears. I get frightened when...? (drawing this fear out makes it less fearful).
- FEELINGS: I feel different because...? (Children don't like being different from others). What would you change about yourself? Others? What do you like about yourself? Draw something you are good at.
- FEELINGS: Draw and colour a sheet with lots of bright colours. Now cover it with darker colour and finally black. Now with a lollypop stick remove some of the dark colours to make a new picture.
- FEELINGS: If I feel angry I can...? Say I am angry because..., punch a ball or pillow, yell into a pillow or when I'm in the shower, stamp your feet, write an angry letter and then tear it up, write into a journal, scribble with a red crayon and then crunch it up, go for a walk with a friend or relative. Use a teddy bear (cushion) and call him angry teddy. Pinch him when you are angry. Kick a ball against the wall. Imagine you are throwing a bucket of water on what makes you angry. Try drawing it. Scream into a wardrobe.

Think of traffic lights. STOP, THINK, GO. Stop – calm down and think before you act. Say why you are angry. Think of some solutions and consequences. Go with the best plan.
- FEELINGS: The goldfish bowl. Using coloured dyes to express feelings and bleach to show what happens when we cope with our feelings.
- FEELINGS: An anger wall. You need potatoes, or water filled balloons or clay, or papier-mâché or eggs. Write or draw the things that make you angry, stick them to the wall and release your energy by throwing objects at them.
- FEELINGS: Can you draw any scary dreams or thoughts that you get? You can change your dreams. Now redraw the dream but add something or someone to make you feel safe. Draw also your best dream.
- FEELINGS: Draw two faces or use mask faces, one that you show to the outside world and one that you keep within.
- FEELINGS: Using a mobile telephone to write text messages as a way to communicate.
- FEELINGS: We all need somewhere that we feel safe. It may be a real place or imaginary. Can you draw it? Draw a bear in front of a cave. What feelings is the bear guarding? Are there any feelings outside the cave? (You could use a door instead of a bear and cave.)
- FEELINGS: Pebbles, rocks and gemstones. Pebbles represent everyday things in life, everyday memories. Rocks represent sharp things in life. Difficult times with the deceased, painful memories. Gemstones represent special memories in life.

Moving on exercises

- MOVING ON: Using a round piece of paper draw three circles within each other. Place yourself in the centre. Think about who is closest to you in the next circle. Then friends in the next circle and others in the community in the outer circle. List the number of people who care for you. Who would you go to if you wanted to talk about the deceased, have a cuddle, talk about the past, talk about the future?

- MOVING ON: Make a friendship bracelet of those who care about and support you.
- MOVING ON: What makes a good friendship? Who do you care for? How can you show your care to those you love? People who experience difficult times can some day help others. Who might you help?
- MOVING ON: The things I like about myself are? The things I do well are? There are things that others tell me I am good at? No one is perfect but we are all good at something.
- MOVING ON: Write a letter about how things have changed.
- MOVING ON. Make a list/picture of positive outcomes of grief: appreciation of life, care of others, strengthening of emotional bonds with others, increased empathy with others, better communication skills, enhanced problem-solving skills.
- MOVING ON: Use a dice to think about what you will be doing in three, five years' times. Then times the number by five and again think about the future.
- MOVING ON: Scribble out. Get the children to think about what feelings they have inside them right now. To draw or colour this in the form of a shape. Remember that endings are a part of life; the children need to leave with positive feelings, wanting to come back.
- If you had five minutes more with someone what would you say/do?
- Write a letter to the deceased including:
    An Apology: Children need to apologise for things they wish they had not done. Because someone has died, it doesn't cancel out the need to complete what is unfinished. Regardless of

belief systems, undelivered emotional communications need to be made indirectly.

Forgiveness: Forgiveness is almost always an essential element required to complete the unfinished and incomplete emotions that attach to any relationship. Children are very susceptible to feeling hurt or slighted. Here, forgiveness is giving up the hope of a different or a better yesterday. It is not condoning, or treating as trivial or thinking it is not important. Remember, forgiveness is an action not a feeling.

A significant emotional statement: Any comment that communicates something important other than apologies or forgiveness.

Fond memories: This is a chance to say thank you for positive things, but not exaggerated or false memories. Otherwise they become roadblocks to the future.

Completing: This is a chance to say goodbye to the physical relationship and to acknowledge that you have things to do in the future.

Ending exercises

- Ending a session: It is helpful to ask for feedback about each session. This could be verbal or by using a drawing aid. It is helpful to inform the group about what you will be doing next week. Children may want to bring something special to contribute.
- Ending the sessions: Allow the children to choose what they would like to do in the final session. Include an opportunity for the children to show/express what they have achieved and learned over the sessions.

Remember: All church workers need to be CRB checked if they are working with children or vulnerable adults

TWENTY-FOUR

The death of friends

A friend shared with me that a distant aunt had died and he was the nearest relative to organise the funeral. The aunt had been a quiet but regular member of her local church. She would sneak in at the back of the church and leave as soon as the final hymn was sung. The nephew did his best at organising the funeral and informing the church members. However a few days before the funeral, a will was found stipulating that only relatives should attend the service. My friend had to inform the community that they were now not required. How are people to express their grief if they are not given an opportunity? We seem to have been better at this in the past.

In 2009, there were just fewer than half a million deaths in England and Wales (Office for National Statistics). If we assume each person had four or five close friends, then we have 2 to 2.5 million bereaved of a friend every year. Friends come in all sorts of shapes and sizes. We have 'good friends, close friends, old friends, best friends, college friends and life long friends'. On top of this, because of internet networks such as Facebook and Twitter we have a network that now allows us to keep in touch with people far more easily than it has ever been. Friends provide stability in life, sometimes they support us, at other times we are supporting them, they are the people we hang out with and find comfort in knowing that they are just there for us. So when we are robbed of this friendship it is not surprising how much it affects us. So much so that many go through life making just casual friends with little depth. In this way we never get hurt when separation takes place. But at what cost to true friendship? In the past, friends might have had a more prominent role at the funeral, perhaps helping to carry the coffin. Today there is no real label of recognition of a friend's grief. It is rarely discussed on TV or in the newspapers. Instead, we see more mass grief for celebrities who we have identified as being relevant in our lives. They almost act as a representative of what friends are meant to be, people who have been around and have helped us identify our true selves.

A biblical example of this is in the friendship between David and Jonathan (1 Samuel). This was a friendship that had to cope with the complexity of Jonathan's father, Saul, who became full of jealousy, hatred and anger for David. But Jonathan maintained his friendship even at risk of his own life (1 Samuel 23:16). Unfortunately, Jonathan was killed along with his father and brothers. David composed a lament to express his loss.

> How the mighty have fallen in battle.
> Jonathan lies slain on your heights.
> I grieve for you, Jonathan my brother;
> You were very dear to me.
> Your love was more wonderful than that of women.
> How the mighty have fallen.
>
> *1 Samuel 25–27*

It is certainly a difficult issue for men in our society to acknowledge the impact of the death of a friend. I can think of a number of men that I know who have lost good friends and colleagues. When I mention their loss and the death of their friend (often years later), I have encountered tears in the eyes such that the men can hardly speak and have to turn away. Here is the depth of friendship, which sadly we find hard to express in grief.

There is also something else going on when we lose a good friend. We are staring into the mirror of our own mortality. I have observed this with some elderly friends who have seen a number of the friends die over the past twenty years. It is as if a small part of them dies with each friend's passing.

There must be a role here for the church to make a significant difference to people's lives. We can offer several things within our Christian community. There is an opportunity to participate in the funeral service or thanksgiving. We have an opportunity to make the close family aware of others who are in loss and who would like to play a part in the proceedings. It may be with a reading, prayers, carrying the coffin, sidesmen duty, helping with the catering afterwards, chauffeuring, etc. We can also produce opportunities for friends to contribute in a Sunday service afterwards. We need to make sure our Sunday services are real and engage people with their current issues. It is all too easy for a Sunday service to proceed that totally ignores a death/funeral that took place in the community that week, or ignore the national tragic news, which equally impacts upon the congregation. We need to remember that national losses, which might seem remote to our community, actually bring back to the mind of the parishioner more personal loss issues of the past.

In any given church there will be a number of people quietly grieving the loss of friends. There is the opportunity of forming short-term homegroups that just look at loss issues. Providing memorial/thanksgiving services throughout the year can also be a useful channel of emotion and reflection. It is here that people engage with their faith and make it real. There must also be opportunities to reach out into the community and put on special events for them, particularly focusing upon the theme of friendship. In a chaplaincy setting, I use a butterfly prayer collage to allow people to express their emotions and prayers in a private yet public way. A prayer book, prayer basket or wall hanging in a church can provide a channel for people to express their thoughts in a safe way. The lighting of candles equally proves to be an effective channel of recognition and release for the mourner. It also says a message about the church being a place that cares and remembers.

It is not always friends that live close to us or that we have seen recently that can upset us so much. Sometimes it is the friend we have known for years who has just always been a part of the backcloth of our lives. Others might find it strange that we are so upset, 'why, you haven't seen him for years', people comment. But the fact that this person has been a part of your life, played a key part at some point on your journey and has always been at the back of your mind can bring a deep discomfort to us. Such losses are often unrecognised by the local church or played down. This can lead to a sense of loneliness and isolation amongst the very community that should be supporting you. Nelson Mandela, in his autobiography, tells the tale of how he had kept in touch with a distant friend whist he was in prison. Not long after his release Mandela's friend suddenly died.

> I felt like the loneliest man in the world. It was though he had been snatched from me just as we had been reunited. When I looked at him in his casket, it was as if part of myself had died.[45]

Mandela hits the nail on the head here as he recognises the fact that the death of any close friend that reflects perceived similarities such as age, interest and experience will have a deep and personal effect upon us. All we can do as a church is to have our antennae out picking up any vibes and then making sure we do not belittle such losses. One thing a pastor can do is to identify anything the two people had in common. It might have been going to a football/rugby match, walking or enjoying a pint together. Offering to do one of these as a token of remembrance can be very comforting. It also provides a setting for further conversation about their journey

---

45. Mandela, N. (1994). *The Autobiography of Nelson Mandela*. Boston: Little Brown.

and experience. Whatever we do cannot be enough to give respect for a life deceased, but we can at least make an effort.

> This cemetery is too small for his spirit but we submit his body to the ground. The grave is narrow for his soul, but we commit his body to the ground. No coffin, no crypt, no stone can hold his greatness. But we submit his body to the ground.[46]

It is worth recognising the difficulty that can occur when being involved in a funeral of a friend or close colleague. I recall moving on from one of my past churches where I had been the vicar for 11 years. I had developed a very close friendship with a retired missionary who had become like a grandmother to me. Only weeks after I had left the church I was asked to come back and officiate at her funeral. With no new vicar in place, I very much wanted to give her the best funeral possible. However, after saying the introductory sentences and turning and seeing my entire congregation I had only recently left, the impact of her death suddenly hit me. I could feel my bottom lip going. On such occasions one can simply acknowledge the toughness of the occasion for yourself and for many others. I then wisely made sure I had a lectern/pulpit to hold, to provide that 'safe place' to allow myself to steer others through this difficult journey. There is nothing wrong with a church leader getting upset at a funeral, it simply conveys our human vulnerability and identifies us with others who are feeling just the same. However, we are there to guide people through the service and therefore must not allow our own grief to get in the way of other people's grief. This doesn't mean we then learn how to hide our grief and feelings, otherwise it simply stores up problems for later as we will see with 'disenfranchised grief' (Chapter 36).

---

46. Abernathy, R. *Spoken at the Committal of Martin Luther King, Jr.*

Reflections

- What impact has a death of a friend or close colleague had upon you?
- How do you think the church can be more open to talk about loss issues?
- What would you value teaching on from the church about one's own mortality?

Part Four

Death arrives at one's door in many costumes. However, two of the most upsetting forms must be in the shape of suicide and murder. Both types of death leave the bereaved in a difficult situation. The suddenness of the death doesn't help along with the fact that there are many unknowns in such a context. A third type of loss that is difficult to handle is when there are multiple deaths within our community. All three events sooner or later knock on the door of the local church, whether it involves people in the church or those outside seeking the church's support at a traumatic time. The next part of this book will specifically look at these difficult situations and outline what the church can do to support.

TWENTY-FIVE

Suicide

Every six seconds someone contacts the Samaritans. Every 60 seconds the contact expresses suicidal feelings. Over five million people contact the Samaritans every year.

Thankfully most of them live to tell the tale. However, every day five men under the age of 35 years dies from suicide. According to the Office of National Statistics, in 2008 in England and Wales, 17.7 men per 100,000 commit suicide compared to 5.4 women per 100,000. Suicide rates have increased steadily since the 1960s but have slightly decreased over recent years. There are more suicides on a Monday than any other day of the week. The commonest place for people to kill themselves in the USA is by diving off the Golden Gate Bridge in San Francisco; however, the majority choose to do it quietly without fuss or attention. There seem to be various reasons for it such as unemployment, drugs, alcohol, money and relationship problems. Although one or two of these issues would not tip someone over the edge, when they come together, it can take just a small thing to lead someone to attempt suicide. This is not including those with ongoing mental health issues. It is estimated that one in four people will experience mental health problems at some point in their lives.

A caring church will inevitably attract people with emotional needs of whatever kind. I can recall one town church, where we had attracted so many people with counselling/mental health issues that I was spending considerable time going to the mental health hospital. I began to wonder whether the church was actually causing some of these problems but was reassured by a psychiatrist who was a member of the church. He expressed appreciation of the pastoral care the church was providing, recognising that this freed up the NHS to handle the more serious cases. There is still a stigma in acknowledging that you have a mental health problem. Some might think it is for the weak-minded and those who can't be bothered to sort out their lives. That's why the church should be a safe haven for such people. People with mental health problems can feel extremely lonely and isolated in the community. If we are to have a ministry for the mentally ill or those bereaved from a suicide, we will need to understand the depth of the complexity of the subject.

When suicide occurs, the shock is overwhelming. Although family and friends may have been very fearful for a relative, when the event takes place it still brings an alarm reaction. There seems to be three areas that affect the bereaved.

- First, all the events that led up to the suicide.
- Secondly, the event itself and the immediate circumstances.
- Thirdly, the long-term effects of the grief.

Pre-suicide events

Someone in mental turmoil may well have imagined themselves dead a thousand times. They will have an urge to end their lives, whether it is by drugs, throwing themselves in front of a car or a train. Some might self-harm to get themselves through the torture of each day's thoughts. This provides a sudden release and a calm for the time being. But it is a huge stress trying not to kill yourself. These feelings can last for many years but it doesn't mean that potential suicides have these feelings all of the time. People can cloak the feelings so well that those who live with them might not be aware. One person can be celebrating their life as they windsurf with the joy of water and wind in their face, while another person can have reached such a low point in their lives that they throw themselves off a bridge to their death. A person can be surrounded by what they think are successful people getting on with their lives while they are feeling inadequate.

> 'Why can't I get a job and get on with my life? It feels as if my head is still in bed. I'm going to top myself. Come on take me away…help, I can't even do this right.'

Others recognise that their relative was 'just not of this world'. They may have tried many times to talk someone around out of their depression. On top of this sometimes the relatives think that the medicine they are taking is making things worse. Here, the body becomes not a temple but a prison to escape from. However, the relatives and friends may have heard a person cry wolf so many times that they cease hearing what is being said. The person can be functioning normally, washing the dishes and emptying the bins on the very day they succeed with their suicide.

I recall when I was cutting my teeth in my early days of learning to counsel, caring for depressed individuals. These were people who came and lived in our Christian community for a few weeks. We had people who had attempted to commit suicide many times. I can recall well their names and picture the scars on their arms. We would get a phone call from one of them saying that they were about to jump into the lake and were just saying goodbye. Off we would go in the car to collect them; it certainly made one hardened to this type of personal situation. Alas, with experience, I have learned that you can never stop taking suicide attempts seriously.

Unfortunately, today there is a new development called Internet suicide. There are people on the Internet who will talk to a suicidal person and actively encourage them to succeed. People offer advice on how to succeed, what to do with their last hour (this is called 'catching the bus'). Some people called Trolls are not interested in suicide for themselves, but they just get a 'high' by inciting and encouraging others.

We all experience black, dark days, but unlike those who commit suicide, we recognise that the next day might be sunny and worthwhile. This is what the suicidal person does not experience; the darkness becomes overwhelming and all-engulfing. They find themselves in a tunnel with no light at the end. On top of this, they also end up knowing others who have attempted suicide and some who have succeeded. This is particularly the case with anorexic cases who meet each other in specialist hospital units. For some, the mental turmoil is made easier by cutting themselves. They then recognise that here is a way of controlling their pain. It is now a small step to hurt oneself completely to resolve their dilemma.

Caring for the survivors

What we need to recognise is that people are not wanting to commit suicide *per se*, what they are wanting is to find a peace from their problems. The good news is that there are many accounts of people who attempted suicide, failed and give testimony of how glad they are now to be alive.

With control of diet, drugs and appropriate care, individuals can control their lives. If they learn to keep within certain bands of control, they have control of their lives rather than have the illness controlling them. This is not as easy as it sounds, particularly for a young person. The relatives and friends are caught as they are 'walking on egg shells' in fear that the person might commit again. This in itself adds pressure and prevents the individual from feeling normal.

Shame is a thin strand that runs throughout this subject. The individual who is having suicidal thoughts grapples with their shame in thinking this way. Those who survive attempts can feel ashamed for trying, failing and now living with their past. There is then the shame of the bereaved relatives and friends who have to live with the feeling that they perhaps could have prevented this scenario. Hopefully they allow themselves to be supported.

> 'The future is definitely better and I am honoured to be alive.
> When you realise that you are not the only person and you are not alone.'

The suicidal event

Often there is a final straw that breaks the camel's back that causes the suicide. It can sometimes be difficult to work out why a person did it at that particular point, but you have to see the whole story to understand why they got to that point and were tipped over into a suicidal crisis. It may be that unemployment is not the issue, or relationships, debt or drugs, but when they are occurring steadily together and increasingly, then that creates the tipping point.

Often the bereaved are treated differently from other bereaved people. They have to deal with the police, an inquest and possibly the media. Unfortunately, a suicidal person's pain is tied to others after they take their lives. At first, people feel disturbed at the news. It is only later that they experience the fullness of the loss and begin to miss the person.

The events of the day of the suicide are often impregnated into the minds of the bereaved. They will be able to tell you where and what they were doing at the time. For some there is the trauma of actually finding the deceased. The impact of seeing someone who has hanged themselves or found them in bed with a bag over their heads is hard to come to terms with. The image lingers for a long time. The bereaved have also got to cope with the knowledge that the deceased probably knew who would find them first. Here the bereaved have been especially chosen out, for good or ill, to cope with the event.

Suicide notes

Not everyone leaves a note when they take their own life.[47] Even if they do, it may create more issues than it resolves. Some contain profound utterances; others are vague, abstract and incomplete. Some appear to be totally false and incorrect to the surviving relatives.

> 'I spent ages wondering what to write or whether I should write a note. And that's because the more you think about it, the more difficult it is to maintain any hope of ever being understood.'

Some letters are left to create guilt; others are offering advice to care for specific people, while others are expressing love and thanks.

Long-term effects

There is one thing that lingers for the bereaved for as long as they live, the unanswerable question 'Why?' that torments so many families. On top of this there is the taboo that we don't talk about suicide, which isolates the bereaved.

There are many 'bad' parents whose children don't commit suicide and many 'good' parents whose children do. But suicide can tear families apart. Siblings can often retreat into themselves; their isolation only causes further pain and fear for the parents. Friends are at a loss to know what to say or do.

The bereaved wonder what other people might be thinking about them, 'what kind of mother, father or family did this person have?' The reality is that the issue of suicide is not usually about the survivors, they are not the focus of a suicidal person's mind. This is hard for the bereaved to accept. This is especially the case if there had been arguments before the death. Often there are arguments before a suicide, when people say things that they later find they didn't mean and now greatly regret.

---

47. Grashoff, U. (2004). *Let Me Finish: An Anthology of Suicide Letters*. London: Headline.

> 'I told him to get out of my house and never come back.
> That was the last words I ever spoke to him.'

Anger is an overwhelming emotion for many bereaved. 'Why did you do that?' is the thought that echoes in people's minds.

The bereaved also sense a relief both for themselves and the deceased. Release from the ongoing torture of living with a suicidal person and the unknown that lingers and release that the deceased is not going to be disappointed or unhappy anymore.

> 'You don't really get over this kind of loss; you just have to incorporate it into your life. It is always there, it always will be, because nothing can change it, it has happened, it is real.'

There is also one other thought that naturally occupies the bereaved: if my relative has committed suicide, does that mean that I might? Some are able to clearly draw a line between the action of their relative and themselves. But others can find that it is a difficult thought to forget.

A Christian understanding

Relatives may not be 100 per cent sure that their relative did want to commit suicide. The thought is just too great to bear especially if they die in a rather spectacular, brave way. If one sees suicide as a sin then this can make it harder for the person to come to terms with what the deceased has done. It is also a big issue for the suicidal person, as they have to grapple with their own beliefs. A 23-year-old woman expressed it this way,

> 'Kill yourself, what's the point, it achieves nothing, precisely, it achieves nothing. Nothingness is what I want.'

The question for the bereaved is 'why?' Was it a warped vision, destroyed hopes? In earlier centuries, the church thought people were possessed by the devil. Then the church said it was a sin, beyond the moral pale, and treated suicides like criminals. They were refused a proper burial and placed outside the churchyard.

Freud thought it was an aggressive conflict within. More recently, scientific thinking sees it as a pathological thought process, a moment of 'crisis problem development'. Today we call it a pre-suicidal syndrome. One thing is clear: suicide is a universal phenomenon. It expresses the reality that human beings have free will.

Today society may have less fear about it but the impact is just as great. David Hume, the Scottish philosopher, said, 'A man who retreats from life does not harm society'. But the truth is far from this, as it's like a terrorist attack that causes ripples to echo through the community.

But is everyone who commits suicide ill? We have an intense fear of the subject; it seems to be a taboo in church that's 'beyond the moral pale'. In the past, they were seen as criminals. Today the fear is less but the after-effects are just as great.

If our parish has a diverse population, poor housing, high unemployment and an increase of drug abuse then we are going to be surrounded by suicidal issues. We need to be aware of the fact that men are less verbal, unlikely to talk about psychological problems or acknowledge that they are depressed to their friends. They also tend to delay going to the doctor with physical symptoms. If we can create groups for men where they have social contact and are able to forge links, then we might have created a safe place for them to seek help. Inviting a local doctor to the church to talk to a men's group may help to break down barriers.

When it comes to funerals, we need to balance fulfilling the requests of the bereaved, while being honest to the community and ourselves. I have been told of situations where a member of a congregation has committed suicide and the church on the following Sunday goes into denial and makes no comment or recognition of the event. Can this type of collusion really help anyone? In an age when we recognise illness, surely we can acknowledge the depth of despair an individual is in to take his or her own life. We also need to recall that a person is far more than the action of their final last moments. We have to be willing to grapple with the congregation about whether the action of suicide is one of a coward or of a very brave person.

What is clear is that we need to recognise that the after-care of the bereaved can be demanding and long-lasting. Once again pastoral workers become carriers of knowledge that is often only shared by a few people. It is here that we can identify with the bereaved both in their pain and their ongoing questioning. It is only when we have stuck with the bereaved that they will eventually trust us to share some of their personal darkest fears.

Reflections

- What do you think your church's attitude is to suicide?
- What kind of conditions in your life would cause you to think about suicide?
- How can the church support the bereaved after a suicide?
- Read the account of Judas' life and suicide in the New Testament. Can we learn anything from Judas?
- How do you think Jesus coped knowing that he chose Judas who would betray him?
- How can we support people who live with relatives who are often threatening suicide?

TWENTY-SIX

Murder

God liked Abel and his offering, but Cain and his offering didn't get his approval. Cain lost his temper and went into a sulk. God spoke to Cain, 'Why the tantrum? Why the sulking? If you do well, won't you be accepted? And if you don't do well, sin is lying in wait for you, ready to pounce, it's out to get you, you're got to master it.'

Cain had words with his brother. They were out in the field; Cain came at Abel his brother and killed him.

Most pastors will come across families dealing with suicidal situations but may never have to deal with a murder situation. But when they do, it can become all-demanding.

It goes without saying that any murder is a shock; but it has the added complexity for the bereaved of the search for the murderer. Hence, the police and media move into their lives. The bereaved family find the police liaison person being assigned to them both as a support and to observe! The reality is that most people are murdered by someone who knows them well; hence the scrutiny on the nearest family members. Over recent years we have had a number of fathers on TV pleading for the murderer to come forward only later to be accused themselves of the crime. This is a huge burden for family members to cope with and to live with, the fact that they allowed someone to become so close to their child only to discover he was the abuser/murderer.

It is no wonder that the grieving process is now delayed in the complexity of the situation. Rather than being able to grieve normally, the relatives are first bombarded by the press and media and become involved in the search for the culprit. Even when someone is charged with the crime, the family tend to have a long wait for the court case. There is then the trial with the possibility that the person charged might be innocent or given a short sentence. There is then the long wait fearing that the person will be released early. All of this delays normal grief as the following diagram shows.

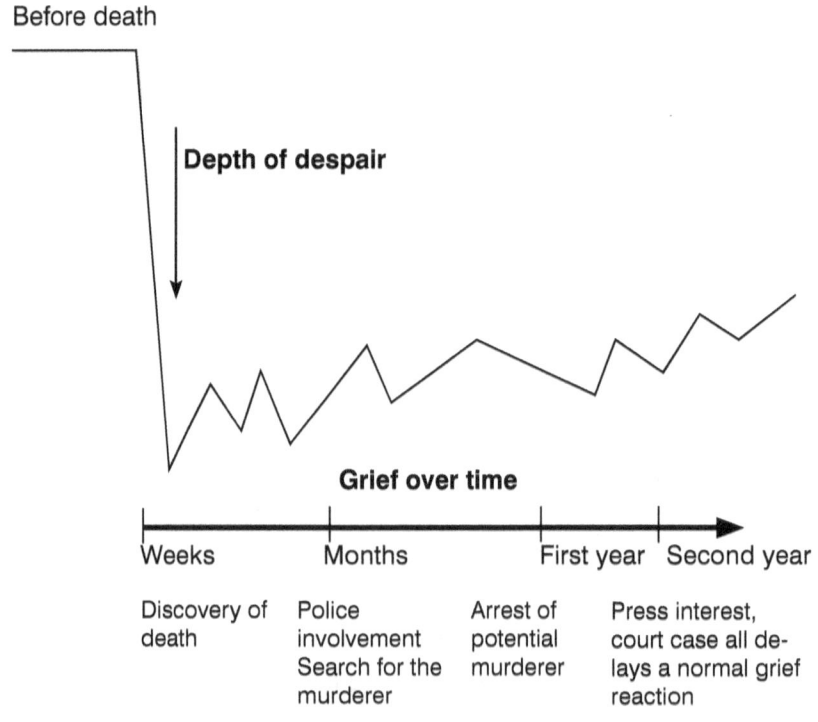

Grief trajectory after murder

We mustn't forget the siblings in these families, who suffer just as much as the rest of their family.

MURDER

'My son is just getting on with life. He doesn't say very much but I think he is very angry, he's a time bomb waiting to go off.'

If a relative has gone missing, the family have to wait while a search is made. In some instances, after many months, these searches are called off. The torment seems as if it will never go away as the family hope and pray that their relative is found. They then have the painful task of identifying the body and later seeing the accused in court face to face. It can feel as if the court case is a pantomime or a farce that they have to sit through, knowing in their hearts that the person is guilty. What is going through the family's mind is 'how can his happen to a normal functioning family?' The court case, which can be delayed and delayed, can then last several weeks. In a few cases, there is the additional pain that their loved one's body is never found, with the accused refusing to acknowledge where they placed the body.

From the church perspective, it can find itself along with the pastoral leader in the media attention. The church itself can become a focus for people to light candles or sign a remembrance book. Whatever the church's tradition, this is an opportunity to open the doors and provide some focus for quiet reflection and prayer. It is not uncommon for caring clergy, who have been supporting the bereaved, to find that they get a large quantity of mail. One has to then decide whether you have the time and resources to answer so many letters, even though it could be a very fruitful part of your church's ministry.

Several clergy over recent years have used their home as a focus point for the bereaved to gather and to share their experience. This is fine provided clear ground rules are agreed at the beginning, otherwise you can find that your home has been taken over for a considerable period of time when you are trying to get back to your normal ministry. There can also be the added complexity that the church is both involved in caring for the bereaved family and the family of the accused. It can be more appropriate for two churches to share this pastoral care situation or at least have different people handling each family.

Death through war

The death of any of our armed force members may not be murder, but it can feel so for the families involved. They have been robbed of a young family member well before their time. A church is probably more likely to have some connection with an armed forces family that has a death in the family than with a traditional murder in the community. The loss of a family member of the armed forces has its own peculiar characteristics. First, how the news is given can be hard to control. With press actively on the front line of any war or encounter, they are very quick to let the world know of a death. Fortunately, there is an agreement that the actual name of the deceased will not be released till the family have been informed. In fact, now the authorities can block any mobile phones working in a conflict zone, until the next of kin are informed. With modern communications the forces try to inform the next of kin within hours of the death. The bearer of the bad news is seldom the one to offer support to the family. Although the forces have now linked up with the bereavement charity Cruse and have over 500 volunteer bereavement carers, the reality is that the bereaved are living in some minister's parish. We can choose to remain at the edge of the care or become more involved over a period of time. If we do get engaged with the situation we need to grasp some of the complexities of such deaths.

The Wootton Bassett involvement in acknowledging the return of fallen heroes came about almost by accident. Normally, the RAF return casualties and the deceased via Brize Norton, it was only because of structural repairs that the flights were diverted. From the simple act of the local British Legion wanting to acknowledge the soldiers by lowering their Standard, the whole community became involved in a ritual act of remembrance. It would be hard for a religious leader not to be involved in some way with the community and how people cope with death entering their streets so publicly and so often. But what if it is just one person returning to our own area that we work in?

The loss of a soldier has its own unique circumstances. There will be attention from the press, parked outside the bereaved home. The death has taken place far away from home, often with a degree of confusion about the events. There is often a wait before the post-mortem and even then the families might be advised not to see the body (although the armed forces do all they can to make the deceased presentable). There is then the question of who to support in the family. These are often young men who may have partners of various degrees of commitment. Who cares for the ex-girlfriend? There is also the complexity of the death itself, with more soldiers being killed in a non-operational situation, often after operating abroad. Those who die after returning home injured will receive less publicity and attention. They will not have their moment of respect at Wootton Bassett. We may also have armed forces personnel that have returned home after losing friends in traumatic circumstances or who have been simply practically involved by carrying the coffin. The impact of the loss spreads like ripples in a pool. Friends of the deceased, who remained in the community with their local careers and friendships, can find it hard to realise their contemporary has been killed. Any death connected with the forces will mean that the death and loss cannot be private but becomes a public death. There will be an inquest and the deceased will be characterised as a hero rather than someone's son and child. There will also be the complexity for children who will have to work through their thoughts of a dad who perhaps is being called a hero but was far from perfect when home as a father.

Often soldiers, airmen and sailors come from families with history and deep roots in the forces. So when death occurs, they not only lose their loved one but also a way of life that had an identity through being a part of an organisation. There is also the regular recall of death that comes about through the media by maintaining their interest in war stories.

In the end, however involved we become, it is very hard to get every aspect of our care right. The funeral services can be complex to get right with different parties wanting their own perspective on things. There is also the perennial question of how long we continue to give specific care to the bereaved.

Reflections

- What Bible stories can you think of where murder took place?
- How did the death affect the characters involved?
- How would the local church react if the minister offered support to the accused?

TWENTY-SEVEN

Disasters – post-traumatic stress debriefing

8.30 a.m. one weekday morning, school children waited for their school bus. Teenagers were busy doing what they do, teasing, chatting, on the mobile phone and yawning. The coach arrived and dashed off to the school four miles away. Minutes later the coach collided with a tanker as they both tried to cross a narrow country-lane bridge. The tanker burst into flames. After the initial shock half the children climbed out of the back of the emergency door of the bus while the rest managed to help the driver out of the front window. Some teenagers tried to help the tanker driver out of his vehicle but his legs were trapped. Unfortunately the tanker burst into flames, killing the driver. By now the teenagers were on their mobiles telling friends and family what had happened. Teachers travelling to school by car stopped and gathered the school children together. Another coach came and they were all taken to the local cottage hospital, which didn't really know what to do with them. Within the hour the press had arrived and were trying to interview the children. It was only in the evening that parents really grasped how fortunate their children had been when they saw on the local news a picture of two vehicles totally burned out. As a local minister and counsellor, when I was asked to meet some of the teenagers, I heard a lot of anger. Anger at the press for interfering, at the school for the way they had handled things, anger at people who were blaming their coach driver and anger at other school children who seemed upset, even though they were not involved in the accident.

Disasters can happen to anyone, at any time, anywhere, unexpectedly in any church community. What constitutes a disaster? While working with a county disaster group where we prepared to offer post-traumatic stress debriefing, the statistics had told us we should expect either a major road accident or a plane crash. However, we began to get enquiries from schools after a teenager had been killed in a road accident or had just died unexpectedly for no medical reason. We began to realise that an unexpected loss is a disaster even if it only affects one person. The reality is that any death causes ripples to go out to the community as people reflect on the fact that 'it could have been me'.

In my own parishes, there have been major road accidents, fires that involved the death of firemen, a school coach crash, a town flood and the sudden death of a schoolteacher. If you pause and reflect yourself, you will be able to recall a surprising number of disasters that come to mind. I won't mention any as others soon replace them. However, the reality is that disasters happen in parishes that we serve and we can quickly find ourselves playing an important role in the weeks, months and perhaps years ahead. Indeed, in the disasters that you can recall, you may also remember the high profile the churches and its leaders received at the time.

When a disaster happens, people lose lives, property, friends and faith; faith in the certainty of everyday life. Although the area quickly becomes inundated with professional services, they become and remain the experts, for now they have the mark of Cain upon their foreheads.

You might think that pastors get involved in tragic situations on a weekly basis. I guess this is true, but what makes these situations unique is that here we get invaded by the press, police, doctors, firemen, council, professional counsellors. At first we can feel rather gazumped by these people coming on to our patch and perhaps rather deskilled. However, we bring three unique factors to bear on the situation.

- We have resources to offer such as buildings and contacts. Churches become places where people in shock and fear can gather and feel safe. If you have a common experience then, together, you realise that you are not alone. It is also a place to look for meaning, express feelings and to find solace. We can provide church halls for accommodation, food and a meeting point to explain what has happened and what will happen. We will inevitably become a place for funerals and remembrance services in the future.
- We already have relationships with the community. We are in a position to link people up with accommodation. We are aware of individuals who will be particularly affected in the community and who would require extra care and attention. We also know people with particular skills that could be useful at such a time. I know of one minister who, after a flood in his patch, went to a fishing tackle shop and got some waders and a pole. He then persuaded a supermarket to give him bread, milk and nappies, etc. He then successfully went around the streets reaching up to the people trapped in their first-floor rooms.
- We will be in the community long after these professionals have come and gone. Indeed we might, in some parishes, be the only professional who not only works in the community but also lives in the area. So when the attention from the media wanes, we will be there alongside the community, both remembering, helping to adjust to a changed situation and bringing hope for the future. The importance of just 'being' with the community at a time of a disaster cannot be exaggerated.

What do families need?

When a disaster strikes, families have time-limited needs and more long-lasting issues to resolve. Initial needs include both practical and emotional concerns. They need privacy, support, someone to listen to them and provide an explanation of what has happened. They may also need practical support such as childcare, shopping, cleaning, money, transport, solicitor advice and help with filling in forms. There will be the more difficult tasks such as identifying a body and registering the death. On top of this they may require protection from the press and interferers.

So at first they need to be made safe, injuries treated, information given, practical help offered and plenty of comfort. But it is not just a matter of offering these things at a critical time but awareness of how they want this provided. People in a crisis time need to be treated with sensitivity. The last thing they require is to be treated as a bunch of numbers. They need to be treated as individuals, with a consistent person dealing with their needs. Most of all they do not want to feel trapped but given the space to be themselves. So they need consistent support at the right time. Finally and significantly for the church, they need someone to remember what has happened to them. It is not surprising that it is difficult to get this right in the midst of confusion and sometimes chaos. But since the church is already established in the community, we are in a better position to offer a consistent and regular support service.

The complexity of disasters

One of the difficulties of offering help early on is that the initial impact is one of shock, numbness and disbelief. At such a point, a person will find it hard to hear any offer of help. What then follows is often confusion and a sense of anger. At this point a person might well resent any offer of help. There is often a second post-impact feeling of euphoria that one has survived such a disaster and along with this a feeling that you are a part of an affirmative community spirit. Once again any offer of help might be seen as irrelevant and unnecessary – until finally a 'what if?' state hits the person with anxiety and possibly depression following. Now the person can feel alone and isolated in their experience with no one understanding how they feel.

Disasters do draw out the best in people and there can be a real, positive community spirit. People do not need counselling in these early stages of shock. It is after the adrenalin has stopped pumping that help is often needed. People can find themselves experiencing the beginning of post-traumatic stress.

People can find themselves re-experiencing events, dreaming and getting recurring thoughts. They may want to talk over and over about the events. This is not easy for those they live with who perhaps did not have this experience. This can alienate the person from their family and they can quickly feel that no one understands because they didn't have their own unique experience.

'People can't possibly understand, they weren't there.'

Avoidance reactions can follow, such as refusing to watch TV or listen to the radio or read newspapers. They feel trapped with strong memories of sight, smell and noise. Lack of sleep, loss of appetite, sudden outbursts, nightmares, nerves on edge, being easily startled are common reactions. People can develop free-floating emotions, which are unconnected or disproportionate to their cause, which can cause panic attack in everyday places such as a car park or supermarket. The person's emotions are now very volatile, and they may become very aggressive and angry, or feel unbearably guilty.

A strategy of help

People need to know what is a normal reaction at a time like this. This can be conveyed as a leaflet or by inviting people to a meeting. This is an opportunity of informing people about what is available in terms of practical and emotional support. The reactions described previously are quite common and normally diminish over time with family support. A smaller number of people will require additional support at a later date. Clearly, those who had emotional issues previous to a disaster tend to exhibit more long-term problems. Debriefing is a simple technique, providing an opportunity for people to express their experiences. It can be done individually but seems to be more effective in small groups. In this way the group dynamic helps both to normalise reactions as well as to fill in any information that an individual lacked that can allow them to make sense of what happened. Together the process is rather like completing a jigsaw. The more one can understand what has happened, the easier it is to recover from the event.

Debriefing

Debriefing is a simple but effective technique that I often use during general pastoral care or bereavement visiting of individuals. It consists of focusing upon three aspects of a person's experience. In a disaster situation, it is usually used about three to five days after the event. People are invited to meet, simply to talk in a controlled way about their experience.

One by one, people are given the chance to talk about what happened to them before the disaster, during the event and afterwards, leading up to the present time. This focuses upon:

- Talking about what they were doing at the time.
- Sharing what their first thoughts were – what did they see, smell, hear and touch.
- Expressing what they felt at the time.

These thee aspects are then repeated as the story unfolds. It is important to keep to the pattern of facts first, senses second and feelings third. This allows a steady unwrapping of a story, leaving no part of it untold, allowing for a steady release of the experience of powerful senses and feelings. People need to talk about the event until they have no more need to do so.

As the story unfolds, people are able to hear other people's accounts, which helps them to put together their own story and to complete any information that was missing.

At the end of the process, it is helpful to affirm that their reaction is very normal and will subside. It is also key to draw their attention to areas where they can receive additional assistance from the local doctors, professionals that have been brought in and perhaps from the church itself. It is essential that people do not feel trapped in any way, with nowhere to turn. It can be helpful to follow this up with a community leaflet or magazine a few weeks later; again pointing out what is a typical reaction that people experience post disaster and to include all the support services' contacts.

In the end the church's task is to stay with the people who are grappling with questions that have no answers. We achieve this by offering remembrance services, setting up memorial sites, providing symbolism and a focus of attention for people to express their grief and loss.

The press and media

A specific role that a pastor or church leader can play for the community is to be a focus of attention for the press and media. A skilled communicator, who can speak in brief sentences, can be able to speak on behalf of the community, conveying the feelings and mood of the community. Here, if we have developed a friendly link with the local press officer, he or she can provide useful guidance when the national press arrive. Most church organisations have regional press officers who can also take the responsibility of handling the press away from you or provide help in thinking through what to say and particularly what not to say. We need to recognise that if we are to be involved with the press at whatever level it requires some thinking through the process. Sometimes we ourselves are chasing the press, as we want our story to be heard. If so, we need to be ready for the sleeping giant that we awaken.

- We need to decide whether this is local or national news.
- We then need to give time to prepare our thoughts about what we want to communicate.
- What questions will we answer and what questions won't we answer?
- Will we choose only to give pre-written statements or are we willing to engage in discussion?
- What is the worst question anyone could ask you?
- What will be the follow on question?
- What is the main message you want to convey? Know it and stick to it.
- Answer your question and not the interviewers.
- Choose your audience, is it to the Christian media, TV or newspapers or web?
- You could decide to not speak to anyone until you have had time to write an article for a magazine, be it Christian or secular.
- Recognise that whatever you say or write, not everyone will agree with you.
- If you enter into an interview with other speakers, be ready for someone to strongly disagree with you. Don't take it personally but have a sentence ready that, without attacking someone, builds on your point of view. For example, 'you may be right but…' or 'that's one point of view, however others…'
- Remember, we don't have to speak to the press but could use our regional press advisor to speak on our behalf.

DISASTERS – POST-TRAUMATIC STRESS DEBRIEFING

The thought of a disaster occurring in one's parish can feel daunting, even if it is a relatively small adversity. But the ability of a community to rally and to draw out hidden talents is remarkable. In the end, you can only react in a way that is appropriate for yourself. The best anyone can offer is to be willing to simple 'be there' with the people in all of your weakness and vulnerability. Some of us are exceptional at organisational skills and taking initiative, but we can be just as much a 'Christ figure' by being one with the people in the midst of a tragedy, revealing our fears and concerns along with everyone else.

As an example to us all, the Lockerbie disaster shows us both the remarkableness of people and how a priest can play an important role. When the aeroplane came down upon Lockerbie, 270 people died with 11 from Lockerbie itself. As one woman put it, 'we just got on with it as if we had a manual of what to do if an aeroplane crashed on us'. Afterwards women voluntarily gave up a year of their time to collect, wash and rewash, iron and identify the clothes and belongings of the deceased to be able to send them back to the families in the USA. There were twenty thousand items to identify and sort of which about 75 per cent went back to the bereaved families. A German film crew, when they saw what was being sorted, said that they had never seen anything like it since the holocaust. Again, a mother expressed what they did in this way,

> 'Their families were a long way from home and if I could help by sending some of the love we have in Lockerbie back with what we were doing, then I would do it everyday.'

Out of something so evil, the Lockerbie community conveyed so much love that its impact of goodness endures today with the bereaved families.

A Catholic priest had just been moved to Lockerbie not long before the disaster. He had been suffering from alcoholism and had felt suicidal at times. At this point in his life he felt that he was just a burden on the people of Lockerbie. Yet by his simple love, and willingness to be vulnerable in the midst of the tragedy, he conveyed a deep humanity and humility to those he cared for. He was one of the first to move back into his house while it still had tarpaulin on the roof.

He would meet people when they visited the area, take them to the makeshift morgue and weep with them. Most of all, he was there to remember in the years ahead as relatives kept on visiting. In his weakness, he mirrored the love of Christ. He conveyed what the event meant to him when he spoke to a television crew. He said that,

> 'There is always a tendency when a disaster happens like Lockerbie, that good comes out of it. And fair enough, a great deal of love has resulted with wonderful friendships forming. There are friendships, which will persist till we die. People have learned a lot about themselves. But at the same time it seems false to say, "here is all this goodness that has resulted to compensate for the bad and so the books are balanced." The books are never balanced. I wish that Lockerbie had never happened. It is a blessing to have these bereaved people in my life but they would rather have their fathers, mothers and children back with them. Given the choice, they would rather have their relative than me and I would rather they had their relative than me.'

This type of disaster raises the important issue of the role of the church in being an agent of remembrance. There will of course always be those who will want to forget and move on. But those who have lost loved ones or have been traumatised will never forget. It is the church's role therefore to be a catalyst in helping people in their grief and providing symbols and occasions to remember. A minister or pastoral leader in such a church becomes an important person over the following years in helping to keep connections with the bereaved. You have something in common that binds you together. We should never underestimate the importance of those who maintain a long-term ministry in one community. More will be said about this in the next chapter.

Finally, we need to be aware of the impact of disasters that occur elsewhere that don't seem to be on our patch yet nevertheless have impact. When a disaster strikes, the media play a key role in broadcasting the event to the world. News breaks into everyone's home. It not only reminds people of their own loss experience but can also make them feel that their loss is insignificant. After all, when we hear on the TV news of someone's death, there will be many at the same time who also lose a loved one of similar age. They, however, get little attention. As time passes, the media keep on broadcasting news that takes the bereaved back into their loss. Here, they can feel no one is interested in their own story. We need to be simply aware when major disasters occur and be sensitive to those you know who might be affected by such news. A word of acknowledgement is often all a person requires.

Reflections

- Imagine the Chilean mine disaster was in your parish, how would you react?
- What role would you play?
- How would you delegate?
- What would your priorities be?
- How would you protect your family?
- How should the church remember the event?
- When would you feel free to move on?

Part Five

When you talk about grief and loss, we naturally assume we are referring to when a person has died. So far this is all we have covered in this book. But the reality is that in an average church and community, there will be more losses that affect people other than death. Remember, a loss reaction can occur whenever we have a break from something we have become attached to and engaged with. We will now look at a range of other losses that we will find ourselves engaged with. This will range from relationship breakdown and divorce to coping with being single and not having children. Inevitably, we will meet people who have become unemployed or have been abused in life. Each will have their own loss account. There are also the losses that particularly relate to the church, ranging from adjusting when the church leader moves on, to actually losing one's own personal faith. All of these types of losses can go unrecognised and can accumulate into what we call disenfranchised grief. The more the church is aware of what is happening with our church members, the more directive our care, support and teaching can be. I hope what follows in Part Five will open our eyes to our own church community.

The hidden losses in a church

Each culture has its own expected 'grieving rules', a particular way to mourn a major loss. Perhaps in our cosmopolitan society these rules are less distinct than previously, but nevertheless they still exist. We all formulate a particular expectation of how a person will or should behave according to the loss. But as we have been finding out, loss can come in many forms. We too quickly assume that loss refers to the death of a person, which we have mainly focused upon in this book. But what about other losses we encounter in the Christian community?

- How should you behave if your foster parent dies or a father you have never met?
- Should you be given time off work if your pet dies?
- How do you cope if your 'secret lover' dies?
- How can a nurse or doctor or vicar cope when handling endless death situations?
- How can the church support you when your children have long-term problems?
- How do you and your church cope if you lose your faith and hope?

It is impossible to deal with all of the possible loss events in a church; however, we need to recognise that a large number of people are sitting in our churches carrying a variety of problems that relate to a loss of some kind. I can recall in one parish at one moment in my ministry caring for a woman whose husband regularly had mental breakdowns, a couple with a son addicted to drugs, a friend whose eyesight had gone in one eye and was at risk of losing the other, another friend who had a secret drink problem and another who kept secret that he was a non-practising homosexual; and I could go on and on. If this is just a small example in the church, how many loss issues are there in our parish?

In one of my churches we used to do a door-to-door visit throughout the parish with a small questionnaire. The final question asked whether the household would like the vicar to visit. Most declined but I was asked to visit a person I had had no previous contact with. After an introductory chat and a cup of tea, I enquired whether there was a specific reason why she wanted to see me. The person finally got the courage to share how she had had a secret affair with a married man with children from work. She had kept this a secret from her friends and family for five years. However, just over a year previously, her lover died suddenly. She was not able to take time off work, go to the funeral or feel able to share her grief with anyone. Finally, from desperation, she was able to share her pain and begin a journey of support and healing.

What all these cases have in common is a loss issue that can be ignored or suppressed and remain unsupported or be caringly upheld by the church and its leaders. Besides this being an activity of Christian love, it is also an act of Christian witness.

In Chapters 28–36, we will draw attention to some of the hidden losses within our Christian community, ranging from complex family life, abuse, moving churches and disenfranchised grief.

TWENTY-EIGHT

Coping with divorce and complex relationships

One Sunday evening at a lively renewal service, I recall preaching about relationships, particularly the breakdown of relationships and divorce. I never forget someone having a strong word with me afterwards that this wasn't an appropriate subject for such a meeting. The person obviously had missed the moment when I asked if people would raise their hands if they had been divorced. Since it was my congregation, I was well aware that almost half of those present had been divorced or were separated from their partner. I had chosen the topic at this charismatic occasion to draw attention both to the denial that exists so often in a church as to the number who have been divorced and secondly to preach in an affirming, accepting way to all who might feel that they are second-class Christians.

Since a breakdown of a relationship tends to lead to a reassessment of life, it is not surprising that the church attracts many who have had broken relationships. A caring church will attract people when they are at a point of need. But do we recognise how those divorced feel within the church? Divorce can be a subject we sweep under the carpet and do not preach about. Or if we do, it can be presented purely from the negative perspective given in scripture.

But for a moment, put yourself in the position of a couple in your church. This might be their second or third marriage or more likely today they are living together without a marriage certificate. I received a letter popped through my door late one night informing me that on a forthcoming weekend church houseparty there would be a couple coming who (in their mid-fifties) were living together, not married, and that it would be inappropriate for them to share a room together as this would set a bad example to the younger members of the church. Since the couple had both been married twice before, it was understandable they had not tied the knot. Scars of the past tend to make us hesitant to go over old ground. Recently converted, they were adjusting to what it meant to be Christians. Fortunately, we resolved the issue amicably and the couple generously took single rooms on this occasion and did eventually get married.

I don't want to go into the rights and wrongs of marriage, divorce and whether you are married in God's eyes just because you have a government piece of paper. We may be very clear about what scripture teaches on the subject of relationships and want to uphold the ideal to the congregation, but how do we relate to this couple at their point of need? It is easy for a church to be very clear about what you represent and what you stand for within the Christian tradition but much harder to be willing to engage with some of the feelings, hurts and pains that people carry into the church.

What are the issues that the separated, divorced and co-habiting couples face within the church?

- The feeling of failure of one's original marriage vows.
- Coping with the ideal being preached while living with the failure of one's marriage.
- Coping with the complexity of feelings about one's ex-partner.
- Wondering whether you are a second-class Christian.
- Grappling with both the forgiveness of oneself and of another who may have hurt you deeply.
- Wanting a new relationship that is physical, emotional and spiritual, yet being told that this can only be fulfilled in marriage.
- Feeling too scared to re-tie the knot with anyone.

I'm sure there are more issues I haven't thought of. I don't claim to have the answer to any of these issues, although we will discuss them more fully in the second book of this series on *Pastoral Care*. All I want to do is to remind us of the type of issues people are carrying within our churches. There is a very complex bag of emotions wrapped up with divorce and remarriage that often get suppressed in the church. When relationships break, they seldom do so without many loose threads. Some of these threads of attachment are like nerve endings, raw and painful to touch. Indeed some threads still remain attached years later and this is without the complexity of sharing the upbringing of children. The emotions of guilt, anger and an enduring sadness are all brought into a church context.

Becoming 'born again' as a Christian doesn't mean that these feelings are all instantly recognised and worked through. In any case, people seldom arrive in church and become Christians on day one. They may be in our church for months and years thinking through issues before becoming a signed up Christian. This may well depend upon how we handle their personal issues that they are grappling with. For example, how do we handle the joy and liberation that comes from being released from an unhealthy relationship?

We are now living in a community with complex patchwork families and relationships. If we seek to reach out and draw people in to the church as well as hold on to them as full members, we need to teach and pastorally care in such a way that recognises the needs of those with complex relationships.

The pain of loss doesn't only occur when a couple separate. What about those in our churches who are holding onto marriages that are chronically ill or have died all but in name? These are often people who are secretly carrying a living pain that they seldom share with another. I have served in a number of churches where there has been a couple whose marriage is stormy and everyone in the congregation knows all about it. Somehow these couples seem to cope with public disclosure of their arguments and troubles. They attract support and sympathy often at the expense of others. But in each church there will be those who bite their lip and hold on to a loveless marriage for various reasons. It might be because of their Christian belief, for the sake of the children, financial reasons or simply from pride and dignity. It is to these individuals that often only a sensitive pastor or care worker will get close enough to begin to understand what it must be like to live in such a situation. If one partner is not a Christian, then often the Christian has others in the Christian community who can sympathise and support them. But it is more difficult if both partners are Christians in the church. Here, there is an incredible tension between all that you believe and uphold, your position within society and the local community along with the gains that you reap from such a position compared to the inner turmoil of being in a kind of mental prison watching your future disintegrate around you. Being in this kind of situation correlates to disenfranchised grief, which is mentioned in Chapter 36.

Reflections

- How does your church make divorced people welcome in the church?
- How does the church policy about re-marriage in church affect people's views about the church and Christianity?
- Betty's new husband left her a week after they got remarried to run off with her sister. 12 years later she arrives in church wanting to be married. How would you handle the situation?
- How can the church tackle mid-life disillusionment about marriage?

TWENTY-NINE

The loss attached to parenthood

I was a guest preacher at a special memorial service where the church had invited members of the community who had experienced a recent death in the family. Afterwards, during the refreshments, a couple came up to me and asked, 'what about those of us who have to cope with a living loss that no one seems interested in?' I was taken aback and wondered what they were talking about. The couple began to share the story of their adopted adult son. He was still alive, but had been in and out of trouble with the police particularly relating to drugs issues. This had been going on for several years. They expressed how they too were in grief, although it seemed to go unsupported by the church. They felt that they had lost not only a son, but also their hopes of what he could have achieved, as well as living with the ongoing pain and fear for the future. They felt isolated in their pain and frustrated at the lack of understanding and support of the church. Each year they would receive Christmas letters from friends giving glowing accounts of their children, all of which simply deepened the couple's sadness. Here was a loss that they had to live with, which had an uncertain future. They were still very involved in the church but carried a sadness that seemed to be under the surface of all their relationships.

Parenthood is one long account of loss. Right from the birth of a baby, the parents have embarked on a path in which the child will constantly be moving on to new experiences. Each new chapter in the child's life is a chapter closed for the parents. On the one hand, this is good news. Children are, after all, individuals who need to go their own way for the good of their own sanity. On the other hand, parents have to learn to let go to allow their children to blossom into independence. That's not saying it is ever easy. Some of the key moments of transition include:

- When a mother ends breastfeeding.
- When the child starts to walk and doesn't need to be carried.
- When the child starts playgroup and then school.
- When the child starts to sleep over at friends' houses.
- When the child begins to speak and think more like his friends than his parents.
- When the child take up interests very different from their parents.
- When the child becomes a teenager with all that goes with it.
- When the teenager doesn't come home as expected.
- When the teenager leaves home for college, etc.
- When the teenager doesn't follow in the career path as expected.
- When the young adult develops habits, beliefs and behaviours that are contrary to the parents' views.

Now all of these changes can be exciting and a very positive sign that a person's own unique persona is developing. Parents may well rejoice at each stage and feel relieved when their child finally reaches adulthood and is off their hands. But for some it can also bring moments of deep pain bringing about the realisation that what was once so special has passed and gone forever. Eventually this might include the loss of hopes and desires for one's offspring. We all want our children to do better than ourselves, but alas it is not always the case. Who do you share such thoughts and feelings with? It might seem selfish and foolish to raise with a friend.

This can particularly be an issue if the parents want their children to mirror their own faith. Some parents are laid back about their child's beliefs while others frantically are praying for enlightenment in their child's life. Over the years I have had a good number of conversations with couples about their concerns, yet, to my shame, I don't think I ever encouraged the church to engage with the issue more fully. Why was this? It might be because I was more relaxed than some about my children finding their own way and not wanting to push 'clergy children' who have enough to cope with living in a vicarage. Some people are more at ease with their children having 'prodigal son' experiences. I also recognise that there would be a conflict of agreement about when a Christian *is* a Christian (if you know what I mean).

The son or daughter growing up with a different belief system to the parents can be a considerable anxiety to some. Others have to cope with greater unknowns. Some parents find themselves in a situation where there is little or no communication with the child. This can range from family arguments and people just not speaking to each other, to where relatives have left the home and have since disappeared all together.

Being a part of a family church with all its children's ministry can be a tough place for parents coping with a handicapped child. There are many benefits, of course, with the social contact for the child and the support for the parents with the child. However, we need to be aware of the daily issues a parent has to face, being aware of lost hopes and dreams both for the child and themselves. This applies equally to grandparents who can feel very helpless in knowing what to do.

Alongside this there will be couples in church that have been unable, for whatever reason, to have children. The church as a whole is very pro-creation, affirming marriage and family life. Not being able to have children is not new to the Bible, although often in the narrative the couple eventually have their special child. What issues are raised if this doesn't apply to you? How open is the church to journeying with you as you grapple with this issue both within your marriage and within your faith?

These issues highlight the point that there are often issues in the church that are 'no go' areas for discussion. Whatever they might be, it does lead to a church that is not functioning as healthily as possible. It is so often these hidden covert topics that people grieve over and this can lead to a gradual withdrawal from the church. Perhaps a preaching series or a home group discussion on the topic 'Things we don't talk about and may disagree on' might be liberating to many in the church, to enable them to feel that they still belong.

Reflections

- How did your parents and grandparents cope with your upbringing?
- How aware is your church of the issues young families have to cope with?
- Do you know how couples without children feel about the church?
- How can we prepare parents for the journey of parenthood?

THIRTY

Singleness in church

Susan was 39 and single. She had been a Christian since 16 when she was converted at a youth rally. Ever since then the church had been her extended family. An only child with elderly parents, she valued the relationships she forged with a range of families. After a spell at university she began her career as a teacher. She had relationships with men but somehow never found the right person. Before she knew it she had turned 30 and was seeing most of her contemporaries get married and have children. It awoke a longing within Susan to be married and have children. She gave up her teaching and began to work full time for the church. Her gifts were well used in administration, children's work and teaching. However, despite the fulfilling ministry she had developed, she still felt a deep ache within her that something, or more specifically someone, was missing in her life. She decided to work abroad for a few years and returned when she was 36. She now became increasingly aware that she didn't quite fit into the church as before. The church was so family-orientated, where did she fit in? There were a couple of other singles in the church of her age but otherwise she felt isolated. She moved from church to church as she re-engaged in her teaching career. One church focused almost solely on their children's ministry, another seemed to have no roles for women, let alone single women. She began to wonder whether she belonged to the church, any church, God's church!

Following on from the difficulties that arise from marriage and having a family lies the issue of singleness in the church. Genesis chapter 2:18-24 is very clear when it say, 'it is not good for a man to be alone'. However, in any church there will be a mixed group of people who would be categorised as single. This will include:

- Those who are single because they have not reached the usual age to settle down into a long-term relationship and marriage.
- Those who are single after the break up of a long-term relationship. This will include those who have now chosen to remain single and those who would be open to a new relationship.
- Those who have never found anyone with whom they could enter into a commitment of marriage and are now likely to remain single.
- Those who choose singleness as a form of celibacy, representing a higher calling in life.
- Those who are single because their career is unsuitable for a permanent relationship. This reflects the apostle Paul's advice when he talks about it being better to be single than to have the pains and cares of a loved one at a time of difficulty.
- Those who are widowed.
- Those who are single because of issues relating to their sexuality.

Scripture seems to present the lifelong relationship of marriage as a reflection of the Trinitarian relationship of Father, Son and Holy Spirit. If this is the case then anything other than this can be seen as second best. This is where the reality of loss arises. There are clearly those who are single and are very content in that state. They are good in their own company and, like Ruth in the Old Testament, will find helpers and friends like Naomi to support them along the way. Here a person has come to terms with what they may be missing from a marriage partner along with having children and recognise that there are equal advantages to being single. Such individuals are to be respected and encouraged to play their full part in the life of the church with their gifts and abilities. But what about those in our church community who feel uncomfortable with their singleness? There are a number of loss issues that they have to face:

- The loss of the hope of a permanent relationship.
- The loss of full sexual activity and fulfilment.
- The loss of the chance of having children.
- The losses of having someone to carry on your name into the future.
- The security that a partner brings in life; be it financial, physical or emotional.
- The loss of companionship in old age.
- Perhaps the loss of feeling fully accepted in the local church.
- The loss of what might appear to be the ideal of Christian lifestyle.

All of this can create a variety of issues for churches. The first relates to the young adults in the church. We can create a situation in our churches that actively encourages our youth to settle down into marriage at an earlier age than the general society. It might be a subtle way of a church handling the subject of sex. Get your young people married early and then there is no problem! This may well have worked well 50 years ago but our society has changed considerably. People are living considerably longer today, they change careers several times and now often live far away from any extended family structure. All of this places increasing pressure on young marriages. Years ago, a young person, by the time they reached adulthood at about 20–23 years of age, had started a long-term career, had worked out their sexuality and were ready to settle down into a permanent relationship.

Today, the average young person hasn't settled down in their career until 28–30 years of age at the earliest. They are hardly in a position to get a mortgage and build their home. Relationship-wise, many are not ready to settle with one partner until other aspects of their lives are settled. All of this simply means there is a higher degree of the unknown in a young 25-year-old's life that creates its own pressure. I don't have the answer to whether our young Christians should get married earlier than the rest of our society. I have heard stories of young Christian couples splitting up simply because they were too young to cope with all the pressures and expectations put upon them by themselves and the community. There is equally the pressure of being a single young Christian living in a permissive society. In many Christian homes, there is simply a silence about the subject. This means that when a Christian couple has grown-up children who are living with partners, the parents simply keep quiet about the subject. It becomes a subject that is not talked about openly in church in fear of being judged. Perhaps the real loss issue for young Christians lies in the church's inability to engage in the issues that they are facing. Some I know have found that the answer is to see the church as much more than the local gathered community. They have formed groups across the country where like-minded single people can come together and share friendship, fellowship and fun together. This enables them to hold into the local church, recognising that their needs are being met elsewhere.

A second group of people in the church represents those who are single in mid-life. They can find themselves caught between still hoping for a relationship while trying to get on with life and plan for a future that is fulfilled within the role of being single. The church again needs to be willing to engage with people as they work out their own calling and state of contentment. The danger is that it can be so easy for a church to present an image that the only right state of being is one of marriage. Where does this leave those who are single? The church rightly makes a great deal about weddings and the birth of babies to church family members. It is good and wholesome to celebrate with others. But we need both to be aware of the language we use in church as well as providing a forum for issues relating to singleness regardless of age, to be openly discussed in a non-judgemental way. Otherwise we are allowing our church members to build up loss issues that can manifest themselves in the form of resentment, anger, loneliness and discontentment. All of this alienates a person. First the person doesn't feel a full member of the body of Christ; and secondly, they can then begin to feel separated from God himself. When the church fails to scratch where a person is itching, sooner or later they move on.

All of these issues equally apply to people who are working out their own sexuality and find themselves at odds with the normal church line. In one parish I would regularly visit a single man who was very involved within the church. He was a homosexual who chose not to practise his sexuality. However, he felt unable to reveal his feelings or views within our church because of the fear of being judged and rejected. Here was someone who felt he had lost the right to be himself in a church environment. Only with a small number of people could he begin to trust his true self to others. There is a great strain in not being able to express yourself among people you count as friends. To be discriminated against within a church is a double loss both for the church as well as the individual.

In all of these different situations, people need to find ways to tell their own story. It is only as we identify and own the narrative of our lives that we can be who God made us to be and to find a degree of contentment. We began by quoting the passage in Genesis that 'it is not good to be alone', but in this fast-changing society, there are many other things that are equally not good for us. Singleness of whatever kind is just one aspect of a person's persona. We need to be a church that is willing to embrace a person's singleness and journey with them. Here we can give an individual space to be themselves; linking them up with others with similar issues and reassuring them that they will never be alone whilst they have the church. This requires an extended family concept within the church that is taught and practised.

Reflections

- If you are not single, can you imagine what it would be like if you were?
- What positives are there in being single?
- What issues do single people face as they get older?
- How can families support single people?
- What are the advantages of having single people in the church?
- How can the church be a companion to single people?

THIRTY-ONE

The problems of age

Kay was the youngest of three daughters and perhaps the most spiritually devout within her Christian family. She decided to become a missionary and served many years in Kenya. She led a very fulfilled ministry teaching in a remote school where the community loved her. This was where she felt she belonged, living out her Christian calling. Her father had died when she was young, so when her mother was diagnosed as terminally ill, she felt she should return home to care for her in her later months of life. This sabbatical dragged on into a year and then two. Her sisters were busy with their own families so it became expected of Kay that she would stick with her mother till the end. Kay's mother lived for another 18 years. Kay had never lost the desire to return to Kenya, but now in her late sixties she felt worn out. Kay had still used her time constructively. As well as caring for her mother, she joined the local church's staff team and was active in pastoral work and helping women's groups. But there remained a deep bitterness in her for the lost years of a fulfilling ministry abroad. She had given up the prospects of marriage and having children but she hadn't expected to lose the one thing she loved dearly. It didn't help her relationship with her mother and in the latter days of the mother's life, their relationship became strained. It wasn't the only tension in the family, as Kay felt that her sisters had neglected their mother and were relying too much upon her to do all the caring.

As we get older, a whole new area of potential losses looms upon us. I think of a couple who were hoping to use their early retirement to go to India and help run a charity only to have an elderly mother ailing and requiring family attention. The mother went on to live for many more years. Here, they had to cope with hopes and dreams fading into the distance as they fulfilled their Christian duty of care of a family member. In a society where it seems we leave the care of the elderly to the professionals, this is a wonderful example of Christian duty. But we can't ignore the cost that these people have to grapple with. Granted, in another culture this behaviour would be seen as just normal and expected. But in our current culture in Britain where the self seems to come first and where we have formulated a level of expectation for ourselves, we have to dig deep to make sense of our calling and circumstances. It is one thing to lose the dreams of what we might have achieved with our lives, it is another to also lose the dream that you feel God had given you to fulfil. Working out Christian guidance and a sense of calling is never as easy as it first seems. God of course is still immersed in our lives; we simply have to work much harder to see the wood for the trees. What helps is if our church is engaged with us in the journey.

This equally applies in situations where a married partner has a deteriorating illness like MS or dementia. There are at least three stages to adapt to. First the reality of the diagnosis, the shock and initial adjustment. At this stage the person who is ill has a full grasp (if they choose) of the impending illness and all that might follow. Here there is the choice to share the news with those in the church and community or to keep it private for as long as possible. This has its own pressures, carrying a secret between just two people. There is then, hopefully, an extended period of remission or limited deterioration. Here, one is living with the Damocles sword hanging over you. Handling the fear of the future while making the most of the present is not an easy balancing act. This makes it awkward for those supporting the family to know how to address issues with them. Do you keep positive and focus on helping them make the most of their abilities or do you encourage the couple to talk about their fears and face the gradual deterioration? The alternative is to choose to not engage in the subject at all and let the couple get on with it by themselves. This calls for more of a long-term strategy by the church in supporting people with this type of illness. Knowing that the church will support both partners through the whole journey can be very comforting and reassuring. For the ill partner it is comforting to know that the church will support their partner when they have deteriorated or died. For the carer, to know that they have support can give them the strength to continue through difficult times. But to achieve this the church has to embrace the ups and downs of this long journey.

This is particularly true when it comes to dementia and Alzheimer's. Here is a living loss where one's loved one is present physically but not mentally or at least in a conventional relationship. Slowly but surely, we have to watch a person drift away from us. Watching this decline is both painful and traumatic. Here, the illness can lead to the person being angry and aggressive with those closest to them.

One of the hardest decisions families have to make is deciding when is the right time for a relative to move to a nursing home. Even when it is clear that there is no other solution, it can be a very traumatic experience all round. I was recently asked to conduct a funeral for a person from work whose father had suddenly died. He had been in his eighties and had had a full life. However, on visiting the family it became clear that he had been the main supporter/carer of his wife, who had dementia. The family was aware of their mother's ailments but it wasn't until dad died that they realised how severe the mother's dementia had become. Her husband had been washing, clothing, feeding and generally keeping his wife safe on a daily basis. Suddenly the family found themselves with a mother who was requiring their 24-hour care. With their full-time jobs and personal health problems it was clear that the children needed to find a nursing home as soon as possible. However, this was not only practically demanding, it required knowledge of what was out there, what they could afford and most of all an emotional willingness to allow the mother to go into care. For weeks the family tried to hold on to their mother, passing her from one daughter's home to another. By now, the mother had totally forgotten about the death of her husband, while the children were still trying to come to terms with the loss of their father. What resulted was increasing disagreements between the children about which home to choose. Once decided, they then had to cope with a mother who was constantly telling them that she wanted to come home (which by now had been sold). It took further deterioration of the mother's health before she settled into the home and two years before the family began to build fresh relationships with each other.

Could the church have helped in such a situation? There are no easy answers but the church has considerable experience of caring for the elderly. In any church there are probably a few families grappling with similar issues although they may not know each other. Finding support from others in the church in similar situations can be very reassuring and supporting in a way that the leadership team simply can't do.

Reflections

- What complications does the fact that people are living longer make for the church?
- How can the church see old age as an asset?
- How can we help people to travel light?
- How can we help people to prepare to die well?
- What are the issues for a Christian in deciding to allow their elderly relative to enter a nursing home?

THIRTY-TWO

The rich, the poor and the unemployed

George was a successful businessman in a large corporate company. He had been with the firm for 21 years, fulfilling a number of roles. He particularly focused upon project work. He seemed to be successful with his regular promotions. As each project ended, there always seemed to be new possibilities on the horizon. During this time George was very involved bringing up his family and actively involved in his church. He had been a churchwarden and was an enthusiastic member of the ministry team. However, at the end of another project, George found that offers of new responsibilities at work had dried up. He continued working for another 10 months before he was finally given his redundancy notice, but during this time he secretly took to the wine bottle. In a relatively successful church, George didn't feel able to share his situation with his church friends. He began to feel trapped and depressed. He found it difficult ministering on the healing team at a time when he felt far from well himself. The church at the time was focused on a preaching series about growth and had a large building project which required the congregation to dig deep in their pockets. George was all for this, but began to feel increasingly remote from the church.

One of the healthy characteristics of a church is its ability to attract a range of people from different backgrounds and ages. It has always been easier to lead a church full of the same psycho-social mix with similar Christian belief systems. However, this kind of make-up reflects more of a club or society than a Christian church that reaches out and welcomes all. However, when we achieve a broad mix of people within our church, we have to be aware of what it is like to be a part of a church community each week where you feel you are the poorer relative. This might be by being less financially endowed or having poorer social skills than those around you. There is always the danger that the leadership of a church falls into the trap of the Revelation churches, where they treat those of similar background to themselves with a greater role in the church. How many times have I heard a curate tell me that the vicar seems to only like doing the funeral services of those who were seen as important in the community? Clearly the church loses something if it fails to treat people equally in the church. Here the loss is both individual as well as corporate. The individual feels undermined as they lose their self-esteem, self-worth and respect of the Christian faith. The church community also loses out by not appreciating the value of the individual with all his or her hidden talent that perhaps just needs to be allowed to blossom in a loving, accepting community. This is often highlighted when churches are having financial appeals to embark on some grand project. As spiritually important as the project might be, it is so easy to ignore those who, week in and week out, hear about the need to support the project, knowing full well that they are just not in such a financial position to contribute. This highlights the importance of recognising the contribution that everyone in a church makes, whether it is financial or practical, however great or small it might be.

Scripture teaches us that we never know what awaits us around the corner. A person's circumstances can change so suddenly, whether it is in relationships or employment.

I was asked as a chaplain to support and journey with a few people who had been told that their jobs were at risk. There were about six people who were not a part of any trade union movement and therefore felt they had no one to support them through the process of what this large organisation was putting them through. It all began with an email from the head of human resources summoning each of them to a meeting. At this stage, all they knew was that they had been 'fingered' for some unknown reason. There was caution about asking others in the team whether they too had been sent an email just in case some personal matter had been identified. All sorts of things ran through their minds, had they misbehaved, fiddled their expenses or performed unsatisfactorily? A brief, three-minute meeting took place in which they were handed a brown envelope with their name handwritten on the front. A large document lay within pointing out that, due to restructuring, their post was at risk. They were told to read the document, email any questions to HR and then there would be both group and individual meetings to allow people to make their concerns known and raise questions. After a month's consultation, they could be given their redundancy notice or have an opportunity to apply for specific posts that were being created. They could also take voluntary redundancy at any point through the process with the promise of favourable terms. All of this took place during a summer period and, particularly, when the line manger of the group was on holiday. He learned about the changes on his return! It was into this mix that I was asked by individuals to go with them to meet HR managers to ask questions and to clarify the situation. Journeying with people over the two to three months before the situation was resolved revealed to me how traumatic the experience was for those affected. This position of potential redundancy let alone actual loss of a job raised so many issues.

- Mortgages and credit cards to pay.
- Competing with work colleagues for fewer jobs.
- Relationships between line management and work colleagues.
- Feeling now insecure within the organisation even if they held on to their post.

- Tensions at home with partners and family.
- Regrets at not taking other offers recently.
- Initiating thoughts about career changes and relocation.
- Extra pressure on a partner to bring in more funds.

The reality is that redundancy fears can linger for a long time. Working in an organisation or culture where you see other staff come and go leaves people feeling very rootless if, regardless of their work contribution, they feel that the axe could fall anytime upon themselves. This inevitably increases people's stress levels both at work and at home. The assumptions of job security and all the many assumptions that go with a steady income are disturbed.

If these are just some of the issues raised with a potential redundancy, what must it be like when redundancy strikes and weeks off work turn into months? A person's self-esteem is very easily undermined. There is then the complexity of finding a new job. This can often result in temporary employment and not always within easy reach of one's home. A provisional existence then exists. Here you now have the strain of additional travelling, perhaps living away from home all week. Being apart from one's family is both financially costly and emotionally draining.

Where does the church fit into this situation? Will we even be engaged in the situation? This will depend upon how a church member perceives the role of the church and those who minister within it. People are very reluctant to share their problems if they don't think they will be supported. However, there is much a church can do to support unemployed people.

First, we can teach the value of an individual based not just on whether he or she earns wages. An unemployed person can easily feel undervalued when they are struggling to find employment in a relatively affluent church. It needs strong but sensitive leadership to make the congregation aware of the issues while not embarrassing the individual.

Secondly, we can develop a church policy that recognises the needs of the unemployed and the responsibility that we have as a Christian community. Christians have been very good at setting up co-operative finance unions to work within a geographical area. But there is nothing to stop a caring church from initiating such an initiative just for the congregation. Some of the more reformed closed religious communities are very good at this. One might suggest that Christianity is far more than just helping your own. At times, though, we can easily have gift days for charities while missing the need right on our doorstep.

Thirdly, we can at least recognise the emotional turmoil a person is undergoing when unemployment strikes. There are so many issues to consider that a friend or a wise owl in the church could be a great support in helping a person reflect upon their issues and decisions. Of course we can't help unless people inform us of what is happening with their work situation, but if we create a more open, caring church, someone will be more likely to share their need.

Finally, knowing that friends and individuals in a church are praying for you can be both reassuring and encouraging. In my own situation, although there was actually little I could change for those potentially being made redundant except speak up on their behalf, I think that knowing that someone else is concerned for you, interested in what is happening to you through a difficult time and praying for you can prove to be very uplifting.

Reflections

- Take a fresh look at the Gospels and see how much is mentioned in regards to money.
- How can the church make sure that it treats the rich and the poor equally?

- How can the local church support those who are unemployed?
- How effective is the church in teaching appropriate use of money?

THIRTY-THREE

When abuse lives in the church

Alice was an attractive 14-year-old whose family had been in the church for many years. Alice was a part of the youth group, although she was very shy and didn't seem to have many friends. The church had a paid youth worker who had been security checked. He built up a good team of helpers and all seemed to be going well with the young people's ministry. However, one day one of the lady youth helpers came to see the vicar. She was very concerned about a male youth helper who seemed very close to Alice. The person in question was a married man in his fifties with two grown up children and one teenager. The vicar assured the lady that this man was very respectable and perhaps there was a misunderstanding. He said he would have a quiet word with the man and nothing more was heard about the situation. A year later a complaint came into the church from a parent of Alice's friend. She informed the vicar that a man of the church was sending inappropriate text messages to Alice that was upsetting her. Alice hadn't told her parents. At first the vicar wanted to keep the police and Social Services out of the situation, but the mother informed him that she would take action if he didn't. The para-church authorities were finally informed and the police initiated an enquiry. The man in question, although didn't have a police record and was clear on the CRB check, had in fact been grooming a number of young girls in the church. When it came to light that the issue had been raised with the church a year previously, the church's reputation was greatly tarnished in the community. The youth leader left and the youth work declined for a number of years.

Abuse comes in many forms. It might be sexual abuse that we have heard so much of recently, particularly in the Catholic Church. However, there are other forms of abuse that take place in God's name that get far less coverage.

Abuse can be physical, sexual, emotional, verbal, social, economic, intellectual and spiritual. All of these can be found in the church. In all of these cases there is an involvement of intimidation or manipulation of another person or an intrusion into another's inner being. The ultimate purpose, whether realised or not, is to exercise a degree of control over another person. It is generally a long-term pattern of behaviour that has developed in an individual, although specific short-term interactions can be labelled abusive.

We mustn't think that abuse is singled out and is to be found only in the church. It can also be found in families, schools, sporting clubs, community organisations and the workplace. However, that is no excuse for its presence in the church that aims to set a higher example to the community. Yet we shouldn't be surprised that it occurs in church. Abuse usually focuses on a weaker person being manipulated by a stronger person. Since churches genuinely seek to care for the weak and vulnerable, it is then understandable that an abusive individual might find the church an easy place to exercise their abuse. It might manifest itself in an individual grooming children. I recall an organisation that particularly cared for boys that didn't excel at primary school. They helped boys to gain their confidence using various sport activities. The leader was a solicitor who had excellent references from school leaders and county youth authorities. The organisation had just begun to rent a church room when they were accused of abusing boys over several years.

As the vicar of the building and the local chairman of the school governors, I was warned that I might get tarred on account of my links to the organisation that was being accused. I wondered what might unfold both for my ministry, my faith, and how it could affect the local church and school. A nervous few months followed. The police and the church authorities told me that I couldn't speak to anyone. I couldn't speak to the accused or offer support to those damaged by the organisation. All I could do was to grapple with feelings of anger at those who should have known better. Guilt for not double- and treble-checking references and carrying a blurred pain for those who I didn't know whose lives had been blighted.

Fortunately and correctly, the church and school were not linked with the case. Here is an example where the church was on the edge of the accusation. But how would it have been if it had been an actual church group? When abuse takes place it destroys not only individuals physically and emotionally, but attacks at the heart of organisations and communities. Ripples go out from the news that shake the confidence of the church. The community naturally reacts with anger and rejection of the church when this takes place. It can take years to rebuild trust and confidence.

But abuse doesn't have to be high-profile to do harm. In fact many people may not fully realise that the church has abused them. They are simply left with a struggling faith, confused feelings for the church and a lack of direction. In the church, abuse might come from a youth leader or the group itself. The youth leader can groom a group of young people not for sexual purposes but to boost their own ego. It is not unusual for young people to feel pressurised to conform to a belief system that they personally don't seem ready for. Youth groups are famous for being cliques and can be quite cruel to those who don't fit in. What results is a young person who is seeking God but feels rejected by him because of poor youth work. It is one thing presenting Christ to young people and another to suggest overtly or covertly that to receive Christ you have to be a part of a particular youth group. The loss experience a young person is left with is one of confusion, not fitting in, wondering whether God is not for them and yet still longing for something more in their lives. This type of loss can linger for decades, unfocused and unresolved.

Since the characteristic of abuse is one of power misused over others, one might expect church leaders to be susceptible to causing abuse. The influence that a preacher or elder has in a church is considerable. Church gatherings like any groups are vulnerable to being led either in a healthy way or in a destructive way. Being a shepherd is a demanding role. Scripture teaches about the high expectation that is expected of Christian leaders, but why? Is it because of the deep damage we can do to people's lives, their faith and ultimate fulfilment of their calling in God's kingdom?

Leaders do damage when they:

- Have favourites within the church.
- Make people feel guilty for non-biblical reasons.
- Perpetually preach sin at the expense of grace.
- Keep on treating Christians as not saved.
- Prevent Christians from growing into maturity in case they challenge their authority.
- Exploit people's financial generosity to build their egos rather than the kingdom of God.

All of these situations cause an emotional reaction within people that damages both their individual lives and the life of the church. Unhealthy leadership leads to Christians that feel undernourished spiritually, lacking in self-esteem and not reaching their full potential within the church. But ultimately the greatest loss is to the church as a whole.

Abuse doesn't just lie with the leaders, a good number of church leaders have been emotionally destroyed by attacks from church members. I can think of one church leader who was told that his children could play in the garden but not in the street and that the congregation wanted access to the toilet in the manse. As months passed, he was then told that he was common person and not up to the requirements of the congregation. Every Sunday he was presented with a religious newspaper with the comment, 'there's a job in here for you'. What kind of impact does this have upon someone who has given up one career, taken a step in faith to retrain and then to be so personally attacked? Some are able to cope with such pressures and see it through, hopefully to a more stable time of ministry. After all, the one we follow was also treated with scorn. But not everyone is suited to such pressures. Here there can be a multiple of losses. There is a loss of that sense of call that took the person to the church and ministry. It now challenges any future calling as to what is the right way forward. There can be an attack to the person's self-esteem as they reflect upon whether it was their own lack of faith that got them into this position. Then there are those who wonder whether God was in this calling in the first place.

We mustn't forget the damage that occurs to a minister's family and the wider congregation when a leader leaves the ministry. I served in one community after a minister left after great divisions. Several years later people were still saying to me that they would support my ministry but wouldn't venture into the church and associate with those in the church.

What does all of this teach us? First that ministry is costly and we shouldn't doubt the full cost that some pay for their calling. Ministers who suffer greatly at the hands of other so-called Christians deserve our love, support and help to find a place within the church where they can find healing and use their gifts for the good of all. When we fail to care for them effectively we simply do further damage to the wider church. Secondly, we have to recognise the fallenness of the Church. We not only attract hurt people to the church but also unfortunately create at times further hurt within individuals. If we can at least acknowledge this within our churches we are allowing the congregations to be honest and truthful. Too often we simply sweep issues under the carpet, which fails to set a Godly example to others. We then wonder why people lose interest in what the church is saying. Thirdly, when any kind of abuse takes place in the church we need to recognise that, as with deep grief, it will take considerable time to bring healing both to the church within and to the wider community. Most churches will now have clear child protection policies guided by their church authorities but perhaps we should also consider some mechanism to handle other forms of abuse in churches such as bullying and manipulation, etc. Any policy that involves more than just the main leader taking decisions has to be a healthy practice.

Reflections

- Has your church a clear abuse policy?
- How would you recognise when a person is being abused?
- What would convince you to report a case to the police or Social Services?
- Has your church completed CRB checks on all who work with children or vulnerable adults?
- How can the church bring healing in abuse cases?
- Would you speak out in the church if there were covert signs of bullying in the church?
- Why not invite a regional specialist to educate your church leaders?

THIRTY-FOUR

Christian hopes unfulfilled

The church minister announced that he was leaving the church to take up a new post. There were some very sad at his leaving while others seemed glad and were excited at the prospects of a new minister. The church said farewell to their minister and began a well-organised prayerful search for a new minister. All seemed hopeful at the induction of the new preacher and leader. However, the honeymoon period didn't last long. The new minister had very clear views that seemed to be contrary to many of the mature Christians in the church. One by one, people began to drift away either to other churches or gave up church all together. All their prayers and hopes seemed to have been washed away. Other churches were blessed with the arrival of some mature Christians and the new minister began to build anew, reaching out to new people in the community. But somewhere along the line, a great deal of hope had been lost.

There can be a tendency in churches today to focus on the modern-day strategy of marketing, to grow and develop the life of the church. This can focus upon success stories, with the worship and atmosphere being rather upbeat. It is an understandable strategy if one is trying to attract newcomers to the church. But at the same time we have to recognise that unless our worship is genuine, people quickly see through the glowing images. If members of a congregation feel that they are unable to share their real struggles in life then it begins to affect their faith and trust both in God and the church. On top of this, if the church never preaches or teaches into these issues, then members quickly learn that this is a church where you do not share your problems or concerns. So the church preaches one story while the congregation lives another. Quietly, one by one, we lose members who just feel that the church doesn't itch where they are now scratching. No wonder at this present time in Britain we have more people who used to go to church than presently attend. A campaign like 'back to church Sunday' has been helpful, but unless we are willing to engage in some of the real honest issues families are experiencing, we will see that their return is short-lived.

The reality is that whenever a person experiences some kind of loss issue, it raises deep questions about their faith. I have known ministers themselves lose the 'way' when they have suffered the death of a child. Six things at least are required if as a church we are to grow mature Christians able to cope with personal tragedy in their lives.

1. We need to acknowledge from the front of the church, that it is okay to have personal issues and still fully participate in the life of the Christian community. In this way people will gain the confidence to be honest about their doubts and struggles. This seems so obvious but is often not said or acknowledged.
2. A leader of the church needs to listen and empathise with individual needs. This does not mean they need to counsel or pastorally support. It is simple recognising people for who they are and making them feel accepted.
3. We need to teach realistic sermons using examples of real people who have suffered and perhaps are still suffering; yet still persevering and believing. It is too easy to preach about the heroes of the faith in a way that makes them out of reach to the average pew filler. We have to recognise that the Christian life, once begun, is a slow journey of sanctification and transformation. All of which comes at a cost.

4. We need to set up home groups that allow people to come together with similar issues so that they can normalise the experience and support one another.
5. We need to appoint people, lay or paid, who are skilled enough to journey with those with long-term issues. I have a dream that one day every church will have a full-time Christian counsellor on the staff who is trained to the highest level. We have the national Association of Christian Counsellors already set up to equip the church when it recognises this need.
6. Finally, we need to be willing to allow people to leave our church graciously. This means not taking the issue personally (although we tend to) and keeping the door open so that the person can return if desired. In one large church I worked in, we were neither conservative, evangelical or charismatic or community-minded or outward-reaching enough to please everyone. There is often a cost if you try and build a broad-based family church. So every now and again someone would suddenly tell you that they were leaving to go somewhere better and more in tune with God. I endeavoured to depersonalise the situation and encouraged people to keep in touch. What was surprising was how many people came back after trying perhaps a number of churches. There was no doubt that if I had 'huffed and puffed' when they left, I would have made it too awkward for them to return holding their heads up high. Often people need a time away to deal with issues in their lives so they can then feel able to return appreciating what the church offers with all its strengths and weaknesses. People would tell me that it was their friendships that they had missed the most. If we had only kept in touch with the many who have left the church, how many would now be back with us?

Reflections

- How can a church allow people to grieve for lost hopes?
- Where do you feel safe enough to share your true Christian feelings?
- Does your church acknowledge when people leave the church or is it too embarrassing?
- Does your church have a policy for keeping in touch with those who move on?
- How can the church bring clarity into real hopes and false hopes?
- How can we help people gain new hope in life, Christ and the church?
- What scripture can you use to renew someone's hope?

THIRTY-FIVE

When the minister moves on

John had been in ministry for 11 years. He had three years as a curate, although it proved to be an unsatisfactory placement with a vicar who was a workaholic who wouldn't delegate any work to John. He put it all behind him when he was appointed the vicar of a town church just three miles away. All went well for the first five years with him building roots in the community and forging many friendships. But things turned sour with a degree of unhappiness within the leadership team. His curate had been complaining behind his back and rallying people against him. Although the curate moved on, John felt betrayed by some of the congregation. He persevered for another two years before being offered a rural post with six churches in a different part of the country. He and his family moved with an initial sense of enthusiasm. The countryside was a new adventure for all the family. However, the role John now played was very different to when he was in a town. He quickly missed the larger congregation and especially the friends he had kept for 11 years. His wife found it difficult to settle. The previous vicar's wife had been very active running lots of activities, whereas John's wife had to work, so she felt she just couldn't compete. John became depressed which meant he didn't get out and about across the parishes. People began to say that they had never met the vicar and a degree of muttering developed in the churches themselves. The previous minister began to get invited back for weddings and funerals. Since he retired only four miles away, was missing the role that he had in the community and had lots of time on his hands, he was ready and willing to oblige. John felt caught, he wanted to tell the old minister he was not wanted, but he was also relieved he didn't have to do some of the additional services. John began to wish he had never left his previous parish and now felt trapped. Who would give him a new church now? Meanwhile, in John's previous parish a new young vicar had been appointed whose focus was purely on the young families in the church. Many of the long-standing members equally longed for John to be back. All in all, it felt a mess.

One issue that so often goes unrecognised is when a minister moves on to another post or retires. We have tremendous welcome services for ministers, particularly in the Anglican Church. We also do reasonable farewells but how much energy do we put into acknowledging our loss. This applies both to the minister and his or her family as well as the church and local community. I have moved on from eight churches in my ministry and now recognise that I have certainly left 'a part of myself' in each parish. I recall returning only weeks after leaving a ministry after 11 years to lead a funeral of a very special missionary and former member of my staff. I was not only upset in losing someone who had become like a mother to me; but as I looked at my old congregation, I felt I had betrayed them for leaving them.

I am sure there are always those who are ready and glad when a minister leaves. I sadly have even known people actively pray for the minister to leave. Unfortunately church members can fail to realise the cost of ministry materially, socially and spiritually. One of the costs for a minister is that he or she rightly grieves for their old congregation and ministry to them. One makes such personal attachments to people whether it is through the hatch, match and despatch part of the job or through week-on caring for the congregation. Ministers are so often quickly thrown into a new ministry with a new congregation that they hardly have had time to work through issues unresolved from their previous ministries. Sometimes this results in ministers who just don't settle after a successful post while others seem to lose their sparkle and enthusiasm for the work. This is less faith-related and more to do with not properly processing their deep losses. I have seen this also in laity who fail to settle in another church for similar reasons. If this applies to yourself or one of your ministers then Part 6 of this book is very relevant and worth considering.

There is also the issue of the effect a minister leaving has upon the congregation and the local community. When he or she leaves, they take with them a wealth of knowledge and experience that can never be regained.

- There is the attachment we had with people who have now died that the bereaved still value and which the new minister can never achieve.
- There are the 'secrets' we have carried and now take with us elsewhere.
- There are those moments when we have been with people at a crunch time in their lives that they will never forget and grieve that we are now not there to support them.
- There are those who were hoping the minister would do their funeral just as he or she did for their partner or baptise or marry their children. It is not surprising therefore that people often try to invite a former minister back to a church to do a baptism, wedding or funeral, all to the detriment of the new minister. Unfortunately ministers' egos get in the way, and congregations fail to see the importance of encouraging people to find a new attachment to the new minister. When we have the need to keep going back we are simply clouding the issue of loss for all concerned, including ourselves.

All of these things need to be addressed from the pulpit. We need to clearly teach what is the psychology of what happens when a minister leaves and a new one arrives. If we can help the congregation to understand their own emotional reactions, we are far more likely to aid in the rooting and settling of a new minister.

What can ministers do to help themselves settle in a new ministry without looking back? There are 12 rules worth considering:

1. First, before you embark on looking for a new parish, ensure you are not just running away from somewhere. I recall asking to see a bishop, as I wanted to resign. The afternoon he was due to visit, I prayed and casually opened my bible to read a chapter in Isaiah, which spoke to me about tightening my tent pegs. I thought I had better not tell my wife about this verse! At the time I felt furious that God might be speaking to me about staying, when all I wanted to do was to run away. Fortunately, the bishop forgot to visit and nothing more was ever said about the matter. I continued in the parish with a new sense of hope for several more years. God works in mysterious ways. There is a right time to move on, but make sure it is for the right reasons.

2. Secondly, make sure the call to a new post is clear and supported by all involved in the appointment. It is easy to be persuaded to take a post by one's leaders simply to make everyone's life easy. However, you, more than anyone, has to live with the consequences. Christian work is never easy, at times it is only the clear call to a post that enables you to continue and complete the task set before you.

3. Before leaving a post, don't just sneak off without a proper farewell. Remember, this is not just for you but also for the congregation and community. It provides an opportunity to say thank you, to recognise the role leaders in the community play in their lives, to begin to adjust, to start to let go and get ready

to re-engage with a new minister. I know some ministers hate farewells but we mustn't have a false sense of humility. Truth needs to be recognised. On top of this, as we have heard earlier with children, some people never have a good experience of positive endings. Here is an opportunity for you to show by your ministry how endings and partings can be healthy.
4. Have a proper break before diving into a new ministry. We all need small sabbaticals to allow ourselves to begin to reflect upon the past and formulate new hope for the future.
5. On arrival at a new post, don't take on the mantle of everything. Issues, problems and hopes have been there since well before you were appointed. Just look at the noticeboards in some Anglican churches of the long list of previous ministers. You are just one in a long continuation of ministry. The issues can wait till you gather a proper perspective on the situation.
6. Don't assume you understand the needs of a congregation for at least six months. Ministers inevitably make the most mistakes in the first six months.
7. Be open with the congregation from day one, that some will miss the previous minister, others will be itching to push on, but inform them, for their good, you require time to adjust yourself.
8. Remind the congregation that you have left many attachments behind and although you are looking forward to forming new links, it will take time.
9. Differentiate between the many people you may be close to from the past church with those you want to continue with as very close friends. There is a limit to how many people you can maintain contact with from the past. Remember, the more people you hold on to from the previous church, the harder it is for you to formulate new friendships and the harder for the minister who is replacing you.

10. Don't be used as a pawn by members of your old church when they ring you up and complain about the new minister who has replaced you. Give your 100 per cent commitment to the new minister and let people know this. The new minister may make a real mess of what you have built up but you must release this to God and others. When you leave a parish, you leave, totally. It's only our ego that wants to dabble and protect the past. It's God's church; leave it to him. Whatever part of your ministry was of God's, it will survive, the rest is just sheaf.
11. Be very clear and firm about what you expect from any previous minister in terms of their involvement in the parish. Let this be known and supported by the governing body of the church. Remember, this is not about you and your ego but about the health of the church. Hopefully, a bishop or para-church leader will support you in this action.
12. Finally, when you do move on, don't be a thorn in the flesh for the next minister!

Reflections

- How can the church support ministers who are moving on to new parishes?
- What can the church do to support ministers retiring?
- What support structure can the church put into place to support new ministers?
- How can we help congregations to be more realistic about what to expect from their ministers?
- What safeguards can we put into church policy to protect ministers?

THIRTY-SIX

Disenfranchised grief

In one of the churches I worked in, we would do house to house calls on everyone in the 4,000-strong parish. We had a team of lay people who would send a letter first of all saying we would be visiting on a particular day. People had the choice to contact the church office and decline the visit. When we did call, we had a small questionnaire which ended with the question of whether they would like the vicar to visit. Most declined, but I was asked to visit a stranger to me. She was a single lady, approximately in her forties. After a cup of tea and a friendly chat I enquired why she particularly wanted a visit. She slowly, hesitantly shared how she had had an affair with a married man who had three children. It was a work colleague and the affair had gone on for about four years. Unfortunately, the man died suddenly of a heart attack. She felt unable to go to the funeral. No one at work knew of the affair and she hadn't shared it with her parents or friends. It was now 18 months later as she finally shared with me how she was feeling.

Much of what has been said in this chapter has been recognised in the form of something called Disenfranchised Grief.

Disenfranchised Grief is where a person experiences a loss that is not or cannot be openly acknowledged, publicly mourned or socially supported.

Some of the signs of this form of grief might be:

- Exclusion of care.
- Lack of social support.
- Exclusion from funeral rites, etc.

A simple example of this was in a church where the minister chose not to be available at the back of the church after the services. Weeks later, one old lady, who was a regular at the church, expressed her unhappiness about this. When the minister enquired why, she reluctantly told him that he was the only person she physically ever touched each week. People's disenfranchisement can come in many forms.

- When people do not reconstruct the story of their lives.
- When we are surrounded by silence.
- When we lose ex-spouses.
- When work fails to recognise our loss.
- When we are caregivers and fail to give time to recognise a loss.
- When nursing home/hospital staff deal with multiple deaths.
- When we can't acknowledge we are broken-hearted at the death of an animal.
- When we have been adopted and our loss is unclear and vague.
- When we have fostered many children, all who have moved on.
- When ministers engage with large number of funerals.

We need to remember that grief is complicated when it is delayed, suppressed, interrupted or merged with additional losses. One of the roles of a pastor is to intervene where appropriate, and in doing so we can prevent this disenfranchised grief from developing. We are able to facilitate grief by our intervention. People don't often raise the subject of loss in a society that tends to deny its existence. But the pastoral worker can skilfully open the floodgates. If one is able to patiently ask open questions in an environment where the person can see that you are genuinely interested and actively listening, then the person gains the confidence to truly share their thoughts and feelings about their loss experience. Tears can often be close to the surface when a sensitive pastoral carer visits. As well as listening skills we can also provide a continuity of care with our regular visiting. We have the skills and knowledge to see when someone is struggling and with our networking skills we can link the grieved up with appropriate support agencies. Unlike other secular community workers we can also help people in their faith struggles and help them to interpret their lives. In this capacity we have an ability to love and to absolve guilt. It has been said that there are regrettable things in life but no regrettable people. Our calling therefore is to work through the negative issues in people's lives such that their own self-esteem is restored. It was Proust who said,

'We are healed of suffering only by experiencing it to the full.'

Therefore good grief means working through our painful experiences and feelings. If we do a bible study of Jesus's encounter with people, we will see that he met a good number of disenfranchised people. To name but a few:

- There was the woman with the flow of blood. Jesus healed her physically but despite the fact that he was rushing on to heal a small dying child, he stopped to hear her story. She no doubt needed not only physical healing but also emotional healing via the telling of her story. Would the healing have been complete if Jesus had not heard her? (Luke Ch.8)
- We are told that Mary, the mother of Jesus, right from his birth stored up all that had happened to her, right up to seeing her grown-up son suffer death on the cross. At the point of death, Jesus directed her to his friend, John, that he might care for her.

Was Jesus providing a channel for his mother to express her long stored-up grief (John Ch.19)?

- Zaccheus was a tax collector who carried the baggage of being a loner; isolated from the very people he collected taxes from. No wonder he had to climb a tree to see Jesus, as no one would let him into the crowd to get a good view. Jesus, however, embraced the man by asking to stay at his house, thus making him acceptable and relevant.
- Jesus engaged with the woman at the well who clearly had a story that others were reluctant to listen to (John Ch.4).
- There was the man who had been ill for 38 years with no one to put him in the pool when the water was disturbed by the Spirit (John Ch.4).
- Apostle Peter, after the death of Jesus, seemed disenfranchised in his grief and from his fellow disciples till Jesus redeemed him (John Ch.21).
- The lepers that Jesus touched and healed had been previously ostracised by the community (Luke Ch.5).
- In the parable of the prodigal son, one might identify a number of people who were grappling with loss issues (Luke Ch.15).
- Finally, the individual that was and is a challenge to us all – was Judas an example of a disenfranchised individual that no one reached out to to save before it was too late (Matthew Ch.27)?

Reflections

- Can you identify other disenfranchised stories in the Bible?
- Have you ever been disenfranchised?
- Can we provide a care system so that our ministers and those in the church who are in the care professions are supported so that they do not become disenfranchised?

Part Six

This final section will look at how pastors can develop a first aid kit to survive the pressures of ministry. I guess most of us don't really know what we are getting ourselves into. Entering pastoral ministry might come through a rigorous interview process for ministers, whereas lay pastoral workers may well find themselves immersed in pastoral ministry after a brief chat by a church leader as they were leaving a church service. However we arrive in this type of ministry, what then follows could never be predicted. This is the wonderful diversity of pastoral ministry. But it does bring its own problems. If we are going to have a long and fulfilling ministry, we need to put into place strategies that enable us to cope. This is about knowing our strengths and weaknesses and putting into place a support structure so that we don't become someone else's pastoral need.

THIRTY-SEVEN

When the pastor weeps

During my first posting in the Church of England, I was in a church which had a large team of colleagues. We would take turns being on call for the local crematorium, which involved doing one week each. When a funeral director failed to find a local minister to do the service, it was our job to step in at late notice and provide a valid form of service that fulfilled the requirements of the family and community. On a Monday morning, we would be given the job sheet for the week and take our packed lunch to the crematorium. I recall a colleague who was on duty for a whole week by himself. He did so many funerals that by the end of the week he phoned in ill, convinced he was dying of cancer.

A recognised occurrence for those of us who are counsellors is something called 'Transference and Countertransferance'. However, it is just as likely to be present for pastors in the role within the community. Pastors can find themselves with a vague sense of hopelessness, guilt, resentment and a spectrum of other feelings that result from a pastoral visit. These feelings can seem hard to pin down and it can be even harder to identify the cause. The pastor begins to find themselves daydreaming when they are with individuals, reducing contact time with people, withdrawing into their working home and forgetting appointments. Others become intensely involved with parishioners and constantly go the second and third mile so that they become unable to switch off from their ministry. With their faith justifying their behaviour, this action can then be affirmed and encouraged by the parishioners.

All of these reactions can simply be an automatic response to the dilemmas we find ourselves in through our involvement in Christian ministry. Ministry is costly and often seems to attach itself to our inner emotions in a way we struggle to understand. We find ourselves struggling to control our feelings and fail to predict how we will react in new situations. This is countertransference, where we tune in to all the pain, feelings and confusion of those we minister to and then project them back to the person. So when, in a pastoral encounter, I am feeling confused, agitated, restless, frightened or angry, I must ask the question, 'our these my own uncomfortable feelings or am I responding to the other person's experience?'

We all have our own transference hooks that dig into us. When I was a maternity hospital chaplain, I was at the stage of life where my wife and I had one baby and my wife was pregnant with our second child. All of this hooked me into the dilemmas of parents of neonatal babies. I could very quickly identify with parents as I reflected upon what it would be like for myself to have a premature baby. This assisted me in the care of others but it also influenced my thoughts of my family. I have many other 'hooks' that I have to be aware of that affect me in ministry. They have evolved over time and reflect my own life experiences – people with headaches, those ill in their fifties, drug issues, and, since all my relatives have died from cancer, just the very word can subtly have influence upon me. We have to recognise that it is normal to get 'hooked'; what is more dangerous is not to recognise the vague gnawing feelings of discomfort that reveal that we are 'hooked' and are unaware of it so fail to take appropriate action. My own life experiences can be a great boost to my awareness of the other person's story. But I also have to be aware of when they interfere with my work.

It has been recognised that this reaction is particularly true when we are dealing with illness and death situations. If the person mirrors our own past experience of life, or the person reflects what could occur for ourselves in the future, or if we see similarities that correlate to our age group, then we are more likely to tune into their situation and experience their pain.

One of the great challenges for ministers is how we can be truly present with people as they struggle with fear, emptiness and trying to make meaning of their lives in the midst of tragedy and pain. As Christians we have the example of Christ who manifests the depth of what it is to share in the world's sufferings. As church workers, we seek to identify with Christ's suffering as we draw close to those suffering in our community. It is only as we empathise and draw close that we are able to bring a new perspective to the situation and bring a glimmer of hope. But this is not easy, which means that we can have a tendency to retreat into our professional objective skin. Here, we can appear to be aloof and distant. It is easy to slip into the mode of discouraging a person from shedding tears. This is the opposite of what many grief specialists would recommend. A healthier practice is to encourage a person to go deeper into the tears by inviting the person to share their thoughts about the tears. It is here that we can begin to get a handle on understanding what the tears represent and therefore where we can offer appropriate support.

Lament is well represented in the Old and New Testaments. It constitutes addressing God, complaining, petitioning and bringing motivation to a situation. The Psalms are full of prayers crying out in difficult situations (Psalms 22, 74, 126 and 143).

At the heart of lament is an ability to give rise to the telling of the narrative about the pain and suffering. Here we are allowing the subconscious suffering and pain to be experienced into consciousness where its power can be diminished. By allowing a person to express their pain and suffering we are helping in several ways.

First, we are offering someone an umbrella of safety, the opportunity to lay out their complaint in a safe managed way that can allow movement and healing. It places the cry in the context of another and of God himself. As we accompany a person in their pain, we are reducing their loneliness.

Secondly, we are making sure that the complaint is not minimised but given its full weight of merit. It is very hard for anyone to move forward until they have been truly heard. Here we are providing a safe space for the person to formulate his or her own language of expression.

Thirdly, we are bringing a painful situation into a relationship dynamic, both with ourselves as well as with God. Relationships are never static, they are always moving in one direction or another. Hopefully it is a relationship that goes from pain, to pleading, to final praise. However, this can be a long drawn-out relationship journey with many twists and turns along the way.

I think of Jesus in the garden of Gethsemane (Mark 14) where he felt alone in the pain he was bearing. The disciples journeyed with him in prayer as they tried to understand what Jesus was going through. But they seemed to struggle to go all the way in comprehending Jesus's burden of pain. There seemed to be an attitude in the disciples of wanting to 'do' rather than 'be' with Jesus. It's a tendency that all professionals can slip into all too easily.

To sit with someone either at death's door or in deep pain and not being able to 'do' anything can be frustrating. It can lead to us fidgeting, looking at our watch, frowning, tapping our foot or hand and relieved when we are dismissed. It is so hard for us to be with people when all we can offer is our presence. So we can easily slip into evasion, false assurance, denial, avoidance and finally flight. All of these strategies provide a way of protecting us from being overwhelmed by feelings of our own mortality, from anxiety and stress and ultimately burn-out. So armed with our fast education, skills and techniques we find ways of engaging purely in our head alone and bypassing the heart. Pastors are encouraged in their ministry to wear the whole armour of God (Ephesians Ch 6:10-20). Unfortunately, we can also put on a defence uniform that might protect us initially but in the long run doesn't help either the parishioner or ourselves or the kingdom of God.

The pastor's armour of defence

EMOTIONS EXPERIENCED	OUR REACTION	A POSITIVE RESPONSE
Helplessness	We become over- or under-involved. Clock watch. Think about other things when with the person. Thinking of reasons why they don't need your visit.	Being willing to acknowledge our helplessness. Sensitively enquiring whether this is how the person themselves are feeling.
Embarrassed	The problem can seem so great we protect ourselves by not fully 'seeing' the person.	Seek to engage so that you can empathise more fully.
Denial	We hope the situation just goes away. We don't talk about the issue, thinking we will just make it worse. We offer misguided advice. Reassure that the problem isn't so bad.	Recognise the feeling of wanting to run away. Acknowledge that you haven't any easy answers.
Anger	We might label the person as a 'problem'. Sarcastic comments. Putting the person down.	Recognise and acknowledge to the person that the situation makes you feel angry. Share this with another person who will listen.
Sorrow	We withdraw into our own deep sorrow and feel sorry for ourselves. We become the sufferer rather than the one we are visiting.	Recognise that as we feel sorry for another, we are also feeling sorry for ourselves. Make sure we do not become a burden to the other person.
Restlessness	Wanting to bring good out of the situation such that we become pushy, dictatorial, seeking some positive outcome that makes us feel better.	Keep on the person's agenda and not your own. Take your restless emotions to a counsellor/supervisor to talk through.

When we learn to tune into these feelings, we can develop an awareness of how to handle them appropriately. This might mean we convey what we are feeling back to the person in such a way that it leads to a deeper discussion of the situation. However, it is not always appropriate to place this discussion on the shoulders of someone who might be already overwhelmed by their situation. We need a protocol of deciding when to share or to choose to take our reactions to a colleague, counsellor or supervisor.

- First, will the information be of benefit to the parishioner? Will it raise information that is new to the person or will bring clarity to his or her own feelings? Here it can lead to a deeper, more open discussion about how a person is truly feeling. This can enrich our theological discussion, inform our prayers and allow a person to feel more fully understood and supported.
- Secondly, if I share my feelings will it lead to a change of focus away from the person to myself and my own needs? It is a common mistake that pastoral visits can become more focused on ourselves, our stories and opinions rather than on the parishioners.
- Thirdly, could we cause harm by sharing our thoughts? Have we the time and confidence to handle what might result? Could the situation become too upsetting for ourselves so that we were unable to continue in the relationship? Perhaps the person already has others who are supporting them from this open emotional perspective. The person may not be looking to you for that kind of support or encounter.
- Fourthly, is this the right time to share and disclose our own feelings? We may prefer to just allow our feelings to educate us as to how the person might be feeling. We have to be ready to acknowledge we could be on the wrong track and have totally misread the situation.

- Finally, when we have recognised the feelings arising within ourselves, we can, without disclosure, raise open questions about whether the person is experiencing feelings of deep pain such as helplessness, confusion, anger, despair, etc.; in this way, the person is free to engage in this line of discussion or not without rejecting your own person feelings.

I recall visiting a dear member of my church in a nursing home. The lady had recently fallen in her own home and was unable now to care for herself. During my hour-long visit, the lady constantly begged me to take her home, she was convinced the staff were punishing her. I had a duty to check that she was being properly cared for, but once assured all I could do was to sit with the lady, offer my presence, pray with and for her and share our humanity in common. I had to fight the urge within to excuse myself and run, to control my fears of being helpless, control my guilt of being unable to change her perspective and control the anger of the mess of it all. Perhaps I was picking up all her inner feelings of fear, guilt and anger. I could either see these emotions in myself as an obstacle and so go and do something that made me feel good or recognise them for what they are, an opportunity to stay connected with a person in their suffering.

It is as we listen and feel another's story that we are able to reflect upon what the situation tells us about the person's view of the world, God, the Church, of their own families and the professionals that care for them.

If we reflect upon Jesus's ministry, he may have helped people with his miraculous interventions, but what took place first of all? Jesus was exposed to people who brought him their shame, rage, trauma, anguish, loneliness and hopelessness. Jesus seemed to be able to draw out of a person how they viewed their illness or dilemma. Jesus at no time gave the impression that he was overwhelmed or uninterested in a person's story. Indeed, he seemed to be able to get beyond people's avoidance techniques. This seemed to come about through developing an intimacy with the person by his compassionate understanding of the situation. Intimacy can be a scary word. We tend to keep it for marriages and very close relationships. Here I am using it to mean 'coming close to a person such that you accept the state of being of that person'. This can be a powerful position to be in and can raise all kinds of feelings within, be they physical, emotional and spiritual.

In the end, the more time we are willing to give in investing into our own healing, the greater we will be able to 'be' with the person in their own sufferings. It is here that we find the beginning of the road that leads to hope, change and acceptance. At the very least we are able to offer a person the reality that they are not alone in their pain.

Offering religion or spirituality

Today the word of spirituality has been claimed as a subject totally separate from religion. Many secular courses in the caring profession may include a section on spirituality. This can seem strange to those of us who are religious (whatever that means); however, there may be lessons we can learn from this differentiation. It has been suggested that spirituality is the whole realm of human existence. This seems a rather grand and all-embracing definition. We are well acquainted with the concept of spiritual formation and reflecting upon our inner and outer journey. From a secular perspective, spirituality can be seen as a shift in mentality. This involves giving up power and knowledge and skills and being willing to move to a new perspective. Here we might be moving from:

Individual to communal.
Isolation to connectedness.

Sameness to surprises.
Static to developmental.
Head to heart.
Competition to co-operation.
Denial to facing monsters.

All of these movements can be seen from a Christian perspective. The more attuned we are to our own spiritual journey of understanding and change, the more we will be led to being attuned to our encounter with others.

What we need to be aware of is when our own belief system clouds the care that we offer the person. Our role is surely to provide an opportunity for a person to speak about their religious beliefs that shape and guide their spirituality while not imposing our own views upon them. Any dogmatic intervention simply closes a person down from exploring their views and you find that they are changing the subject as soon as possible. Of course it is very natural as a religious person to believe that you have something 'other and holy' to offer that is different from the other carers. It is certainly true that when we are asked to pray for someone, so often more is really being asked. People can see us as God's representative who will bring healing, physically, emotionally and spiritually. Others can see us as someone who is going to inflict on the person religion and dogma. We need to stay true to our calling and not perform according to role or expectation but engage as a whole person. This means being truly present as another sojourner. There are often multiple layers of meaning going on when we enter pastoral care.

- To sit and pray.
- To be willing to raise important issues.
- To represent the organisation that sent you.
- To show that you along with the rest of mankind care.

- To empathise with the situation.
- Fulfilling our own need to be needed.
- To assist in helping a person to find their own meaning and purpose in the situation.
- To bring a quick 'fix' to the situation.
- To remind ourselves we haven't all the answers.
- To reflect upon our own fears in the situation.
- To hear what God might be saying in the situation.
- To wrestle with the unknown.

The list goes on. Perhaps we can pin down what we are actually doing to four areas.

1. Relatedness
2. Meaning
3. Forgiveness
4. Hope

First, our very presence is giving a message – you are not alone. Simply relating to a person in suffering is giving an unconscious message that someone cares. This alone makes our work worthwhile. Suffering of course affects how we relate both to those close to us, the wider world, God and even to ourselves. It is inevitable that our care will engage at some level with this discussion.

Secondly, we are called to grapple with the person as they seek some kind of meaning in the midst of their suffering. This doesn't mean we have the answers, how can we as we don't truly know what it is like to sit where they are? But we can endeavour to journey with them and listen to their questions without coming up with quick answers. We need to remember that they are always the experts in understanding where they are sitting with their problem.

Thirdly, forgiveness is so often apart of our work. But the question is how do we engage in it? Do we want the person to find forgiveness for their sake or ours? If it is a concern for the individual then we have to recognise that it is their understanding of forgiveness we have to relate to and not ours. Here, perhaps, prayer comes to our aid. Often, when people are asked what they would like us to pray for, they are able to express what they are struggling with. Issues around forgiveness need to be handled delicately. People behave more like cats than dogs with this subject. A cat will only sit on your lap when they are ready but if you push they will run away. Issues around forgiveness with themselves, others and God will surface if we are patient and gentle enough.

Lastly, hope is very much a part of our ministry. But hope is not a static thing, especially for someone seriously or terminally ill. Hope has many colours ranging from wanting to get better, to having the pain controlled, to concern for others and finally commending our loved ones and oneself to God. We must be willing to understand these spectrums and move with the person through the colours of hope.

So the more we are able to make our own unconscious reactions to ministry conscious, the more valuable we will be to the other person. This, however, often requires support or supervision to help us to see the wood for the trees.

Reflections

The armour of God (Ephesians 6:10-20)
Paul talks about being strong and powerful because of what we have received from Christ. How does this affect our pastoral ministry? He gives us seven pieces of advice.

1. Pastoral ministry is about spiritual battles. In any conflict, the soldiers, as we see too often in Afghanistan, are in an environment

of harm and danger where they can become severely injured. We mustn't think that our pastoral work has no dangers. We can do damage to others if we fail to take situations seriously. But what about ourselves? Too many pastors leave ministry because of burn out. Beware, Paul is saying, don't take this form of ministry lightly (v.12).

2. Paul secondly tells us that we are called to stand right until the end of the task by using the full armour of protection. In a pastoral context this involves being trained as much as possible. I am constantly being challenged by new situations that force me to go on with more training, learning and reflection. It is also about using good management techniques, skills and abilities (v.13). The more I learn, the more I become aware of when I am also out of my depth or I am taking on too much work for the good of my health.

3. The belt of truth and the breastplate of righteousness are the first pieces of armour to put on (v.14). They both go so well together. For any encounter to be right requires a serious look at what is the truth of the situation. This is the truth that we perceive in others but also what we perceive in ourselves. Reading our own inner reactions is so important if we are to get to the truth of what is happening to both parties. The opposite to the truth is lies. We need to be aware when we are colluding in lies when we say we are okay but are clearly struggling or when we are lying to ourselves about the volume of work we can actually cope with.

4. Next comes the shoes of the gospel of peace (v.15). This is about being both sure-footed and ready to move lightly and quickly. Sometimes in pastoral situations I have felt an internal ill-at-ease when about to visit someone. We need to listen to our inner spiritual antennae that warn us when we might find ourselves being knocked off balance. We need to be humble enough to take another person with us when we feel unsure. Travelling with

light, agile shoes means we are ready to engage with situations. I have found that the sooner I have reached out to an individual, the greater the influence I had in gaining their respect and their willingness to appreciate my ministry.

5. The shield of faith was a large piece of wood that covered all aspects of the Roman soldier's body (v.16). It provided almost total protection and was made to take any darts of fire aimed at it. Our faith is our shield of protection in ministry. It is there to absorb all the wrongs that might be thrown at us. It is not uncommon for people to hurl all sorts of angry words at us from their own frustrations. It is our faith in Christ that reminds us why we entered this ministry.

6. The helmet of salvation is about the past and the future. Salvation covers all that has happened in the past and gives us the sure hope of a saviour who awaits us. This gives us confidence in ministry that there is no situation that is beyond God. We enter pastoral situations with confidence that we are his child and his wisdom is above all worldly problems. We need to remind ourselves of this before and after any pastoral encounter. The sword of the spirit is the only attacking implement, it is short and cuts to the point. This of course is the word of God, which, at the right moment, spoken in love, can make a transforming difference to an individual's life. It remains long after you have left the situation and, like yeast, quietly works within a person.

7. Finally Paul rounds it all off with prayer (v.20). He calls us to prayer in all encounters. This marks us out from all other ministries, works and employment. This includes all types of prayers: supplications, thanksgiving, praise, confession and intercession. Pastorally we are praying with our eyes open, adjusting our prayers according to the situation. Using all types of prayers is a safeguard to us becoming trapped just with intercession. It means that, at the end of the day, we can still

praise and give thanks, even in the most difficult of situations. Also bringing in a different type of prayer to a pastoral situation can take a person's focus away from something they were obsessionally focusing upon. We can often forget how Paul ends this letter. He sends Tychicus (v.21) to offer support and to bring encouragement. We all need to be reminded in ministry, of whatever kind, that we minister only with the help of others. It is in God's strength that we minister and often that comes from support from others. May we never be too proud to ask for help.

THIRTY-EIGHT

Support and supervision

Over the past four years I have been running what is called 'Work Based Learning Groups' (WBLGs). These consist of about five or six ministers who commit themselves to meeting monthly for two years for sessions lasting two-and-a-half hours. As the facilitator, my role is to develop clear ground rules of confidentiality, commitment and keeping the sessions safe, while initiating a deeper level of reflection and challenge. Generally we try to gather people who don't know each other or work in the same geographical area. These groups are very different from groups such as clergy chapter meetings, as we can achieve a greater degree of openness and confidentiality with less competitiveness being present. What I have observed over this period is how isolated ministers can become. They can feel undermined by senior management in the church while trapped with some members of their congregation eating into their self-confidence. There can develop an illusion that one can't take a day off (or even two days like their congregation), that the phone has to be answered at all times and that no one understands the pressure a minister is under. These symptoms come from the isolation that is created by the post with often the lack of clear management structures of responsibility and support. This may well change as the churches begin to see ministers more in terms of employment but for now there are a good number of ministers who feel unappreciated. I've noticed this is particularly true for ministers in the later stages of their career. By now there can be a fading of their original calling and their faith can be rather worn down. They find themselves feeling trapped in tied houses, with weakened opportunities of finding a new post. With the pension pressure in our country, there is little prospect of taking early retirement and indeed many are being told that they will have to work extra years to get their full pension. Having no one to share these issues with seems a common problem. It is not surprising therefore that some end up ending their ministry with sickness. The purpose of the WBLGs is to prevent this sense of being isolated. The group provides both a safe place to receive empathy from others who understand but also a place where we can challenge false assumptions and expectations we place upon ourselves. If we can help individuals regain their true identity as a whole person without the label of being a minister, then it can be liberating for a person to find a new identity in the ministry and outside it. These groups take time to formulate where people trust each other. It can be a difficult lesson to learn that the group comes before funerals and meetings and should be seen as work and therefore not as a day off. But gradually I've found people find it a lifeline to have a place where they can be their 'true selves', bringing issues they are grappling with and reflecting over the following month what has been said. Whenever I have gone for my counselling supervision sessions or being a member of a support group, I've always been surprised with what I have suddenly shared. Just reflecting upon my own sharing has given me a chance to see things in a new light and gain a fresh insight.

When I began my ministry nearly 30 years ago, I was totally unaware of my gifts and abilities except a need calling to want to love God's people. Gradually through my theological training, and working in city, town and country churches, I acquired skills and learning along the way. I am, by nature, a gatherer of techniques and so gradually I attended a whole range of courses that seemed to fit my need in each ministry I found myself in. When I was in a large church, I suddenly found that I needed to be far better trained in the area of management issues. As a hospital chaplain and encountering serious pastoral issues in parishes, I was out of my depth and so began learning as much about healing and counselling as possible. At a difficult time in a church's life, I surrounded myself with a small group of trusted prayer partners and later initiated a long-term prayer triplet. The reality dawned that I could not do this ministry without ongoing support, whether it be with a prayer group that I trusted, yearly professional development courses, a spiritual director and, when a trained counsellor, a supervisor.

All of this might seem over the top but the reality is that when you are almost self-employed, you are personally responsible for your own spiritual and professional development. Who else will see that your ministry lasts for 30–40 years? As I became more involved in the counselling and the psychological world, I began to realise how other professionals had safety factors built into their working practice. A counsellor cannot be accredited unless they see a supervisor regularly, usually at a financial cost. Now as an accredited supervisor of counsellors, I have to have supervision both for my counselling and my supervision. I have come to not resent this but to fully endorse its benefits along with its provision of safety both for my clients and myself. One has to ask why ministers, who finds themselves in just as many if not more compromising situations, are not required to have this kind of regular supervision? I have discovered that a supervisor and a spiritual director provide an opportunity to be supported, challenged, corrected, protected, stretched and encouraged. I now could not function without it. Unfortunately I got here by the long route of experience and making mistakes on the job that at times could have cost me my ministry and my marriage.

There is no doubt that as all counselling professions are being more closely regulated, ministers themselves also need that oversight of accountability. In the past, ministers enjoyed the freedom to formulate their ministries in their own image and style. This, however, historically reveals itself to have been precarious in light of the problematic issues that often arise between churches and their ministers. The child abuse issue is just one area that should ring alarm bells and make us question whether our style of functioning is honourable to the church or God. If one only looks at the issues covered in this book, one will see that anyone involved in this ministry is very vulnerable to physical and psychological burn-out. They are also at risk of potentially crossing the line of working in a safe way both for the parishioner and themselves. Whenever you are dealing with emotionally upset individuals who are not thinking or reading a situation clearly, we are putting ourselves at risk of being misunderstood. We can also potentially be making ourselves open to becoming overly emotionally attached to individuals. It is in this context that all kinds of transference of feelings can take place, twisting our normal rational judgement. It is in the light of this that I highly recommend any minister to find someone outside the local church to be a supervisor of his or her pastoral ministry. In this way we are saying that we take our ministry, our family and our church seriously and we are recognising humbly that we are as vulnerable as the next person in getting this wrong.

One of the underlying beliefs of doctors and counsellors is that we are not there to make people's lives worse. A key way of achieving this is to be able to bring situations to a supervisor who can challenge us about whether our practices are Christian, ethical, human and professional. The church needs to recognise how important this is for the reputation of the Christian faith and how it is their duty to protect their minister from harm. If there is a cost (and usually if the supervision is professional with clear ground rules, there is) then it should be borne by the church.

I cannot commend this practice more strongly for anyone seriously engaged in any form of pastoral ministry but especially when dealing with people with loss issues. In the end, if we don't find a healthy way of looking after ourselves, we end up leaving ministry early, which is a great loss to the wider church.

Reflections

- How can a minister ensure he or she has a support structure and routine that will enable them to have a long ministry?
- How can we as ministers model a behaviour that sets an example to the congregation?
- How healthy is it that the church relies on ministers who are well past their retirement date?
- What does scripture teach about our relationship with our leaders and elders of the community?

THIRTY-NINE

Know yourself

I recall seeing my spiritual director one day and sharing the pressure I felt I was under. She quickly suggested that I had what was called the Jesus Syndrome. At first I was about to take it as a compliment until she explained, 'you think you are Jesus with all that you are doing'. At this point I began to cry as the stress poured out. I went back to the parish and signed up for a 'how to delegate' course.

Church ministry should come with a health warning. It is a privileged role that allows you to minister right at the heart of the community's soul. However, there is also a cost. Often without a clear job description and, as previously outlined, usually without adequate professional supervision, we can find ourselves working very long hours. When a job becomes a way of life it brings with it great satisfaction but with the added sting that there seems to be no end to what is required of you. Over the years I have asked clergy to fill in various questionnaires so that I could carry out stress analysis. The conclusion I have found is that most clergy are 'A' type behavioural, in other words they are prone to be 'workaholics', the type you find in coronary care units. Ministry clearly has an impact upon us and may affect particular character types more negatively. It is interesting to note that in one Anglican diocese, they recently found that the greatest job satisfaction came from non-stipendiary ministers rather than the stipendiary posts. Perhaps this lay in the fact that these people were doing their roles almost as a hobby (I say this in a positive and creative way) compared to their main financial career that had very different pressures. Whereas the stipendiary ministers carried the responsibility for the overall ministry. When someone is 'carrying the can', it inevitably leads to greater pressures. On top of a demanding role comes the psychological pressure of always having to relate a ministry to one's own personal belief system. This endless self-analysis is wearisome. When you then add onto this a whole range of emotionally draining grief and loss issues within the parish, it is easy to see where the stress comes from. So when it comes particularly to dealing with bereavement issues, we really need to 'know ourselves' if we are to not only survive in the ministry but thrive and last the course set before us.

One of the first requirements in ministry is to know what your gifts are and to make sure you use them well without distraction. In my understanding, everything else comes second. It is here that you find your fulfilment in your ministry. Everything else in ministry then has to be managed effectively. So what happens if funerals, counselling and all of this grief work is just not you? We need to remember that not all church leaders want to be involved in funerals or bereavement work. This is perfectly fine provided the church therefore appoints others to do the role in a professional way. This is not just abdicating responsibility to whoever seems interested but seriously appointing a trained or 'willing to be trained' individual who will be a credit to the church and wider community. The professional example we offer at funerals is a huge marketing opportunity that is not to be just passed to any retired priest or lay reader who might not have their heart and commitment in the task. We therefore need to budget a cost to this ministry and ongoing training costs. If this is effectively managed then the minister can learn to 'let go'. Although being the overseer, he or she does not need to be responsible for every situation.

Whether a minister is involved in loss issues in the parish or not, they need to be responsible for themselves. This includes respecting the needs of one's own family and setting a Godly example to the congregation. If we simply copy the laity and become workaholics, what example are we making? In most Anglican churches we have the tradition of placing a plaque of all the names of previous vicars going back to the church's birth. In some instances, the names go back a thousand years or more. It brings a sobering realisation that the church was there before you and will be, long after you have moved on. We therefore need a better framework of mind that recognises the importance of looking after oneself. We need to set the example to the congregation of the importance of days off and holidays both for oneself as well as the family. One very quickly becomes aware in the church ministry of when you are feeling stressed, exhausted and ready for a break. After a year or two it should be clear how the pattern of ministry affects your health. We are then in a position to plan ahead and book breaks well before a crisis point. This not only applies to our long-term ministry but also on a daily basis. I have known ministers who cope fine with several funerals each week while others find that just one drains them physically and emotionally.

We need to recognise our own psychological make-up and, if required, book time after such events to restore ourselves spiritually. Otherwise we may find that 'disenfranchised grief' soon builds up within us. Here, we may not recognise why we are feeling this way or what these feeling are connected with. Who else can look after ourselves but ourselves? To love our neighbour requires us to first love ourselves and to formulate a healthy self-esteem for the good of our families, the congregation and ourselves. In this way we will have a long and fruitful ministry.

Reflections

- Does your church recognise your minister's gifts, abilities, strengths and weaknesses?

- Does your church delegate or abdicate responsibilities?
- What care is in place to support the lay people who take responsibilities within the church?
- When was the last time your minister took a spiritual break?

FORTY

Developing a pastoral policy

If we are to take the loss issues seriously in our church, then we need to do more than just appoint a Cruse counsellor, as useful as that might be. We need to think through a strategy of care that is Christ-like. We need to be able to care for both members of the church and those in our community. This needs to be carefully planned out in such a way to make it sustainable. We will only do more harm if we attempt to take on more than the church can adequately manage. But if it is seen as a serious long-term strategy then it will not only build up the church's body in Christ, but also prove to be extremely outward reaching. Churches that are able to engage with people's real problems in a sensitive way become very attractive churches to join.

So let me outline twelve possible aims for a church to have pastoral care at its heart.

1. Validate people's struggles. How do we do this? We simply engage in listening to our people about how they are truly feeling. This takes time, as Christians can be very reluctant to truly share unless they believe that the person offering help is doing so in confidence and is trustworthy. Alas, the church has a lot to learn about what we mean about confidentiality (look out for the *Christian Handbook to Pastoral Care* that goes into further details).
2. Help people to find appropriate resources. We can too easily think that the church is the only place to turn to for help at difficult

times. But we don't have the numbers to get together a group of people who have experienced a particular type of loss. That's why we have groups like the Compassionate Friends and Sands, etc. We need to be willing to have their leaflets and contact details in churches. As educated resourceful people, our support in linking people with support agencies will be greatly appreciated. Our church members will be able to return to the church both encouraged and perhaps with stories of outreach. But we as church leaders have to have the courage to let our people go!

3. We can provide rituals to say goodbye. This needs to be planned into the calendar life of the church. We have Remembrance Sunday and All Saints/All Souls Day in the established church calendar and these are good opportunities to engage with the subject of loss. But I find that a thanksgiving service in the spring can be very effective. These are opportunities of inviting people in the community who have experienced any kind of loss in recent months or years. With good record-keeping, a church can send sympathy cards on a yearly basis to families. This then gives you a base to invite people to a special service. Such services need not just be reserved for a Sunday afternoon session. We need to incorporate into our regular services themes that show that we are not just interested in the bereaved but also in those who are struggling with singleness, divorce and separation, family problems, etc. Our weekly prayers need to demonstrate this.

4. We need to explore spiritual stories with those who are in a loss situation. The Bible is full of such stories, many of which our people will know well. If they grapple with their grief without engaging in the spiritual aspect of their lives we will be causing a chasm to form between their experience and their faith. The more they look to scriptural stories concerning loss, the greater the spiritual awareness and insight will be found. We need to

do this with them without providing quick shallow answers. Journeying with someone is to be alongside while they find the spiritual answers that are appropriate for them. They will amaze you with the insights they will come to, without us doing it for them.

5. We need to link the bereaved and those with loss issues with others on the same journey in our church or community. A home-group setting is ideal for this. It is no good putting a person in an 'ordinary' home-group where people are just giving standard biblical answers. This only closes people in grief down and they soon stop attending. But if a group is created with clear ground rules where people can say anything without being judged, there is hope that a real engagement with their problems will be shared and explored and prayed over (any study on Job brings this out).

6. Whatever particular churchmanship we come from, we need to acknowledge that we do not have all of the best spiritual practices. When a person is bereaved or going through a difficult time, they will often find that their traditional methods of Bible reading or praying or worshipping is inadequate. Let us not chastise them or feel they are rejecting us or that they are necessarily losing their faith. We need to be mature enough to release them to find new Christian spiritual ways of communicating with their Lord God. Perhaps we need to recognise our own ignorances here. The history of the church is full of a variety of ways of studying scripture and praying. Let us be brave and encourage them to find ways that are right for them in their spiritual practices such that they will bring back to us new spiritual insights.

7. We need to develop a congregation that asks difficult questions, allows real dialogue, grapples with tough questions and be at ease with not always having the answers. Leaders of churches find this difficult. You are expected to preach and communicate

in a clear and confident way to build people up in the faith. But that doesn't mean we cannot be human and vulnerable from the pulpit. Indeed, it is often when a pastor shares their struggles from the heart that people remember the sermon. The application of scripture and the Christian faith is often lacking in our churches. No one really wants to join a church that thinks it has all the answers. It simply leaves no room for ordinary human beings. We need to plan sermon series that are asking the questions the congregation are grappling with. Perhaps we need to ask them what they want the preachers to expound. It might be helpful if we encourage home groups to then discuss and be allowed to disagree with the sermon. Then we are truly creating an open church.

8. If we are engaging lay people to be caregivers, we must be professional enough to then care for the carers. This means helping them to formulate a resilient faith that encourages them to look at how this ministry is affecting their faith. You cannot be at the crunch end of people's lives and it not affect you spiritually. When people are asking the big questions when they are going through the 'dark night of the soul', it is inevitable that the carers, if they are truly engaged and empathising, will journey that way themselves. I can assure you that I could not have focused on ministering to bereaved families over thirty years without having to seriously think and reflect what losing a child would mean to me. At the time I was bringing up three children. On many occasions, I would pause and have tears in my eyes as I realised what the impact would be on my life and my family. Just because it hadn't happened to me, didn't mean it did not shake and shape my faith. If we fail to recognise what our carers are going through, then we find that they collapse with burn-out, feeling unclear why they are struggling in their faith. They become our own disenfranchised carers of the church.

9. We can provide emotional support to people in loss simply by having a trained bereavement counsellor on the staff. I had a Christian Cruse trained counsellor, who voluntarily had a wonderful ministry following up the bereaved. She would offer the bereaved a chance to visit regularly and also invite them to our special services where she would then meet and greet them. She became skilled to then know when someone should be referred to other professionals for help.
10. We need to protect the bereaved especially when they seem helpless. This might be from well-doers who want to 'lay hands' on them at inappropriate times. Church is a vulnerable place to be. We need to create space for those who are struggling in life to be able to sneak into church during the first hymn and leave during the last. There is nothing worse than wanting to escape a church service only to be stuck at the back of the church for ten minutes in a queue of people who can't leave without saying goodbye to the minister. We have to give the bereaved room to breathe in church and allow them to be themselves. Remember the church is there for the lost and weak to feel safe, not trapped or exploited by those who want to experiment on them with their ministries. This is especially true for those who do not recover as fast as we might want. I have heard too many bereaved parents who have given up church because people cannot cope with the fact that they are not behaving as others wish. Strong leadership is required to protect these vulnerable lambs.
11. We need to assist in helping the bereaved and the church to form new models of understanding as they cope with change. It is too easy to rely on the first model one is taught about bereavement and then repeat it for thirty years. Funerals and sermons on a Sunday are an opportunity of making people aware of new grief models, as well as recognising the unique journey that people experience. If we engage with the grief issue at a funeral, the

congregation is far more likely to listen to what we might then say spiritually.

12. Finally, we need to help our congregations to plan for the future. This means sowing seeds of good practice. I would often encourage a WI or Mother's Union group to think about talking to their children about their own funeral. By encouraging their grandchildren to help plan their funeral is a way of equipping the children for future losses in life. Otherwise they will as adults suddenly be faced with their parents' funeral, or worse, their partner's, with no coping mechanism formulated. A child copes with a funeral as a child ought to. If a sensible carer supports them, they will cope naturally and will then not feel neglected from the grieving process. Remember, we can't protect children from being upset, as they are already upset when someone dies. We can also encourage our congregations to be ready for death by preparing a will. In the past the church was very good at helping people to think about how to die well. We need to break the taboo of our present society and its denial of death by helping our congregation be mature, responsible Christians that set an example to the community.

Reflections

Draw up your policy to include:

- Who will do funerals?
- Who will follow up funerals?
- How will we show care to the bereaved?
- Who will do the administration?
- Who will plan the yearly calendar?
- Who will teach these issues in our schools?
- Who will gather people with similar experiences together?
- Who will remember?

FORTY-ONE

A time to listen

When you are listening to someone, completely, attentively, then you arelistening not only to the words, but also to the feeling of what is being conveyed, to the whole of it, not just part of it.

Jiddu Krishnamurti

Jesus said, 'someone touched me. I felt power discharging from me.' When the woman realised that she couldn't remain hidden, she knelt trembling before him. In front of all the people, she blurted out her story – why she touched him and how at that moment she was healed. Jesus said, 'Daughter, you took a risk trusting me, and now you're healed and whole. Live well, live blessed.'

Luke Ch 8:46-48

Listening has to be one of the most important aspects of being a good pastor. Yet it is something we so often take for granted and assume we are all experts at. Unfortunately, both in the clergy and the counselling world, too often one can hear comments that the very person who should be listening seems too full of their own ideas. So let us briefly just remind ourselves of what good, active listening involves.

POSITIVE LISTENING INVOLVES:

- Warmth and Caring – this is being concerned for the individual, accepting them in a friendly manner.

- Empathy – trying to understand how it feels to be in someone else's shoes and conveying this to the person so that they feel you want to understand.
- Non-judgmental Acceptance – this is not being shocked with what is shared or finding yourself judging the person. This is easier said than done and requires real practice to achieve. We have to learn to accept the feelings of the individual regardless of what they may be.
- Respect – here we allow someone the dignity of having the right to feel any emotion and the free choice to choose any action.
- Genuineness – being real, not just someone 'playing' a role.
- Limit your own Talking – this is difficult for those of us as preachers when we are expected always to have an answer for everything. The reality is that you can't talk and listen at the same time.
- Clarifying – if you don't understand something, or feel you may have missed a point, clear it up by asking a relevant question.
- Summarising – periodically check back with the person that you have heard them correctly by summarising the main points of what has been said. You may wish to encourage them to do the summary or to ask them to clarify if they think you fully understand.
- Questions – always use open-ended questions, the questions which cannot be answered by just 'yes' or 'no'. These types of questions close a person down and can make them feel that they are being interrogated.
- Don't interrupt – a pause, even along pause, doesn't mean the person has finished saying everything they want to say. The art of being able to sit with someone in silence needs to be developed. It is often in the silence that we are allowing God to work. Such silence nearly always bears fruit with an individual finding the courage to share deep concerns.

- Turn Off Your Own Words – personal fears, worries, problems not connected with the person easily distract from what they are saying.
- Listen for Feelings – don't just concentrate on the facts as these are often less important than the feelings. Convey back to the person the feelings you perceive in them and see if they agree.
- Don't Assume or Jump to Conclusions – don't complete sentences for the person either verbally or in your mind.
- Listen for Overtones – you can learn a great deal from the way the person says things and what they do not say. We can also learn a lot by the mannerisms of the person, how they use their hands, fidgeting, etc. We can communicate more by the tone and non-verbal actions than we do by just the speech.
- Concentrate – focus your mind on what the person is saying. We need to practise shutting out distractions. This means asking for the TV to be switched off or turned low, turning off your mobile phone and not looking at your watch and thinking about your next appointment. If we are clear about how much time we have available and make it clear at the beginning, then we don't get embarrassed when we have to excuse ourselves to move on.

NEGATIVE LISTENING INVOLVES:

- Displaying boredom, impatience or hostility.
- Being condescending or patronising.
- Devaluing by minimising the problem or disbelieving them.
- Jumping to premature identification of the problem.
- Passing judgment.
- Distracting body gestures (e.g. fiddling with your pen, keys or mobile phone or looking at your watch).
- Filling in a silence too quickly.

- Asking too many questions, when the person is trying to think something out. (A good check is to ask yourself, 'why are you asking this question?' Will it help the individual or is it just because you are curious?)
- Interrupting. There is an 'art' to listening between the lines to pick up what is really being said.

Reflections

Try the following exercises over one week:

- Day 1: See how you can develop an ability of listening without interrupting anyone.
- Day 2: See if you can increase your observations of the people that you encounter through the day. Observe what people are wearing, their mannerisms, their tones of voice.
- Day 3: Try listening to what is not being openly said, but possibly being felt.
- Day 4: Listen to yourself and how you are feeling throughout the day.
- Day 5: Try and create longer pauses and silences in your conversations.
- Day 6: Try paraphrasing what someone has just said to you and see if they agree.
- Day 7: See if you can put all the exercises together throughout the day.

Remember: Advice is seldom welcome; and those who want it the most always like it the least.

FORTY-TWO

Conclusion

Death is outside of life but it alters it: it leaves a hole in the fabric of things, which those who are left behind try and repair.

How did the minister we began this book with cope with his new church? Well, after a difficult time, he decided to go and seek some external counselling. This enabled him to begin to deal with some of the emotions he had hanging around from the last church. He also realised that he wasn't the only one who needed support, there was his family and his parishioners. He decided to work five days a week (yes, it is possible) and give more time to his wife and children when they needed it. In regards to the various pastoral issues in his church, the first thing he realised was that he wasn't equipped to handle all these needs nor had he the time. So he decided to be more honest with his governing body in the church explaining how he was feeling. Together, they recognised and appreciated his gifts (different from the last minister) and theirs, so began to create a church that released others in their talents. From out of the congregation, they appointed a skilled social worker to become their pastoral worker who in turn began to train others in pastoral ministry. It wasn't a perfect church, but people began to feel cared for in a new way, which allowed more people to use their pastoral gifts. With an able administrator/ secretary the minister also put into practice a remembrance scheme that meant that no one felt forgotten in the church. The family would always miss some things from the old parish but they had begun to put down roots and build new relationships. By sharing in people's lives they became an important part of the community.

Throughout a person's ministry, there will be many highs and lows both with individuals and with congregations as a whole. I have had the privilege of experiencing preaching to very large congregations with all of the buzz and the challenge. However, looking back, I think the most special moments of my ministry have been sitting with a mum and dad at the point of death of their premature baby or sitting and praying through the night with an elderly member of the congregation during their last days. These are the events I can recall clearly. Partly because it is in such situations that one feels totally ill-equipped and rather helpless. But there is also a great honour at being with people at crunch moments of their lives, be it for the dying or the bereaved. One can always preach another sermon or run another teaching course, but one has only one opportunity to get it right for a person at the end of their life.

One cannot produce a book that captures all of the many situations and encounters that a pastor experiences in his or her ministry relating to grief and loss. But I hope, as you have meandered through this book, that you have caught a flavour of the high calling of this ministry.

I have never forgotten the day I went to work voluntarily before ordination, in a large residential home for the mentally handicapped. I was a part of a group of European students about to live in the home for four months. On the first day, as the manager took us round, I observed situations and the conditions of the mentally ill individuals. At one point, one young resident jumped out at us from behind a wall. My heart pounded in fear and terror. At the end of the tour, the manager said that if anyone was feeling uncomfortable, then they should say so now and they could be released from the post with no embarrassment. I was feeling embarrassed, afraid and totally unskilled for such a calling but I didn't have the nerve, surrounded by my peers, to say so. In the end, it was a completely rewarding four months that I will never forget and I made friends with the residents that I can now still picture and recall. Perhaps you might be feeling about grief work the same as I did on my first day at the home? If so, there is actually no embarrassment in saying that this is simply not your calling. By allowing others to do it, you are releasing yourself to fulfil your own calling. But if you are willing to engage at a deep level in the lives of the bereaved and those grappling with loss issues, then I believe you too will be greatly rewarded and will make long-lasting friendships with many people. If, during a time of deep pain and agony in a person's life, we can help that individual to find peace, comfort and hope, then it will have all been worthwhile. And if people can come to have a deeper, more robust faith through it, then all the better.

We have discovered that we cannot enter church and community ministry without being challenged about our own mortality and self-awareness of how loss issues affect us. It can produce the full spectrum of emotions out of us. This means we need to learn our own boundaries, workload and awareness of how many people we can support without doing ourselves harm. The reality is that if we fail to recognise our own limits in ministry, we will inevitably begin to carry 'sadness' within, which in turn will lead to burn-out and perhaps a premature end of our ministry. This condition is not new, Elijah experienced it and it plunged him into depression. Fortunately, God sent an angel to Elijah not to pray more, make him work longer hours or change church, but to feed him and allow him to sleep. The physical needs were required to be met before the emotional and spiritual. I have always wondered why ministers work six days a week when the rest of society do five on average. Yes, God made the world in six days and rested on the seventh, which we try and emulate. However, that was with the concept of natural daylight before the days of electricity and emails that arrive at 11pm with the expectation of a reply by midnight. How many times I have heard it said that it is impossible to do the role in less than six days. But is this really what the Bible talks about when it says 'take up your cross and follow me?' Are we really indispensible? It affects us physically as well as bringing a negative impact upon our families and settling an example to a congregation that we all have to be 'workaholics'. Unless we care for ourselves, how can we truly care for others? This perhaps means we need to walk away, take time off, allow others to give to us and allow ourselves to be kind to ourselves.

To be in ministry requires a sense of calling. Here we recognise that our work is more than just a job. We give because we know we have been given to, we care because we know a greater force has cared for us, we hope in all situations because we believe in a God of hope and we love because we have tasted the depth of God's love through Jesus.

It is a privilege to care for other human beings but it is also just as much a calling to allow others to care for us. In the story of the Good Samaritan (Luke 10), the good deed would not have taken place without the Jew and his injury. I have always previously assumed that the Jew survived his injuries and recovered in the inn. But in fact the story doesn't tell us. All we know is that both the Jew and the Samaritan were blessed through each other. Sooner or later, we will be in the position of both of the characters. May we have the good grace to see that whatever our calling becomes, God is able to use us for good.

We hope according to our dreams,
But we live according to our fears.

Resources

Child Bereavement
www.childbereavement.org.uk
Supports families and educates professionals both when a child dies and when a child is bereaved.

Childline
www.childline.org

Compassionate Friends
www.tcf.org.uk
Supporting bereaved parents and their families after a child dies.

Cruse Bereavement Care
www.crusebereavement.org.uk
Confidential help for bereaved people.

Jigsaw4u
www.jigsaw4u.org.uk
Child-centred charity supporting children and young people through loss and trauma.

National Children's Bureau
www.ncb.org.uk
The leading national charity supporting children, young people and families, and those who work with them.

RD4U
www.rd4u.org.uk
Supporting young people after the death of someone close. Part of the Cruse Bereavement Care's Youth Involvement Project.

Winston's Wish
www.winstonswish.org.uk
The charity for bereaved children.

Glossary

BEREAVEMENT – is what happens to you
GRIEF – is what you feel
MOURNING – is what you do

Acute grief: grief occurring during the period when somatic, intrapsychic, and behavioural reactions are most intense.

Anniversary reaction: increased grief reaction precipitated by a special day related to the deceased (such as a birthday).

Anticipatory grief: grief experienced prior to the death of a loved one.

Bereavement: state of being that results from a significant loss.

Bereavement overload: extreme degree of grief triggered by multiple losses in a relatively short time.

Cathexis: investment of psychic energy in an object.

Chronic mourning: grief that is unusually intense and extremely long lasting (beyond one to three years).

Complicated grief: a complex distortion, or failure of one or more tasks of grief work.

Delayed grief: relatively extreme grief reaction long after the original loss that the person is actually mourning.

Disenfranchised grief: situations in which the larger society does not socially sanction and/or recognise certain bereaved persons' right, role or capacity to grieve.

Grief: the outcome of being bereaved: a variety of reactions that constitute the grief response.

Grief work: process by which individuals resolve their grief.

Hypercathexis: investment of an extreme amount of psychic energy in an object.

Idealisation: distortion of reality regarding deceased: only the positive characteristics are remembered.

Identification: manifestation by a survivor of symptoms; problems, or behaviours similar to those of the deceased.

Inhibited grief: prolonged absence of acknowledged grieving: however, physical symptoms are often manifested.

Intrapsychic: pertaining to the emotions and mind.

Libido: energy of love and pleasure.

Loss orientation: focus is on concentrating on, dealing with, and processing some aspect of the loss experience.

Memorialisation: phenomenon where the survivor pays homage to the deceased through a particular frequent ritual.

Mourning: social prescription for the way in which we are expected to display our grief.

Mummification: phenomenon whereby the bereaved attempts to leave things just as they were when the deceased was alive.

Object loss: loss of a loved one.

Obsessional review: extreme preoccupation with the deceased.

Preventability: belief that factors contributing to the death might have been avoided.

Restoration orientation: adjustment to numerous changes triggered by the loss.

Ritual: a specific behaviour or activity that gives symbolic expression to certain feelings or thoughts.

Role loss: loss of one's position or status in society.

Somatic: related to the body.

Thanatologists: professionals who specialise in the study of death, dying and grief.

www.ingramcontent.com/pod-product-compliance
Lightning Source LLC
Chambersburg PA
CBHW020349080526
44584CB00014B/948